Corporations, Classes and Capitalism

John Scott

Lecturer in Sociology,
University of Leicester

St. Martin's Press
New York

ISBN 0–312–17011–4

Library of Congress Cataloguing in Publication Data
Scott, John P.
  Corporations, classes, and capitalism.

  Bibliography: p.
  Includes index.
  1. Capitalism.   2. Corporations.
3. International business enterprises.
4. Industry and state.   I. Title
HB501.S47   1980   338.7′4′01   80–5097
ISBN 0–312–17011–4

For Jill, Michael and Susan

Contents

Tables

Acknowledgements

This book was originally to have been written jointly with Mike Hughes who, unfortunately, had to withdraw at the beginning of the project. I am nevertheless indebted to him for his help and for the many discussions which we have had on the topics covered in this book. Tony Giddens first suggested that I write the book and has read the whole manuscript. His comments were always useful, even when I did not fully accept them. Garry Runciman's objections to interlocking directorship studies have been important in the development of the argument in Chapter 4. A long interchange of letters forced me to clarify this argument considerably. Sections of the manuscript have been read by Dominic Strinati and Terry Johnson, and many of the ideas have been discussed with my co-workers in the Research Project on European Companies: Rob Mokken, Frans Stokman, Meindert Fennema, Bert Schijf, Rolf Ziegler, Beth Mintz, and Mike Schwartz. My final academic debt is to Maurice Zeitlin, whose path-breaking article (Zeitlin 1974) did much to stimulate my work in this area.

Preface

The aim of this book is to discuss some of the main issues involved in the development of the modern business corporation. The issues covered are not those of the internal administration of the corporation but those which relate to the wider significance of the corporation in capitalist society. I discuss the patterns of ownership and control in the corporate system and the relation of the corporation to the class structure, the state, and the world economic system. These issues are discussed in terms of two general theories. The theory of industrial society, based on a liberal and pluralistic political viewpoint, is drawn from the mainstream of American and European sociology. The theory of capitalist society, based on a Marxist political position, is drawn from the textbooks, pamphlets and monographs of orthodox Marxism. These two theories have raised most of the issues analysed in this book and have stimulated much of the empirical research which is discussed. My argument is that neither theory is adequate, and I show that developments at the empirical and theoretical levels point beyond these theories to the need for a new interpretation of industrial capitalism. Much new empirical work has been produced in recent years, and this has led to the need to reinterpret previous research. At the same time, both theoretical traditions have broken down. For example, Marxist writers such as Poulantzas, Offe and Habermas have been severely critical of the orthodox theory of capitalist society. The work of these theorists has complemented the development of empirical research, and my aim in this book is to lay the foundations for further advance.

The two theories are presented in Chapter 1 and are discussed as ideal types, taking no account of more recent theoretical positions. Chapter 2 discusses the concepts of ownership and control, and Chapters 3 and 4 relate these concepts to empirical data on the major capitalist societies. Chapter 5 shows how ownership and control are related to the structuration of a propertied class, and Chapter 6 analyses the economic role of the state. Chapter 7 completes the analysis by looking at the international dimension and, particularly, the emergence of the multinational corporation. Finally, Chapter 8 draws together some of the main conclusions of my analysis.

JOHN SCOTT
November 1978

1 Contending theories of industrial capitalism

The central feature of industrial capitalism is, undoubtedly, the large business corporation. In contrast not only to pre-capitalist forms of economic activity but also to those of 'classical' nineteenth-century capitalism, all the major economic activities today take place within large 'joint-stock' companies.[1] In the 1870s the joint-stock company was still a new social form; by the 1970s it has become established as the dominant feature of the economic landscape. In the mid 1970s the top 1000 British industrial corporations had a total turnover of £95000m., employed a total capital of £52000m., and earned total profits of almost £10000m.[2] A considerable proportion of these amounts, moreover, was accounted for by a relatively small number of the largest companies: the top 100 companies accounted for 62 per cent of turnover, 64 per cent of capital employed, and earned 69 per cent of profits; the top fifty companies accounted for 48 per cent of turnover, 49 per cent of capital employed, and earned 56 per cent of profits. The ten largest companies ranked by turnover (British Petroleum, Shell, British American Tobacco, Imperial Chemical Industries, Unilever, Imperial Group, British Leyland, Shell Mex and BP, General Electric, Bowater Group) had a total turnover of £22000m. – 24 per cent of the total turnover of the 1000 largest industrials. Looking beyond the industrial companies, there was considerable concentration in the financial sector: the two largest banks (National Westminster, Barclays) had deposits and assets greater than all the other banks together, though the next two largest (Midland, Lloyds) approach them in size; the top four life insurance companies (Prudential, Legal and General, Commercial Union, Standard Life) had life funds comparable with the capital of the top industrials. Such a high degree of concentration is not unique to Britain, but is common to all the major capitalist societies. The top ten European companies[3] (Royal Dutch Petroleum, IRI, Philips, Volkswagenwerk, Unilever NV, BASF, Daimler Benz, Siemens, Farbwerke Hoechst, Bayer) had total sales of £30000m.

In the USA, the top ten corporations (General Motors, Exxon, Ford, Mobil, Sears Roebuck, Chrysler, General Electric, Texaco, IBM, ITT) had total sales of £70000m. While the largest British and European corporations were of comparable size, the top US corporations were between two and three times as large, and held a similar position in relation to Japanese, Canadian and Australian companies.

The growing importance of the very largest firms has led writers such as Holland to speak of a new 'mesoeconomic' sector[4] which 'controls the commanding heights of big business in the national and international economy' (Holland 1975, 15). The top 100 British firms and the top 500 American firms comprise the high-profit sector of the economy and dominate a periphery of relatively small firms operating in restricted low-profit markets (Averitt 1968; Miller 1975; Nettl 1965). The largest firms 'are mainly diversified multi-product companies, with modern multi-divisional management structures. They are, in many cases, multi-company companies which have grown through the takeover and absorption of other concerns in related product lines' (Holland 1975, 51). The major trend in advanced industrial capitalism has been towards the concentration of more and more areas of economic activity in the hands of the largest companies of this kind.[5]

There are, broadly, two main interpretations which have been placed upon this process: the themes of 'industrialism' and 'capitalism'. The theme of industrialism refers to the transformation of human labour through the application of inanimate sources of energy to productive activity, and the associated physical proximity of workers and machines in a system of factory production (Giddens 1973, 141; Turner 1975). On the other hand, the theme of capitalism refers to the organization of production in terms of a search for the realization of profit for privately owned capital and the broader system of market exchange for which commodities are produced (Giddens 1973, 142). While capitalism in its broadest sense precedes industrialism, the conjunction of the two processes is what characterizes modern economic history (Weber 1923; Sahay 1974). The interplay of industrialism and capitalism has generated two further consequences: the *concentration* of production in ever larger technical units, and the *centralization* of money capital in ever larger financial units (Blumberg 1975). Each of these themes has provided the basis for a different theory of the development of industrial capitalism: the theory of industrial society, and the theory of capitalist society.

While the theory of industrial society has dominated sociological analysis, it has always been countered by radical, Marxist analyses.[6] The aim of this chapter is to present an outline of each of these theories. The theory of industrial society is drawn from the work of mainstream sociologists, economists and political scientists during the period since the Second World War, while the theory of capitalist society is drawn from the mainstream of orthodox Marxism. Each of these approaches has a fairly coherent internal structure and involves a systematic account of the development of industrial capitalism. The remaining chapters of this book will discuss the empirical basis of the arguments raised in these theories. While each theory has illuminated one aspect of the total process, each has concentrated on this aspect beyond all reasonable limits. Neither the theory of industrial society nor the theory of capitalist society can adequately explain the conjunction of industrialism and capitalism. Nevertheless, the interplay of the two approaches has generated much research and has produced a solid body of empirical knowledge concerning the nature and significance of modern industrial capitalism. My aim in this book is to draw out and make explicit the main outlines of this body of knowledge.

The theory of industrial society

Giddens has recently argued that much sociology since the work of Saint-Simon and Comte has centred around a concept of modern society as a specifically 'industrial' society (Giddens 1976*a*; 1971, 245 ff.; 1973, chapter 8). In many respects, argues Giddens, this theory is the substantive correlate to structural-functional sociology, although its influence extends beyond Parsons himself to writers such as Dahrendorf, Aron and Kerr.[7] The theory holds that the fundamental contrast in the modern world is that between traditional agrarian societies and urban industrial societies. In contrast to the traditional, religious legitimation of pre-industrial societies, industrial societies are characterized by the diffusion of power between competing elites within a democratic state, and by the solidarity of economic exchange and the division of labour. Industrial societies are depicted as essentially harmonious, in contrast to the Marxist view of a society based upon antagonistic classes:

The theory of industrial society recognizes the phenomenon of class conflict but holds that it is characteristic of the transitional phase in the emergence of industrialism out of traditional society and that it becomes transcended (read 'regulated' or 'institutionalized') when the industrial order reaches maturity [Giddens 1976a, 719].

This argument is based upon a view of social development as the unfolding of tendencies inherent in the social type itself (Goldthorpe 1974, 265–6). These inherent tendencies flow from the level of technological and economic development, and thus the society which is economically most advanced shows to other societies the image of their own future.

The clearest statements of the theory of industrial society are to be found in a number of works produced in the 1950s and 1960s, in particular those works of Dahrendorf, Kerr, Aron and Galbraith.[8] Both Aron and Dahrendorf have expressed the connection between industrialism and the value of 'rationality', or the 'scientific spirit'. Aron remarks that 'Industrialization arises from the application of science and the scientific spirit to the exploitation of natural resources' (Aron 1967, 16, 55; Dahrendorf 1959, 58). Aron emphasizes that, while industrialization involves the purely quantitative features of economic growth, it also involves the inculcation of 'rational habits which run counter to immemorial custom and are indispensable for the achievement of a high output' (Aron 1967, 12). It is the permeation of the whole society by the spirit of scientific rationality which makes it a specifically 'modern' society:

Modern societies are defined first and foremost by their organization of labour; that is, by their relationship to the external world, their use of machinery, the application of scientific methods, and the social and economic consequences of the rationalization of production [ibid., 15].

This model, adds Aron,

. . . corresponds in striking fashion to the conception of modern society that Auguste Comte, following Saint-Simon, worked out. . . . Both of them realized the prodigious increase in the means of production. Both saw the crowding of workers into factories as a symptom of modernity, as an original feature of the social organization that was coming into being. Both believed that the new working methods were at once the cause and the essential characteristic of modern society [ibid., 15–16].

Common to all variants of the theory of industrial society is the argument that the basic features of culture and society are to be explained in terms of the determining role of the economy. In contrast to Marxist theory, however, the economy is not defined in terms of its relations of production but in terms of its scientifically organized technology of production (Lenski 1966, 298–9). Galbraith is perhaps the most forceful advocate of the view that in advanced industrial society this rational technology finds its expression in the large corporation. The core of the economy, the 'industrial system', is composed of the 500 or 600 'technically dynamic, massively capitalized and highly organized corporations' (Galbraith 1967, 9; Pavitt and Worboys 1977, chapter 4). The industrial system, which is the basis of the 'industrial state', follows from advanced technology and, in its turn, leads to further technological progress. Such is the 'logic' of industrial technology (Kerr *et al.* 1960, 42–3; Aron 1968, 53).

The theory of industrial society involves six main themes: the separation of ownership from control in industry; the bureaucratic differentiation of management; the technical specialization of management; the social responsibility of management; the end of ideological politics; and the modernization theory of development.

The solid backbone of the theory is the idea of the separation of ownership from control in industry (Berle and Means 1932). As a consequence of the increasing scale of production, corporations must become more and more capitalized, and it becomes beyond the wealth of most individuals to maintain anything but a minimal stake in the ownership of the large corporation. The number of individual shareholders in a corporation increases until no individual or group of individuals can mobilize a controlling interest. The continuous long-term process of dispersal creates a power vacuum which can be filled only by the professional management. While in principle the stockholder 'owns' the corporation, he has little effective 'control' over it. As Galbraith characteristically argues: 'Corporate size, the passage of time and the dispersion of stock ownership do not disenfranchise the stockholder. Rather, he can vote but his vote is valueless' (Galbraith 1967, 80). The changing role of private property and the rise of a managerial group have important implications for the social-class structure of an advanced industrial society. The clearest formulation of these changes can be found in Aron, who argues that the class structure is no longer a rigid system of antagonistic classes, but is a more open and flexible system of strata. Industrial societies continue to generate inequalities, but at the same time industrialism is an equalizing force. The inherent logic of industrialism and its law of development break down the rigidities of the old class structure: 'The operation of the tendential laws weakens the reality of classes in many ways, but so long as social stratification exists (and it appears to be inseparable from industrial society), an interpretation in terms of class will always be possible' (Aron 1968, 36; 1964). Aron argues that

... most contemporary observers see social evolution as moving towards less heterogeneity between one stratum and another, hence towards less homogeneity within each stratum; towards less inequality in education, hence towards a greater degree of ascending social mobility; towards less solidarity within the strata, hence towards a decreasing penchant for an apocalyptic interpretation of the class struggle and the movement of history [Aron 1968, 37].[9]

It follows that 'In whatever sense the idea of class is understood, an industrial society does not tend toward the model of a *class* society' (ibid., 38; Dahrendorf 1968).

As the industrial system develops, so the managerial hierarchy becomes more differentiated and bureaucratized. Bendix explains this in terms of an increase in the scale of corporate production: 'As the enterprise increases in size, it becomes necessary for the owner-manager to delegate to subordinates responsibility for many functions, which he has performed personally in the past. Subsequently, it becomes necessary to delegate further managerial functions' (Bendix 1956, 226). At each stage of development along the size dimension, the extent of delegation increases. But not only does management become more extensive, it also becomes more specialized (Lenski 1966, 313–14). Technically educated specialists are required in increasing numbers by the advanced technology, and so management becomes more 'professional':

As industrialization reaches an advanced state, the enterprise emerges as an organization of high-talent managerial resources, with product development specialists, production engineers, and planning departments, all coordinated and directed by divisional and top managers [Kerr *et al.* 1960, 146].

Galbraith has christened this technical bureaucracy the 'techno-structure'. Not only is the technostructure an essential technical element of the industrial system, it is also the locus of power within that system and the wider society itself. Power in the economy is an attribute of that factor which is hardest to obtain or replace – and nowadays capital is relatively abundant, while specialized talent is in short supply. Power has passed from organized capital to 'organized intelligence' (Galbraith 1967, 56). The technostructure

. . . is the association of men of diverse technical knowledge, experience or other talent which modern industrial technology and planning require. It extends from the leadership of the modern industrial enterprise down to just short of the labour force and embraces a large number of people and a large variety of talent [ibid., 56].

The definition of 'management' used in the theory of industrial society follows from its view of the inherent requirements of an advanced industrial technology. Aron argues that any industrial society, capitalist or communist, requires an extensive professional management. 'There are certain leading roles to be performed in any industrial society, and consequently the same kinds of men appear to perform them' (Aron 1968, 59). The composition of the 'technosphere' of professional management has been spelled out by Kerr *et al.*: 'The managers in this context include entrepreneurs, administrators, engineers, and specialists who hold top positions in public or private enterprises. Collectively, they form a hierarchy of functions and people which is called management' (Kerr *et al.* 1960, 143; Galbraith 1952; Bell 1953).

To the extent that management attains control of the corporation, important shifts in the motivations of business leaders are held to occur. By contrast with the profit motivation of capitalist entrepreneurs, managers are able to exercise a 'sense of responsibility', since they are no longer constrained by the demands of the shareholders. This is the basis of the idea of 'soulful' or 'benevolent' corporations. Management sees itself as exercising a trust or fiduciary role on behalf of the community as a whole, and Berle labels the new form of society 'People's Capitalism' or 'Collectivism' (Berle 1960). The growth of 'institutional' share-ownership[10] makes little difference to this. The financial institutions do not normally wish to interfere, and will permit corporate management to go its own 'soulful' way. The corporate economy tends towards an economy in which 'management' is the dominant social force.

Just as the profit motive is held to disappear from the orientations of business leaders, so political ideologies disappear from the sphere of politics. Politics becomes more and more concerned with the technical administration of social affairs within an accepted economic framework, and political decisions are the outcome of competition among a plurality of interest groups. The state becomes a powerful agency which regulates the conflict of political groupings

(Kerr *et al.* 1960, 274; Aron 1960; Lipset 1960; Lenski 1966, 304).[11]

All of the processes described above are held to follow directly from the technological progress which is the core of industrialism. It follows that they are not merely descriptions of processes which have occurred in Western industrial capitalism; they also describe the pattern of development which any industrializing society will experience. While the details of the process will vary with national, cultural and political differences, the core features and the end result will be the same (Aron 1967, 35). The orthodox approach to 'the sociology of development' has operated in terms of the transition from 'traditional' to 'modern' societies, which is seen as arising from processes internal to particular nation-states. In Parsonian terms, the transition has been from the diffuse, particularistic and ascriptive role structure of pre-industrial society to the specific, universalistic and achievement-oriented role structure of industrial society (Hoselitz 1960; Hoselitz and Moore 1966; Hoogvelt 1975). The transition to industrialism begins when the rational entrepreneurial orientations which are central to industrialism begin to develop (McClelland 1961; Rostow 1960). It follows that the activities of the 'advanced' industrial societies in relation to the 'developing' ones cannot but be helpful in setting the logic of industrialism in motion. The industrialization of developing societies can be speeded up through the process of the transfer of technology. Turner argues that 'it is unrealistic to expect countries with little industrial background to be able to create a computer, car, aircraft, or chemical industry from scratch without help from foreign companies which do have experience' (Turner 1970, 106). The soulful corporation now operates worldwide. The multinational corporation can help to close the 'technological gap'. As Aron argues, 'there is no contradiction between the interests of under-developed countries and those of advanced countries': progress in one promotes progress in the other (Aron 1967, 24). The consequences of this for the developing societies are not purely economic; they will acquire all the other features of industrial society, including its political organization.

The theory of industrial society offers a clear and systematic account of the development of industrial capitalism. I shall discuss its empirical foundation in later chapters, but first it is necessary to outline its main rival as an explanatory theory – the Marxist theory of capitalist society.

The theory of capitalist society

The starting point for the orthodox Marxist theory of the development of capitalist society is the work of Marx himself.[12] The joint-stock company was still a fairly new device at the time of Marx's death, and there are only scattered remarks on its significance in his posthumously published works. Nevertheless, Marx's discussions of the various forms of capital and of the divisions within the capitalist class have provided a source of material for later writers. In this section I shall examine the orthodox Marxist attempt to construct a theory of capitalist society on this basis. This theory has been constructed in orthodox Marxism through the early works of Lenin and Bukharin, and has acquired the status of textbook knowledge in Soviet Marxism.

The theory of capitalist society involves five main themes: the separation of money capital from productive capital; the monopolization of production; the dominance of finance capital; the rise of state monopoly capitalism; and the imperialism theory of development.

The joint-stock company rests upon a separation between the ownership of money capital and the 'function' of capital as a productive force (Kuusinen *et al.* 1959, 252; Menshikov 1969, 11 ff.; Ryndina and Chernikov 1974, 112 ff., 186–9; Mandel 1969, 229). In contrast to 'real' productive capital, shares, bonds, mortgages, etc., are merely entitlements to a regular interest or divided income. This latter 'fictitious' capital gradually outstrips real capital as the dominant form of capitalist property (Ryndina and Chernikov 1974, 113). Although property owners may be withdrawing from directly productive activities, this does not alter the basic relations of capitalist production. Lenin, for example, sees it as a feature of the incipient transition from capitalism to socialism. It is a process which 'drags the capitalists, against their will and consciousness, into some sort of a new social order, a transitional one from complete free competition to complete socialization' (Lenin 1917*a*, 23). This 'highest stage' of capitalism is merely a partial transcendence of capitalism: 'Production becomes social, but appropriation remains private' (ibid., 56, 119).

In *Imperialism*, Lenin traces the growth of industrial concentration and combination from the apex of competitive capitalism in the 1860s to the growth of monopoly capitalism from the 1890s onwards. Monopolization occurs through the growth of individual corporations and through various link-ups between corporations: cartels, trusts, shareholdings, interlocking directorships, etc. (Lenin 1917*a*, 39, 45 ff.; Ryndina and Chernikov 1974, 183; Mandel 1969, 401–3). Alongside industrial concentration there is monopolization of banking. The banks 'grow from modest middlemen into powerful monopolies having at their command almost the whole of the money capital of all the capitalists and small businessmen' (Lenin 1917*a*, 28; Eaton 1963, 191). Similarly, Bukharin claims that monopolization, as a necessary feature of the development of the forces of production, occurs both within and between particular branches of production, so creating a tendency for the entire national economy to become 'a single combined enterprise with an organization connection between all the branches of production' (Bukharin 1915, 70). Thus monopoly capitalism is an 'inevitable outcome of the nature of capitalism' (Aaronovitch 1955, 14).

If the core of the theory of industrial society is the separation of ownership from control, the central theme of the theory of capitalist society is the dominance of finance capital. Lenin and Bukharin both point to the fact that monopolized capital in banking and manufacturing fuses into 'finance capital', i.e. capital which is not restricted to one particular sphere of activity.[13] The major banks own shares in industry, and industrial combines own shares in banks. Finance capital is that part of fictitious capital which is in the hands of the monopolies, and the growth of the credit system – which is manifested in the development of savings banks, insurance companies, pension funds, investment trusts, and so forth – consolidates the dominance of finance capital over real capital (Ryndina and Chernikov 1974, 179–80; Mandel 1969, 403 ff., 411 ff.; Rochester 1936, 13). Aaronovitch argues that this 'proceeds partly by way of fusions and coalitions of industrial and financial organizations, and partly by way of financial organizations entering industry and industrial firms becoming financiers' (Aaronovitch 1961, 37–8; Menshikov 1969, 159). The normal form of appearance of finance capital is 'financial groups', each of which is a centre of coordination and control over subordinate production units. Interlocking directorships, cross-shareholdings and other types of connection create 'associations of capital which at most have a common direction and at the least a common interest in avoiding conflicts of interest' (Aaronovitch 1961, 79, emphasis removed). Perlo (1957, 15) claims that the 'ties which interlock the monopolies have become tighter and more complex. The control of corporations is more and more centralized in knots of financial power.' The controllers of the financial groups concern themselves with general policy, not with the actual operations of the units of production. Menshikov (1969, 205–6) argues that 'The activities of such companies are coordinated at a higher level, outside the companies themselves. Such coordination deals with the more general and broader problems: it is effected not so much by those who directly manage the companies, as by men connected with the wealthiest families, the big banks, and so on.' Similarly, Perlo argues that the network of finance creates a complex 'spider web':

Strong ties of ownership cemented with interlocking directorates link financial institutions of different kinds in an inner circle of coordinated power. Similar strands extend from the inner circle to the great corporations of industry, transport and utilities, through which billions of profits extracted from the population of this and other countries are funneled to the central oligarchy [Perlo 1957, 61–2; Ryndina and Chernikov 1974, 182ff.; Bukharin 1915, 72].

The rise of finance capital involves the separation of money capital and productive capital at the level of the economy as a whole, and so leads to the dominance of a 'parasitic' financial oligarchy:

It is characteristic of capitalism in general that the ownership of capital is separated from industrial or productive capital, and that the rentier who lives entirely on income obtained from money capital, is separated from the entrepreneur and from all who are directly concerned in the management of capital. Imperialism, or the domination of finance capital, is that highest stage of capitalism in which this separation reaches vast proportions. The supremacy of finance capital over all other forms of capital means the predominance of the rentier and of the financial oligarchy [Lenin 1917a, 56; Bukharin and Preobrazhensky 1920, 141–8; Rochester 1936, 85].

The financial oligarchy is a clique of 'a few hundred or at most a few thousand men of wealth' (Perlo 1957, 13; Eaton 1963, 193) who comprise the dominant social class in the society (Aaronovitch 1961, 70; Haxey 1939, 42). There is an internal division within the capitalist class between the monopolists and the smaller capitalists (Kuusinen *et al.* 1959, 242; Ryndina and Chernikov 1974, 24–5). The monopolists as a group continue to control the most important parameters of the system, but actual decision-making within these parameters is delegated to top managerial employees:

The financial oligarchy . . . does not, as a rule, itself take part in the direction of the hundreds and thousands of industrial companies, banks, railways and other enterprises which it controls. The 'activity' of the financial groups comes down more and more to expanding its domination by way of the acquiring of controlling blocks of shares in ever new companies and by various financial machinations. The immediate direction of the enterprises passes over gradually into the hands of hired directors [Kuusinen *et al.* 1959, 252].

Thus the finance capitalists became more 'parasitic' on the manipulation of fictitious capital. While they play an essential role in the reproduction of capitalist relations of production, they no longer have any significant contribution to make to the technical development of the forces of production:

After all, the real power over production remains with the owners and not with those who in their name are directing technological progress, etc. The engineers and clerical employees of a monopolistic company cannot throw its owners out nor force them to surrender a portion of the profits in favour of the workers. The owners, on the other hand, can hire and fire engineers and clerical workers and dictate their will . . . just as they could a hundred years ago [Kuusinen *et al.* 1959, 292; Menshikov 1969, 88–91, 132–4, 318–20].

While monopolization leads to a reduction in the extent of competition between monopolistic groups, the intensity of this competition increases and is the driving force towards further monopolization. The end result of this process of monopolization is the elimination of competition within the national economy, except among those small firms which are dependent upon the continuance of the monopolies. Competition is displaced from the national level to the international level. Monopolization is associated with an interlocking between finance capital and the state, and the state then becomes an instrument for the international expansion of the national monopolies. In this way, the national economy is transformed into 'one gigantic combined enterprise under the tutelage of the financial kings and the capitalist state' (Bukharin 1915, 73–4, emphasis removed). The conflict of national capitalisms produces a world economy in which the 'anarchy' of capital production is reproduced at the international level. Bukharin argues that

State power has become the domain of a financial oligarchy; the latter manages production which is tied up by the banks into one knot. This process of the organization of production has proceeded from below; it has fortified itself within the framework of modern states, which have become an exact expression of the interests of finance capital [Bukharin 1915, 108].

According to the theory of capitalist society, the increasing importance of the state leads to a system of state monopoly capitalism. This is the system appropriate to the period of the 'general crisis' of capitalism. The general crisis was initiated by the First World War and the Russian Revolution, and was deepened by the Second World War. It is more pervasive in time and space than the periodic economic crises, since it is 'an all embracing crisis of capitalism as a social system, characterized by progressive disintegration of capitalism, the weakening of all its internal forces, economic, political and ideological' (Kuusinen *et al.* 1959, 258; Aaronovitch 1955, 66, 73 ff.; Rochester 1936, 287 ff.). It is precisely because the general crisis will not allow the monopolies to pursue their interests in the same way as before that the state becomes a progressively more important instrument of capitalist policy. Varga argues that the tendency towards state monopoly capitalism

. . . is brought about by the necessity for socializing certain economic functions such as power supply, a necessity which grows more urgent with increasing technical development; it is also brought about by the accentuation of class antagonisms in the different capitalist countries, which makes it essential for the bourgeoisie to concentrate their forces more strongly in their struggle against the workers; by the increasingly bitter struggle for the world market, which necessitates State support of the bourgeoisie in this struggle; by the necessity to concentrate all capitalist forces for the coming fight for the re-division of the world [Varga 1928, 66].

Not only does the state take on more and more economic functions, such as maintenance of profitability, creating demand, reallocation of national income, direct state enterprise, international military and policy involvement, etc., but there are important changes in its internal structure (Kuusinen *et al.* 1959, 267–9; Mandel 1969, 498 ff., 501–7). The period of monopoly capitalism marks the end of the liberal parliamentary system of democracy. Writing in 1928, Varga claimed that the rise of fascism in Italy and Spain was an indication of the future of the capitalist world:

Parliamentary democracy serves as the state form of the bourgeoisie as long as it is a historically progressing class, as long as it can claim to serve the interests of the people as a whole. The Fascist State, organized terror in the interests of the capitalists, is the form of government adapted to the period of decline, when the rule of the bourgeoisie is seriously threatened [Varga 1928, 12].

The fascist state represents the extreme form of the changes in the state which are required by monopoly capitalism. The state must reflect the interests of the 'small clique of monopoly capitalists' (Varga 1928, 67; Kuusinen 1959, 264–6). The interests of the capitalists are directly represented in the government and its centralized agencies, and parliament becomes more and more 'decorative', a formal body with little power. Dictatorship is more appropriate than democracy for monopoly capitalism (Bukharin 1915, 128). However, it is held that, even when things have not reached this extreme situation, the state and state policy are determined by the interests of finance capital. State monopoly capitalism is the situation in which 'the state machine, acting in the interests of the most powerful capitalist groups, subjects the entire economy and resources within its reach, to serve the interests of monopoly capital' (Aaronovitch 1955, 75). This occurs through the direct connections between big business and the state:

Finance capital is not one interest among many which may lobby an impartial government and whose legitimate rights such a government should seek to satisfy. It is built into and controls the entire government and administration of this country for its own profit and against the wider interests of the nation [Aaronovitch 1961, 162].[14]

To the extent to which the tendency towards the formation of state capitalist trusts develops, so the degree of international competition increases. Owing to the lack of profitable investment opportunities in their own economies, the monopolistic corporations export capital throughout the world. The competitive struggle for colonies in which to invest brings about the greater likelihood of conflicts involving the military power of the states. The industrial development of the colonies is subordinated to the needs of the imperialist powers (Lenin 1917a, 77). An international division of labour develops, in which colonial territories are subordinated to the imperialist nations:

Capitalism planted from above does not seek to satisfy the requirements of the local, national market. Its main aim is to ensure the reproduction of capital in the metropolitan countries. . . . For this reason it is mainly used for producing mineral raw materials or agricultural products for the imperialist powers, and only a very small part is used for the development of branches which satisfy national needs [Ryndina and Chernikov 1974, 277; Jenkins 1970].

The consequence of the imperialist division of the world is a heightening of international conflicts of interests. While the imperialist powers as a whole have contradictory interests to their colonies, the former group is itself divided into warring national factions.

The two approaches discussed in this chapter – the theory of industrial society and the theory of capitalist society – are probably the most influential perspectives on the corporation and industrial capitalism to be found in the social sciences. Each offers a relatively coherent interpretation of the main developments in industrial capitalism, and each has a certain credibility. Yet neither theory can be accepted or rejected in its entirety. Much of the empirical material available and most of the more restricted interpretations of aspects of industrial capitalism can be seen as products of attempts to grapple with the implications of these two contending theories. The interplay between the two theories, and the attempts by protagonists of each theory to reject their rival, have resulted in the accumulation of a large body of empirical knowledge. Further advance in our understanding of modern industrial capitalism now depends upon the recognition that it is only through the synthesis of aspects of each of the contending theories that an adequate interpretation of the available empirical material can be carried out. The rest of this book is a contribution to that task.

2 Property relations and the mediation of control

Few concepts in the social sciences would seem to be so self-evident as 'control', yet there is little consistency in its usage. The notion of the 'separation of ownership and control' has been hotly disputed, much of the dispute being concerned with the interpretation of generally accepted 'facts'. In later chapters I shall examine the status of these 'facts'; in the present chapter I shall attempt to clarify the concept of control itself by placing it in the context of a broader model of property relations. Despite its importance, there is little work on the sociology of property. While lawyers and philosophers have investigated the nature and justifications of property (Becker 1977), sociologists have, by and large, neglected it. The one outstanding exception is Karl Renner, who has endeavoured to construct a model of property relations from within the Marxist tradition. Despite its failings, Renner's work provides a useful framework for discussing the complex issues of ownership and control.

Legal forms and social relations

All social orders require that there be some sort of regulation of access to objects, particularly those involved in the production of goods and services. Renner (1904, 53, 73–4) defines the institution of property as the set of legal imperatives relating to the power of disposition and possession of social objects. Property regulates the 'detention' of such objects through the legal relation of ownership, 'a person's all-embracing legal power over a tangible object' (ibid., 81). But to concentrate on purely legal forms is insufficient, since the actual social relations which constitute a society rarely correspond exactly to codified legal representations. While legal forms are one of the basic conditions of actual social relations, they are not the only such conditions. To forget this is to commit the error of 'fetishism', to transform a social relation into a thing. Thus ownership has a dual character as both legal relation and social relation, and the sociologist must realize that, while in legal theory 'ownership is reduced to a mere legal title' and is thereby fetishized (ibid., 147), in reality it is the 'social function' of legal forms that is crucial. A legal relation of ownership can have varying social meanings depending upon the social order of which it is a part. The social relation of ownership – the actually effective power of disposition – may diverge from the legal relation of ownership, even though the latter is an essential condition of the former. Renner argues that effective possession and disposition can be structured in a way which does not correspond to the prevailing legal forms, and that in such a situation rights over objects become relations of social power:

Without any change in the norm, below the threshold of collective consciousness, a *de facto* right is added to the personal absolute domination over a corporeal thing. This right is not based upon a special legal provision. It is a power of control, the power to issue commands and to enforce them [ibid., 107, 117].

Similarly, Schumpeter has argued that the legal institution of private property and capitalist social relations are not at all the same thing. He argues that

. . . the capitalist process pushes into the background all those institutions, the institutions of property and free contracting in particular, that expressed the needs and ways of a truly 'private' economic activity. Where it does not abolish them . . . it attains the same end by shifting the relative importance of existing legal forms . . . or by changing their contents or meanings [Schumpeter 1943, 141–2].

This approach to the sociology of property is, of course, based on the scattered remarks which Marx made on this subject, particularly his statement that 'relations of production develop unevenly as legal relations' (Marx 1857, 109), which recognizes the continuing importance of Roman private law to modern capitalist production. To possess something (*besitzen*) is not to have a legal title to it; it is not to have 'property' (*Eigentum*). Relations of possession, argues Marx, are always part of a 'more concrete substratum' (*konkretere Substrat*) and, in consequence, 'The influence of laws in stabilizing relations of distribution, and hence their effect on production, requires to be determined in each specific instance' (Marx 1857, 98, 102). Study of law in the abstract is inadequate, since law must be related to its concrete context. The precise meaning of this prescription is not clarified by Renner's somewhat obscure restatement that actual social relations are the outcome of an interplay between legal forms and their 'external, technico-natural substratum' (Renner 1904, 58). My discussion above, however, shows the nature of the method: the social relation of ownership – the effective power of possession – is a deeper and more basic resultant of the conjunction of the various social forms (including legal institutions and relations) present in a society (Cutler *et al.* 1977). In order to analyse this social relation further, it is necessary to examine the legal form itself in more detail. I shall use Renner's concepts to show that, while the legal and social relations of ownership once coincided, this correspondence has gradually dissolved.

What Berle and Means (1932) term 'the traditional logic of property' involves two aspects: the right to determine the use of the object and the right to benefit from this use (Macpherson 1973, 123; Tawney 1920). With the legal recognition of the corporate form (Levy 1950; Thompson 1976) there is a dissolution of these traditional property rights, since those who supply the capital of a joint-stock company need not be identical with those who determine the uses to which it is put (Berle and Means 1932, 4333 ff.; Berle 1955, 17). When the two aspects of property rights are dissociated, it is possible to distinguish 'nominal ownership', which is the right to receive revenue as a return for risking one's wealth by investing in a company, from 'effective ownership', which is the ability to control the corporate assets.[1] Before the rise of the corporation, the owner of industrial property had full rights of both use and benefit over his property, but in the era of the corporation this has changed. Stocks and shares give their owners an interest in an enterprise, but they are not necessarily associated with control of the assets. The joint-stock company involves 'the surrender and regrouping of the incidence of ownership, which formerly bracketed full power of manual disposition with complete right to enjoy the use, the fruits, and the proceeds of physical assets' (Berle and Means 1932, 8). As Macpherson (1973, 154) argues,

. . . individual investors of all sorts become *rentiers* and become aware that this is what they are. Their property consists less and less of their ownership of some part of the corporation's physical plant and stock of materials and products than of their right to a revenue from the ability of the corporation to manoeuvre profitably.

According to Berle and Means (1932, 339), 'we are no longer dealing with property in the old sense' and, in a similar way to

Renner, they argue that it is necessary to go beyond the law to the 'economic and social background of law'. The corporation is, in Veblen's terms, 'the incorporation of credit' (Veblen 1924, 93), and its nominal, legal owners 'become no more than creditors' (Westergaard and Resler 1975, 154) who can be treated 'as legitimate claimants to some fixed share of the profits' (Bell 1974, 295). The corporation itself is the unit which is legally recognized as having ownership of the assets (Thompson 1977, 258; Cutler *et al.* 1977, 249, 307). Being legally recognized as the owner of the assets, however, is not the same thing as actually being the locus of effective possession.

A bewildering confusion of terminology has arisen among those who have attempted to clarify this evolution in property relations. Unfortunately, Renner's discussion of the problem is of only limited value. Renner argues that in the large corporation the link between the owner of money capital and the corporation is reduced to a relation of interest, the interest which can be earned from profitable investments (Renner 1904, 142–3). As a consequence, the link between the legal owner and the locus of effective possession is no longer direct or straightforward. Legal ownership of company stock gives 'economic ownership', the right to benefit from corporate activities, and this is gradually separated from 'technical ownership', which refers to actually using the means of production (ibid., 198, 268, 275). The confusions inherent in Renner's argument have been partly clarified by Bettelheim and, following him, Poulantzas. These writers employ the term 'legal ownership' for the nominal right to benefit, and they define 'economic ownership' as the power to appropriate the product and to control the labour process (Bettelheim 1970, 69, 134–5; Poulantzas 1974, 18). Economic ownership corresponds to what I have termed effective possession and disposition.[2] The most useful attempt to elaborate these definitions has been that of Cutler *et al.*, who argue that effective possession is the capacity to control the functioning of the means of production and to exclude others from their use, and that this is vested in the corporation itself (Cutler *et al.* 1977, 249, 275).

There is a fundamental problem with such arguments. If effective possession is predicated of the corporation itself, then it would seem to be predicated of a legal form, and legal forms cannot have effective possession because they cannot act. There is an ambiguity as to whether the concept of the 'corporation' refers to the legal device defined in commercial law, or to the collective social actor

B

which is structured in terms of such a legal device. Clearly, only the latter may have effective possession as opposed to legal ownership. Thus the shareholders in a corporation have nominal ownership of that corporation and the right to revenue, and the corporation itself has nominal ownership of the assets. Effective possession of the means of production rests elsewhere. One possible solution is that given by Cutler *et al.*, who argue that effective possession rests with the corporation considered as a social actor, that is, as a locus of economic decisions (ibid., 1977, 277). In this they seem very close to Berle, who argues that, while the corporation emerged as a purely legal form, it rapidly became a 'social institution' to which the law had continually to be adapted. The corporation is not a mere creature of the law; it is 'not fictitious, but factual' (Berle 1955, 9). The social reality of the corporation gives it an autonomy as a social actor. This autonomy rests upon its ability to engage in a distinct 'calculation' irreducible to the calculations of its constituent individuals.[3] This calculation is 'effected by an organizational apparatus involving both individuals and machines (e.g. computers, tabulators, and sorters, etc.) so that the products of calculation can in no way be reduced to the work of any human individual' (Cutler *et al.* 1977, 277). What Cutler *et al.* fail to realize is that effective possession may rest with any actor, individual or collective, and that the enterprise is not necessarily the only collective actor capable of effective possession.[4]

The significance of the rise of the corporate form is that it creates the possibility of a greater or lesser degree of dissociation between shareholders and the agents of effective possession. As a social relation, effective possession is always an attribute of real social groupings, but this need not be the body of shareholders as a whole. The locus of effective possession is no longer obvious, but must be discovered empirically. While Cutler *et al.* designate the corporation as the most important locus, Poulantzas, like many others, suggests an alternative:

. . . not every share or interest taken by a shareholder in a firm's capital corresponds to an equivalent or proportionate share in economic owner-ship and real control. This ownership is wielded as a whole by a few large shareholders, not necessarily a majority, who by various means . . . con-centrate in their hands the powers that derive from it [Poulantzas 1974, 119].

That is, a sub-set of the shareholders may have effective possession. The join` stock company can involve 'the simultaneous development of diffused ownership and of concentrated control' (Cole 1948, 124). As De Vroey argues, 'the relationship between ownership and control can be viewed as one consisting of several *degrees of separation* determined by the extent of the effective involvement of the owners in decision-making' (De Vroey 1976, 12). Large shareholders may 'retain real ownership through a partial legal ownership' (Carchedi 1975, 49). The legal forms are not eliminated, but remain as essential conditions of actual social relations. The social function of the law has changed and has allowed a degree of dissociation between nominal ownership and effective possession.

When the object of an ownership relation is a corporation operating within a system of corporations, effective possession pertains to units of *capital*. The corporation is not merely an 'industrial' unit; it is primarily a 'pecuniary unit' (Veblen 1924, 82 ff.; Braverman 1974, 257–8; Fitch 1972, 97). What unifies such a unit of capital is its 'strategy', that is, 'the determination of the basic long-term goals and objectives of the enterprise, and the adoption of courses of action and the allocation of resources necessary for carrying out these goals' (Chandler 1962, 13; Ansoff 1965). Effective possession is manifested in the corporate strategy in relation to finance, markets, products, mergers, and so on. Because corporations are frequently related to one another in a hierarchical way as parents, subsidiaries and associates, it follows that the strategies of the various corporations will be hierarchically arranged. For example, a wholly owned subsidiary may have its strategy totally determined at the level of the parent company, or a parent company may be partly subjected to the strategies of other corporations. The ultimate unit of corporate strategy is the basic unit of capital; it is the 'economic subject', i.e. 'whatever money funds are operated by a single direction' (Cutler *et al.* 1977, 307). Corporations are the means through which such a unit of capital operates, and its operations are determined by the strategy it follows. Effective possession and the unit of capital are, therefore, two sides of the same coin. Effective possession is the basis upon which the strategy of the unit of capital is determined: only those standing in a relation of effective possession to a unit of capital have the capacity to affect its strategy in a significant way. I propose to use the term 'strategic control' to refer to this power over corporate strategy. As a capacity, strategic control is a potential which is inherent in effective possession, although the agents of effective possession may intervene to a greater or lesser extent in the actual determination of strategy.

I have argued that, in relation to the functioning of capital, effective possession takes the form of strategic control. It is now necessary to examine further the ways in which capital functions. Marx has argued that the joint-stock company involves the separation of 'capital as a function' from 'capital as property', and his analysis makes it possible to extend the above discussion of the partial dissociation of effective possession from nominal ownership. With the joint-stock company, the function of capital in the process of production – which is to subordinate the process to the expansion of the capital – is 'institutionalized' and so separated from the individuals who supply the capital. Those who actually carry out the 'work of management and supervision' which is involved in the capital function need not be those who are the legal owners of the corporation (Marx 1894, 372, 376, 378–9; Renner 1904, 198).[5] As Marx (1894, 428) puts it, 'In stock companies the function is divorced from capital ownership'. As I have already shown, this is no absolute divorce: 'Stock companies in general – developed with the credit system – have an increasing tendency to separate this work of management as a function from the ownership of capital, be it self-owned or borrowed' (ibid., 380). The function of capital finds its concrete embodiment in the corporate strategy, and it is, therefore, necessary to discuss what is meant by 'strategic control'.

Berle and Means (1932, 69) define control in terms of direction over the activities of a corporation as manifested in the ability to determine the composition of the board of directors. This has been the working definition adopted in numerous other studies. In their study for the Temporary National Economic Committee, for example, Goldsmith and Parmelee (1940, 99) defined control as 'the power of determining the broad policies guiding the corporation', and Larner (1970, 2) follows this usage. However, using 'control' in this general sense gives little idea of the precise range of decisions which are the object of control.[6] I wish here to adopt and to elaborate the ideas of Eisenberg (1969) and De Vroey (1973) in order to specify the meaning of strategic control.

De Vroey demarcates two 'spheres of decision': the strategic and the operational spheres. The strategic sphere involves decisions related to investment, finance, executive recruitment and the legal structure of the corporation; while the operational sphere involves control of particular plants, sales activities, appointment of middle management, setting wages, budgeting, etc. (De Vroey 1973, 82–3). Similarly, Eisenberg defines 'structural decisions' as relating to the constitution of the business, to matters such as mergers, liquidation, combination, sale of assets, changes in voting rules, etc. These structural decisions are distinguished from 'business decisions' which are made in the course of business or within the general framework of the business as it exists – matters such as selection of suppliers, hiring and firing, extending plant capacity, union recognition, etc. (Eisenberg 1969, 11–13). Taking these definitions together, it can be seen that strategic control relates to that sphere of decisions which concerns the basic parameters within which the corporations forming a particular unit of capital are to act. To exercise strategic control is to be involved in setting or altering these parameters.[7] By contrast, I shall designate as 'operational management' all those activities which relate to the sphere of decisions concerning the implementation of corporate strategy and hence to the immediate day-to-day administration of company operations. Following Cutler *et al.*, it can be said that strategic control is based upon an 'economic calculation', a calculation in relation to the setting of objectives, as opposed to the 'technical calculation' of implementation involved in operational management (Cutler *et al.* 1977, 309).[8]

Under the traditional concept of property, the capitalist entrepreneur as an owner-manager held the right to revenue and performed the function of capital. The capital function aspect of this role relates to effective possession of industrial property, that is, to both the strategic control and the operational management of capital. The emergence of the legal form of the joint-stock company involves legal recognition of the corporation itself as the owner of its assets. Only then does strategic control become a problem: with nominal ownership passing to the corporation itself, the question of who is able to control corporate strategy becomes all important. It is possible that the stockholders, or a portion of them, will continue to exercise strategic control – since the 'separation' is one in law, not one of fact – but it is also possible that those who are employed as operational managers will exercise strategic control. Berle and Means argued that a transition from stockholder control to manager control was occurring. Marx recognized a similar transition but held that share-ownership, through the credit and banking system, remained a centrally important factor in the exercise of strategic control. To assess questions of this kind, it is necessary to examine the mechanisms through which strategic control is exercised.

Modes and mechanisms of control

I have argued that the legal forms of property and ownership are the framework within which effective possession arises. Strategic control is *mediated* through legal institutions and relations (Giddens 1973, 121; Clement 1975, 13). It is important to look at the various modes of institutional mediation and the associated mechanisms through which legal ownership is translated into strategic control. The most influential attempt to do this has been the Berle and Means classification of types of control. They distinguish those situations in which control rests upon the legal right to vote the majority of the stock from those in which control rests upon some additional 'extra-legal' basis. Under the first category they include ownership through almost complete share-ownership, majority ownership by a single individual or group, and majority ownership through a 'legal device' (i.e. through the 'pyramiding' of inter-company shareholdings). Under the second category they include minority control and management control (Berle and Means 1932, 70). In all those situations where control rests upon the ability to vote the majority of the stock,[9] the degree of dissociation between nominal ownership and effective possession is not very great – a single ownership interest holding in excess of one-half of the outstanding shares stands in a position of effective possession. In those situations where a single interest is not able to vote the majority of the shares, 'control is more often factual [than legal], depending upon strategic positions secured through a measure of ownership, a share in management or an external circumstance important to the conduct of the enterprise' (ibid., 79).

Minority control exists, say Berle and Means, where a small group with less than a majority of the shares has 'working control' owing to the absence of any other holdings large enough to oppose them. Berle and Means set the amount of stock required at 20 per cent, and later writers have suggested that, with a wider dispersal of share-ownership, minority control is possible with 10 per cent, 5 per cent or even less (Larner 1970; Burch 1972; Scott and Hughes 1976). Similarly, Blumberg has criticized Berle and Means for concentrating their attention on only the single largest holder or small group of associates. He claims that this may underestimate the extent of minority control, since the method does not uncover 'the behind-the-scenes alliances which can accumulate the necessary critical mass' for control (Blumberg 1975, 93). The situation of the minority shareholder is buttressed by factors such as their hold over the voting machinery, which reinforces their position as the current members of the board of directors. Minority control is, however, inherently unstable, since there is always the possibility that another holder may increase his holding, force a vote and engage in a 'proxy fight' to gain the votes of the majority of normally uninvolved shareholders.[10] Zeitlin *et al.* have argued that a situation of minority control is the most characteristic mode of control in modern industrial capitalism:

Minority control is one of the most important consequences of the development of the corporation as the decisive unit of productive property: the great majority of shareowners are stripped of control by a small segment of the capitalist class made up of the principal shareowners of the large corporations, who are thus able to extend their control of capital (and of the political economy) far beyond the limits of their ownership [Zeitlin *et al.* 1975, 92].

Management control rests purely on the advantages of incumbency. No stock interest has sufficient shares to gain minority control, and so the members of the board, who may have only minimal holdings in the company, will be a self-perpetuating control group which is almost totally divorced from legal ownership (Berle and Means 1932, 80–4). In such a situation, 'challenge to management comes only from the occasional shareholder or group of holders who together possess a relatively substantial minority position that can serve as a base to offset the advantages inherent in management's position' (Baum and Stiles 1965, 12–13). That is, management control is based primarily on control of the proxy-voting machinery and is unstable for this reason. If a proxy fight occurs, if a group of shareholders can form an alliance, or if a major holder is able to increase his holding, the incumbent management may lose control.[11] Berle and Means argue that the change in control status from owner to manager control has definite consequences for corporate strategy:

The separation of ownership and control produces a condition where the interests of owner and of ultimate manager may, and often do diverge, and where many of the checks which formerly operated to limit the use of power disappear [Berle and Means 1932, 6, 121–2].

That is, those whose control rests upon legal ownership of the majority of the company shares have an interest in the value of these shares and the dividend which they can earn, while those whose control has little to do with share-ownership have no such interest. Larner has claimed that management control 'simply means that the management, in the absence of gross incompetence or serious misfortune, has open to it a wide range of discretionary behaviour in which it can, without fear of punitive action by stockholders, pursue policies which serve its own interests at the expense of the owners' (Larner 1970, 3). The interests of the stockholders 'serve as a constraint rather than as the dominant motivating factor' (ibid., 4). This argument conflates two distinct ideas: that the management acquires an autonomy from the *particular* ownership interests of the company's shareholders, and that management acquires an independence from *any* ownership interest. Berle and Means have established that management control involves a partial autonomy from the large mass of shareholders in the company which they manage, but they have not established that 'the managers' are a distinct social grouping from 'the owners'. Furthermore, the managers of a particular company may not be unduly influenced by their stockholders, but they may be subject to influence from 'outside' the corporation. That is, the managerial group may not be internal professional executives (the operational managers), but may be representatives of propertied interests external to the particular corporation. The manager-controlled corporation may be a part of a broader unit of capital:

A powerful interest group, because it is powerful, possesses a certain degree of *influence* in the affairs of a corporation; that is, its desires, opinions, advice, remonstrances, or cajolings tend to be heeded by management. However, this sort of pressure is not decision-making if management itself . . . makes the final decision [Gordon 1945, 151].

The Berle and Means classification is based on the principle that, as share-ownership becomes more and more dispersed, so control passes from majority ownership to minority control and finally to management control. The managers have control because the outstanding shares are so widely dispersed that no individual or group of associates holds sufficient shares to counterbalance the power of the entrenched management. It is, however, possible to see dispersal of share-ownership as enhancing the power of those who have substantial holdings (Child 1969, 45), even if this may not be sufficient for minority control. The ten or twenty largest shareholders may, collectively, hold a block of shares which is large enough to give minority control (or even majority ownership) to a cohesive group, yet the major shareholders may lack the basis for a collective organization which would enable them to act as such a group. Gordon (1945, 36, 44) has argued that the successful exercise of minority control requires that the major shareholders comprise a small compact grouping which is willing and able to intervene in pursuit of their interests. To the extent that the major holders are not associates of one another, such a coalition is unlikely. Furthermore, no one of the major holders will have sufficient shares to exercise minority control on its own, and any coalition of a sub-set of the major holders is likely to be countered by a coalition based on a different sub-set. In this situation, any coalition will be unstable since there is no community of interest among the large holders over and above certain minimal stockholder interests which are, in any case, shared with owners outside the group of major shareholders. If shares are more or less equally distributed among the major holders, then each share has a greater power than it would in a situation of inequality, since it competes on equal terms with all the other major holdings (De Alessi 1973, 844). This relative equality precludes the formation of stable alliances, yet makes some sort of *modus vivendi* necessary (Morin 1974, 22).[12] Therefore, in situations where the major holders are in a position of effective possession but do not constitute a coalition of associates, the mode of strategic control must differ from both the minority and management control situations. No coalition can achieve minority control, but the board cannot disregard the interests of those in effective possession. It is likely that the major shareholders will be able to cooperate in order to agree on the composition of the board, this composition depending on the power balances among the major holders. I propose that this sort of situation may be termed 'control through a constellation of interests': effective possession is an attribute of the major shareholders collectively, yet this constellation of ownership interests has no unity and little possibility of concerted action. Zeitlin *et al.* (1975, 102, 106) have argued that owing to the 'congeries of intercorporate relationships' and the 'intricate interweaving of interests' many corporations that appear to be management-controlled are in fact minority-controlled. To this I would add that in many cases 'control through a constellation of interests' may be a more accurate description. The board will reflect the constellation of interests (though it does not necessarily reflect this in an immediate and direct manner) and so controls strategic policy in a characteristic way. The board cannot achieve the autonomy from particular stockholder interests which is characteristic of management control, yet neither is it the mere instrument of a cohesive controlling group.

The basis for management control is that the distribution of shareholdings is such that no individual or group of associates can be a serious threat to management. Similarly, minority control requires that, apart from the controlling holding, there is a wide dispersal of shares. Control through a constellation of interests requires that a substantial block of shares be concentrated in a small but diffuse group of shareholders and that the remaining shares be widely dispersed. While minority and management control are phenomena which arise as share-ownership becomes 'democratized' – and this was indeed the claim behind such notions as 'People's Capitalism' – control through a constellation of interests is a phenomenon which arises when 'democratization' is replaced by a movement of concentration. This is precisely what is involved in the growth of so-called 'institutional' share-ownership. The increasing importance of insurance companies, pensions funds, and investment and unit trusts has led to a new form of concentration in share-ownership. Individual persons tend to invest in these financial intermediaries rather than investing directly in industrial companies themselves. As a result, the 'institutions' become the most important holders of company shares and so acquire a position of effective possession (Berle, 1960; Child 1969, 46). As such, investment institutions are an extension of the principles of the joint-stock company and the stock exchange: the growth of a market for securities allows investors to attain 'independence of the fate of the particular enterprise in which he has invested his money' (Sweezy 1942, 258; Hilferding 1910; Parsons 1958, 112), and the growth of indirect investment is the completion of this process so far as the individual investor is concerned (Cole 1948, 125).

Majority ownership, minority control, management control and control through a constellation of interests are all *modes* of strategic control, and it is now necessary to examine in more detail the *mechanisms* through which control is exercised.[13] At the most general level, all shareholders have an interest in the income and capital gains which their investments can yield, and company policy is necessarily constrained by this interest (De Alessi 1973, 843; Peterson 1965, 18). The larger shareholders will tend to be a much greater constraint than the small shareholders, since any dissatisfaction that the former feel could lead to substantial share sales and so have a considerable effect on the share price. A rapid and sustained decline in the share price will lead to considerable difficulties for a company hoping to raise new capital. The shareholders – and particularly the major holders – are 'a part of the environment of which those actively responsible for policy must continually take cognizance' (Gordon 1945, 57). As Westergaard and Resler (1975, 160) argue, influence over corporate strategy 'does not require active participation in control. The power . . . to sell a large block of capital can be enough – *if* clashes of policy between major shareholders and company directorate should occur'.

Additionally, the major shareholders tend to be better informed and to have greater access to the company, and will be able to ensure that their opinions and advice are brought to the attention of the management. Those making company policy are bound to be influenced by this advice. As Eisenberg (1969, 45–6) argues,

Is it not likely that many of these major holders will own substantial blocks in particular corporations – substantial either in percentage or absolute dollar terms – and will either be skilled investors or under the guidance of investment professionals? Is it not likely, in other words, that while 'the average shareholder' may not be highly interested in structural changes, those shareholders who own the bulk of the shares held by individuals will consider such changes with some care and will expect to have a role in such changes.

Eisenberg points out that the growing role of the 'institutions' means that they too, as large shareholders, will be well informed and will wish to make their views known to the company management. As institutional holdings grow, 'the predisposition to vote in management's favour seems to be breaking down' (ibid., 52). Baum and Stiles, in their study of institutional investment, make the general point that 'As an influence in the corporation, the large shareholders have been better able to obtain, analyse, and act on information to protect their economic interests. At times they have enhanced their own position at the expense of the uninformed smaller shareholders' (1965, 156).

These first two mechanisms are both found in situations of minority and management control wherever there is a diffuse group of substantial shareholders excluded from direct participation at board level. In situations of minority control, argues Gordon, control by those in effective possession is often 'passive' or 'negative':

'Control' in these cases usually implies approval rather than initiation of decisions, and may imply merely an indirect influence rather than direct approval or veto. The purpose of control is normally to further or protect particular interests of the controlling group, and this may be done without participating in the formation of many, perhaps most, policies [Gordon 1945, 173].

These mechanisms are also characteristic of control through a constellation of interests where the board is drawn from the operational managers or from, say, a previously controlling family. In these situations board members continue in office subject to the acquiescence of those with effective possession, and these control mechanisms may be the main ways in which strategic control is ensured. The absence of direct involvement by the major ownership interests, as Beed (1966, 13) argues, 'may point to an identity of interest or lack of dissatisfaction'. Blumberg recognizes that the major shareholders may express advice and opinions in a concerted way, even though they are not intended as pressures upon management:

> Concerted action . . . need not reflect formal agreement. It may arise as an objective phenomenon produced by congruent pressures leading to common patterns of conduct. Thus, one may inquire whether the existing pattern of management control with the acquiescence and support of the institutions does not constitute a *modus vivendi* representing an accommodation of the interests of these groups [Blumberg 1975, 94].

Concerted action, that is, may be an unintended consequence of the 'congruent pressures' which the major shareholders experience rather than resting on 'an economic alliance or other intentional association to achieve common objectives' (ibid.).

There are also more 'active' mechanisms of control. If some or all of the board members are direct appointees of the major shareholders, then the advice and opinions of the latter may be regarded as instructions. Gordon argues that influence is transformed into actual decision-making 'if the advice or opinions of the interest group are taken by management as orders which they must obey' (1945, 151). This is because

> The power of minority groups stems from the ability, inherent in their collective voting strength, to change the management of a company. The mere existence of this power, quite apart from any threat to use it, cannot help but be an important conditioning influence operating on management [ibid., 187, 57; Monsen *et al.* 1968, 437].

The major shareholders do not need to intervene in order to exercise strategic control. Under most conditions 'a milder sort of continuing pressure is needed, plus reserve power to act when the occasion requires' (Peterson 1965, 20).

The most 'active' mechanism of control is actual intervention by the ownership interests. The major interests may intervene and dictate board policy or replace the board. Intervention is especially likely in 'crises', i.e. where the company has run into serious financial or legal difficulties. When intervention occurs it is likely that the composition of the board comes more and more to represent the constellation of interests among those in effective possession. Board members formerly in office under sufferance will tend to be replaced by others who are more representative of the major interests. Intervention is the most 'active' mechanism of strategic control available to the major shareholders, since none of them has a holding large enough for the exercise of undisputed minority control. The rarity of intervention 'indicates that such intervention is not often necessary because, in the generality of cases, such shareholders are satisfied that their interests are reasonably well-served' (Nichols 1969, 104). The more routinized are the decisions, the less likely are the controllers to wish to intervene. It is when strategic issues arise that the controllers will strive to influence the board and to see that its wishes are carried through (Zald 1969, 107). The rarity of intervention is exceeded only by the rarity of proxy fights. Generally, intervention can be handled without open conflict. As Peterson argues, 'Far from being an ordinary election, a proxy battle is a catastrophic event whose mere possibility is a threat, and one not remote when affairs are in conspicuous disarray' (1965, 21). Intervention, therefore, need not involve a dramatic struggle; it may consist in the gradual but firm imposition of the interests of the controlling group over the company's management. In situations of minority control the minority interests will gradually come to dominate the board and to use it as their direct instrument; in situations of control through a constellation of interests the major holders will gradually find that the power balance among themselves is reflected in the power balance on the board (Clement 1975, 23).

The 'active' mechanisms of control are, perhaps, most characteristic of control through a constellation of interests, since the balance of power has to be constantly reasserted whenever necessary. The boundaries between minority control, management control and control through a constellation of interests are variable, depending, as Morin (1974) emphasizes, on the changing pattern of share distribution resulting from the constant restructuring of company capital. New issues, mergers, acquisitions, and so forth, create a complex and shifting pattern in the distribution of shareholdings. In the course of this restructuring, certain groups may be eliminated from positions of strategic control and new alliances may arise to positions of minority control. For example, control through a constellation of interests may give way to minority control if some of the holders merge with one another or if the company itself enters into an association with a company in which one of its major shareholders has a stake. Similarly, if the number of large and relatively equal holders increases, a company may move from control through a constellation of interests to management control, though the opposite movement is perhaps more likely.

An important point to emphasize is that all the mechanisms except the first are also available to non-shareholders with a substantial interest in the company, such as the holders of a company's loan stock and its bankers. This emphasizes that strategic control relates to the use of capital, and any groupings which are related to a particular corporation in the overall flow of capital may be able to exercise control over that corporation. Share-ownership is the most crucial form of capital, though its importance in relation to other forms of credit can never be merely asserted. The importance of this point is that, say, banking interests may be able to exercise considerable influence over minority- and management-controlled companies in which the control status would otherwise seem straightforward (Chevalier 1970, 45–6; Morin 1974, 35). Very often, however, those who are creditors of the company in this way are also owners of the share capital, either as direct beneficiaries or as trustees. This is particularly likely in companies controlled through a constellation of interests, where the major creditors will be represented among the constellation.

To conclude, 'control' is by no means a straightforward self-evident concept. There are various modes of control and a number of mechanisms through which this control can be exercised. Some mechanisms of control are obvious and direct, while others are 'passive' and indirect. As Zeitlin has emphasized, the control status of a corporation can be decided only if it is examined in relation to 'the concrete situation within the corporation and the constellation of intercorporate relations in which it is involved' (1974, 1091,

1107–8).[14] In the era of the joint-stock company and its associated features, strategic control is mediated through a complex of social forms. While the legal structure of property relations is a central part of this institutional mediation, it is never the sole part.

3 Capital ownership and strategic control

In this chapter I shall examine the argument which lies at the heart of the theory of industrial society – the argument that strategic control in industry has passed from capitalist families to professional managers. This process of separation of 'ownership' from 'control' is seen as an inexorable consequence of the development of industrial society. As Parsons and Smelser argue, 'the kinship-property combination typical of classical capitalism was destined, unless social differentiation stopped altogether, to proceed toward "bureaucratization", toward differentiation between economy and polity, and between ownership and control' (Parsons and Smelser 1957, 289; Bell 1957). Similarly, Lenski (1966, 343) claims that while the propertied class is still important there is a 'slow but certain decline' in its power. In the theory of industrial society, classes are seen as generated by the distribution of administrative power in the industrial enterprise. The clearest statement of this can be found in Dahrendorf, who attempts to reconstruct the Marxist account of class in such a way that it is no longer restricted to the specific historical conditions of nineteenth-century capitalism. Dahrendorf claims that Marx assumes a narrow, legal definition of property in the means of production and that this must be broadened out to cope with changes consequent upon the separation of legal ownership from strategic control (Dahrendorf 1959, 21). From a similar point of view, Bendix (1956, 13) has argued that 'All economic enterprises have in common a basic social relation between the employers who exercise authority and the workers who obey'. For Dahrendorf, classes refer to 'the relations of factual control and subordination in the enterprises of industrial production' and can be defined in terms of the 'exercise of, or exclusion from, authority' (1959, 21, 136). While Dahrendorf's discussion is less complex than that given in the preceding chapter, his meaning is clear:

Control over the means of production is but a special case of authority, and the connection of control with legal property an incidental phenomenon of the industrializing societies of Europe and the United States [ibid., 136–7.[1]

The separation of ownership from control is regarded as an integral feature of the transition from 'capitalist' to 'post-capitalist' society. It is the empirical basis of this argument which must now be examined.

Ownership and control in the USA

The study by Berle and Means (1932) has been a model for similar studies as well as being an object of sustained critical attention. Their study of American corporations must be the starting point for any empirical assessment of the 'separation' between ownership and control.[2] Berle and Means begin their analysis by pointing to the fact that modern corporations typically exhibit a wide dispersal of their shares to a large number of shareholders. As Table 1 shows, almost half of the top US corporations in 1929 had more than 20000 shareholders.

Table 1 *Shareholders in the largest US non-financial corporations (1929)*

No. of holders	*No. of corporations*	*% of corporations*
Less than 5000	20	14
5000–20000	53	37
20000–50000	39	27
50000–100000	22	15
100000–200000	7	5
200000–500000	3	2
Totals	144	100

SOURCE: adapted from Berle and Means (1932), 49.

This wide dispersal of shareholdings creates the possibility for strategic control to pass out of the hands of the majority of the stockholders. During the period 1914–28, majority ownership gradually gave way to minority control, and Berle and Means see the 1930s as the period in which management control becomes a prominent feature of the economy (Berle 1960, chapter 2; Berle and Means 1932, 84–9). While they make it clear that they are writing about a process of development, not a process which has come to an end, they do claim to have found evidence to suggest that 'management control' is the characteristic form of strategic control. Table 2 presents this evidence.

Table 2   *Ultimate strategic control in the 200 largest US non-financial corporations (1929)*

Mode of control	No. of corporations	% of corporations	% of corporate assets
Private ownership	12	6	4
Majority ownership	10	5	2
Minority control	46·5	23	14
Legal device	41	21	22
Management control	88·5	44	58
In receivership	2	1	0
Totals	200	100	100

SOURCE: Berle and Means (1932), 106.

NOTE: 'Private ownership' is defined as a holding with 80 per cent or more of the shares; minority control is defined as a holding with between 20 per cent and 50 per cent. One company was classified as joint minority and management control and so Berle and Means allocated half to each category.

On the basis of this evidence Berle and Means conclude that the traditional capitalist forms of private ownership and majority ownership, which together account for fewer companies than any other mode of control, are disappearing. Their significance in relation to the proportion of corporate assets held is even less, managerial corporations accounting for more than half of all corporate assets. Berle and Means claim that 'the separation of ownership and control has not yet become complete. While a large body of stockholders are not in a position to exercise any degree of control over the affairs of their corporation, those actually in control are usually stockholders though in many cases owning but a very small proportion of the total stock' (Berle and Means 1932, 343). As share-ownership becomes more dispersed the proportion of stock, represented on the board will drop even further.

Numerous problems have been raised in relation to the data which Berle and Means present. The category of control through a 'legal device', for example, has been questioned. If one corporation was majority-owned or minority-controlled by another company which was itself subject to majority ownership or minority control, then the corporation in question was classified as controlled through a legal device. Thus the forty-one corporations classified in this way might better be classified in the same category as their parent – i.e. as subject to one of the forms of proprietary control (Larner 1966; Zeitlin *et al.* 1975, 97). This re-classification would cast some doubt on the notion that traditional owner control was disappearing. Much of the classification is, in any case, based on estimation and guesswork. For example, half of the managerial corporations were 'presumed' to fall in this category on the basis of little or no information at all (Zeitlin 1974, 1081; De Vroey 1976, 16 ff.). The extent of the separation between ownership and control in 1929 may have been considerably less than Berle and Means suggest.

A re-analysis of the Berle and Means data by Burch does indeed suggest that the extent of management control had been exaggerated. This study estimates that between 37 and 45 per cent of the top 200 non-financial companies in 1929 were family-controlled, many of these being classified as 'managerial' by Berle and Means. That is, Burch argues that corporations could still be subject to the control of particular families, even if the latter had only a small block of shares (Burch 1972, 114–15). This view is confirmed by a study carried out during the 1930s on behalf of the Temporary National Economic Committee (Goldsmith and Parmelee 1940; Anderson *et al.* 1941). Goldsmith and Parmelee argue that in 1937 just under two-thirds of corporate stock was held by individuals, estates and trusts, and just over one-third was held by other companies. However, although share-ownership appeared to be widely distributed, large holdings were concentrated: 'not much over one per cent of the holders are required in most cases to account for the majority of the stock outstanding or for voting control' (Goldsmith and Parmelee 1940, 15, 9). As Table 3 shows, the overall distribution of shareholdings in share issues of the top 200 in 1937 was not dissimilar to the figures for eight years previously (see Table 1).

Goldsmith and Parmelee show that 88 per cent of the holdings analysed in Table 3 comprised 100 shares or fewer, and only 0·25 per cent were holdings larger than 5000 shares (ibid., 36). The twenty largest holdings in share issues of the top 200 companies were investigated (Table 4), and it was discovered that these holders had a majority of the shares in more than a quarter of the share issues. In one-half of the issues, the top twenty shareholders had a substantial minority block. Owner control was therefore apparent in at least three-quarters of the share issues.

A detailed analysis of the twenty largest shareholdings shows that

Table 3   *Shareholders in the largest US non-financial corporations (1937)*

Number of holders	No. of issues	% of issues
Less than 1000	24	12
1000–10000	62	30
10000–100000	109	52
More than 100000	13	6
Totals	208	100

SOURCE: Adapted from Goldsmith and Parmelee (1940), 27.

NOTE: The 200 largest companies had a total of 208 issues of common stock. Of the 24 issues with fewer than 1000 holders, 14 were wholly owned by parent companies.

Table 4   *Holdings by the twenty largest shareholders in the largest US non-financial corporations (1937)*

Proportion of shares held by top 20 holders	No. of issues	% of issues
Less than 10%	46	22
10–30%	69	33
30–50%	36	17
More than 50%	57	28
Totals	208	100

SOURCE: Adapted from Goldsmith and Parmelee (1940), 81, table 5.

there were only three share issues in which the largest single holding was smaller than 1 per cent. In half of the issues the largest holding amounted to at least 9 per cent. Of the fifty-seven issues with more than half of their shares held by the major holders, thirty-two had a majority held by the largest single holder, and in thirteen of these the largest holding comprised over 95 per cent. In over a third of the issues a controlling position was held by individuals rather than companies (Goldsmith and Parmelee 1940, 89–91). It would appear that the proportion of management-controlled companies was far less than Berle and Means had estimated. Many of these companies should more accurately be seen as minority-controlled or as controlled through a constellation of interests, or even as majority-owned. Table 5 gives the basic information on modes of control.

Table 5 *Strategic control in the 200 largest US non-financial corporations (1937)*

Mode of control	No. of corporations	% of corporations
Majority ownership	42	21·0
Predominant minority	37	18·5
Substantial minority	47	23·5
Small minority	13	6·5
No dominant shareholders	61	30·5
Totals	200	100·0

SOURCE: Calculated from Goldsmith and Parmelee (1940), Appendix XI, 1486.
NOTE: Control is measured by proportion of voting stock held and by representation in the company's management. The dividing line between 'predominant' and 'substantial' minority is set at 30 per cent and that between 'substantial' and 'small' is set at 10 per cent.

Over two-thirds of the 200 largest companies were subject to some kind of owner control. Single families held control in forty companies (eight majority and thirty-two minority), and groups of families had control in thirty-five companies, generally through a substantial minority holding. Some sixty companies were controlled by other companies, some of the latter themselves being family-controlled. Thus family control was present in about two-fifths of the companies, Of the thirteen family groups identified, four (Ford, Du Pont, Mellon and Rockefeller) were particularly important (Anderson *et al.* 1941, 172–3). Burch's re-analysis of these data also comes to the conclusion that between 37 and 48 per cent of the large companies were family-controlled, a figure broadly the same as that which he calculated for 1929 (Burch 1972).

Part of the discrepancy between the Berle and Means study and the Goldsmith and Parmelee study can be explained by the fact that the latter did not exclude from their analysis the subsidiaries of other companies included in the study. This would lead to an overstatement of the extent of owner control as compared with Berle and Means, who looked only at 'independent' corporations. Similarly, Goldsmith and Parmelee classified companies by their immediate control status and not in relation to the control status of the companies which controlled them (Larner 1970; Gordon 1945, 43). While the results are not conclusive, it is unnecessary to go as far as De Vroey, who argues that 'procedural choices are almost shaping the very nature of the conclusion' (1976, 29). The careful and extensive studies carried out by Goldsmith and Parmelee and by Burch definitely show that management control of large corporations during the 1930s was not as extensive as Berle and Means had suggested and that majority ownership and family control were still persistent features of the economy.

Relatively few studies were carried out in the 1940s and 1950s, and those that were carried out were not as systematic as those discussed above. However, it is possible to get some idea of the changes which were occurring in this period. Villarejo (1961*a*) reported on the increasing dispersal of share-ownership, and Table 6 shows that the 'average' corporation in 1951 had a fairly wide share distribution. The majority of the shareholders have small holdings (an average of just over thirty shares each), and they account for only 10 per cent of the outstanding stock. On the other hand, a small number of large shareholders (averaging almost 5000 shares each) accounted for more than half of the outstanding stock. Villarejo estimates that in 141 of the 232 corporations that he studied (61 per cent) a controlling block of shares was held by the directors and/or other major interests (1961*a*, Appendices I and II).

Table 6   *Share distribution for 'average' US corporation (1951)*

No. of shares held	No. of holdings	No. of shares per holder	% of stock held
1–99	3360	31·1	10·1
100–999	1755	194·5	33·1
More than 1000	118	4968·8	56·8
Totals	5233	197·1 (avge)	

SOURCE: Villarejo (1961*a*), 49.

Perlo confirms Villarejo's general findings when he argues that 'The important stock-owners are numbered in the hundreds of thousands rather than the millions. And the decisive stock-owners are numbered in the tens of thousands' (Perlo 1958, 29). Perlo suggests that the proportion of stock held by the twenty largest holders actually increased between 1937 and 1954 (ibid., 29–30). A particularly important trend identified by Perlo is the growing number of financial institutions which were represented among the largest shareholders. The share of these financial intermediaries in total corporate stock rose from 8 per cent in 1900, to 14 per cent in 1929, 24 per cent in 1949, and to 33 per cent in 1954 (ibid., 30). Indeed, it was this growth which led Berle (1960) to suggest that the 1950s were the period in which the trend towards management control was replaced by a counter-trend towards control by fiduciary institutions.[3]

In a study carried out in 1957, Kolko analysed those companies in the top 100 which had also been analysed in 1937. He found that these seventy-two companies showed a continuity in their principal stockholders over this period of twenty years. In twenty-two of these companies the same families remained dominant, even though the proportion of shares which they held had fallen (Kolko 1962, 62). Evidence that the major shareholders were in controlling positions in many corporations is given by Eisenberg, who shows that in 1961 even the largest corporations (those with more than 5000 shareholders) had at least 20 per cent of their stock held by the ten largest shareholders in about 40 per cent of cases. The proportion held by the ten largest holders increased steadily to the point at which corporations with fewer than 1000 shareholders had more than half of their stock held by the major interests in at least half of all cases (Eisenberg 1969, 43–4).

A number of studies undertaken in the 1960s enable the picture to be brought up to date. The most influential of these was that carried out by Larner, who explicitly intended that his results should be comparable with those of Berle and Means. On the basis of the figures in Table 7, Larner claims that 'it would appear that Berle and Means in 1929 were observing a "managerial revolution" in process. Now, thirty years later, that revolution seems close to complete' (Larner 1966, 786–7).

Table 7 shows that 84 per cent of the top 200 corporations were controlled by their managements, and Larner adds that 70 per cent of the next 300 were also management-controlled. However, Larner recognized that old controlling families remained important, even in some 'managerial' companies. In fact, he argues that 14 per cent of the top 200 companies were subject to family control. These figures were confirmed by Sheehan, although he arrived at the slightly lower estimate of 11 per cent of the top 100 companies as being family-controlled (Sheehan 1967). The study by Larner has been criticized in the same way as the Berle and Means study on which it was modelled. Burch has argued that 40 per cent of the 1965 top 200 were subject to some degree of family control, another 18 per

Table 7   *Ultimate strategic control in the 200 largest U S non-financial corporations (1963)*

Mode of control	No. of corporations	% of corporations	% of corporate assets
Private ownership	0	0·0	0·0
Majority ownership	6	3·0	2·0
Minority control	18	9·0	11·0
Legal device	9	4·5	3·0
Management control	167	83·5	84·0
Totals	200	100·0	100·0

SOURCE: Adapted from Larner (1970), 12–13, table 1.
NOTE: Larner uses 10 per cent as the cut-off point for minority control.

cent being 'possibly' family-controlled. However, the proportion of management-controlled companies was held to be greater among the larger than the smaller companies, 58 per cent of the top fifty being management-controlled (Burch 1972, 68). A study by Palmer confirms the view that Larner had overstated his case. Table 8 shows that, while the top 500 companies included a majority of 'managerial' corporations, the top 125 companies were significantly different from the rest of the 500.

Table 8   *Strategic control in the top 500 U S industrial corporations (1965)*

| Mode of control | Rank by sales | | | | |
	1–125	126–250	251–375	376–500	*Totals*
Owner-controlled	24	45	48	44	161
Management-controlled	101	75	73	78	327
Unknown	0	5	4	3	12
Totals	125	125	125	125	500

SOURCE: Adapted from Palmer (1972), 57, table 1.
NOTE: The cut-off point for owner control is 10 per cent.

Chevalier has carried out a major study which takes account not only of the proportion of stock held but also of the identity of the shareholders and directors. As a result, he gives perhaps the most accurate picture of ownership and control in the 1960s. Tables 9 and 10 show the pattern of strategic control and its association with size.

Table 9 *Strategic control in the top 200 US non-financial companies (1965)*

	Rank by size				
Mode of control	1–50	51–100	101–150	151–200	Totals
Majority ownership	1	3	3	4	11
Minority control	14	24	25	30	93
Predominant influence	5	6	4	1	16
Management control	30	17	18	15	80
Totals	50	50	50	50	200

SOURCE: Chevalier (1970), 67.

NOTE: Minority control involves more than 5 per cent of shares as well as representation on the board. 'Predominant influence' is the situation where there is strong influence on the board, even if there is no evidence of a 5 per cent holding.

Table 10 *Identity of controllers on the top 200 US non-financial companies (1965)*

	Type of controller					
Mode of control	Families	Banks	Other financials	Board	Other	Totals
Majority ownership	7	0	0	0	4	11
Minority control	58	14	5	16	0	93
Predominant influence	4	12	0	0	0	16
Management control	—	—	—	—	—	80
Totals	69	26	5	16	4	200

SOURCE: Chevalier (1970), 67.

According to Chevalier's study, it is the top fifty companies which are most marked by management control in the strict sense. Families directly control sixty-five companies, are a predominant influence in four, and are influential in a further twenty-three companies controlled by other groups. Of these twenty-three companies in which families are a subordinate influence, fourteen are classified as management-controlled by conventional methods (Chevalier 1970, 71). In twenty-eight of the management-controlled companies, banks exert a secondary influence, the same being true for seven of the minority-controlled companies. Altogether, the six largest banks control or influence forty companies (ibid., 115). Chevalier also examined the top 1937 corporations which were also in the top 200 for 1965. He discovered that the number of management-controlled companies among the eighty-five companies involved had increased from thirty to only forty. His main finding was that both majority and minority control had given way to situations of 'predominant influence', or what has above been called control through a constellation of interests (Chevalier 1969, 166).

Burch has estimated that family control is even more extensive among merchandising and transportation companies than it is among industrial companies. Whereas 20 per cent of the top fifty industrials were 'probably' family-controlled, 58 per cent of merchandising and 36 per cent of transportation companies were in this situation (Burch 1972, 96).[4] In order to establish that family control was real rather than apparent, Burch examined the degree to which members of the proprietary families hold executive posts and the extent of continuity in family representation. Table 11 shows that more than three-quarters of the large companies classified as family-controlled had family representation in their top management, and that in most cases the families had remained in control for more than a decade.

Table 11   *Family control in top US corporations (1965)*

	% of family firms with family executives	*% of firms with family control for more than a decade*
Top 50 industrials	80	90
Top 50 merchandising	97	83
Top 50 transportation	77	56
Top 50 commercial banks	80	100

SOURCE: Adapted from Burch (1972), 101.

On the basis of the figures presented, it is clear that the period from the 1930s to 1965 saw a diminution in the extent of family majority ownership and a concomitant increase in the extent of minority and management control, though Chevalier's findings suggest that the predominant trend may have been towards control through a constellation of interests, with many families remaining on the board only because the effective possessors permit them to do so. In 1937, between 44 and 49 per cent of the top 108 manufacturing and mining companies were family-controlled; by 1965 the corresponding figure was 36 per cent. Burch concludes that 'it would certainly appear that while there has been a definite trend toward managerial control of big business over the years, the magnitude of this shift in economic authority has generally been overstated' (ibid., 102). He estimates that 'America's big industrial corporations have been shifting toward a professional form of managerial control at a rate of from roughly 3 to 5 per cent per decade, which many would argue is fairly slow' (ibid., 105). Palmer has confirmed this estimate in his study of changes between 1965 and 1969. During this period, six of the top 500 companies changed from owner control to management control, most of these being found in the top 125. This shift was offset by the disappearance of management-controlled companies through mergers: while very large firms which disappeared through mergers were just as likely to be owner-controlled as manager-controlled, overall 'Management-controlled firms are more likely to be merged out of existence than are owner-controlled firms' (Palmer 1972, 59). There is much evidence, however, that the trend has not been towards management control, but towards control through a constellation of interests. Burch argues that his findings 'do not really take into account the now truly vast blocks of corporate stock held by the big institutional investors, particularly the top fifty commercial banks and trust companies, a number of which are controlled by various wealthy families' (1972, 17). A trend from direct family ownership to effective possession by financial 'institutions' involves no straightforward separation of ownership from control. Control by ownership interests may not disappear, but may occur through different modes and mechanisms (Sweezy 1942, 261–2).

The American evidence suggests that the development of the legal form of ownership from the exclusive possession of a real asset to the right to receive revenue has been associated with a development in the sphere of effective possession. This has been from 'personal possession' by particular families and interests to 'impersonal possession' through an interweaving of ownership interests which breaks down the direct link between particular interests and particular companies. Correspondingly, strategic control has shifted from private, majority ownership to control through a constellation of interests. The period of the 1930s seems to be transitional in these respects, and it is not surprising that minority control and management control were important at this stage, since these forms of control seem to correspond to situations in which particular ownership interests are diminishing their holdings but have not been completely replaced by the 'impersonal' holdings of the financial intermediaries. The continuity of families in top management positions in companies which formerly belonged to them must be seen as evidence that they remain on the sufferance of the large institutional shareholders who now possess these companies (Fitch and Oppenheimer 1970a, 82–3).

Ownership and control in Britain

The first major study of ownership and control in Britain was that of Florence, who examined shareholdings in English companies in the 1930s (Florence 1947; 1953; 1961). His investigations show that, at this time, family and private control were of similar significance in the USA and in England. It can be seen from Table 12 that at least half of the largest companies in each country were controlled by a dominant ownership interest. Florence's detailed figures show that most of the 'marginal' cases in England were companies in which the top twenty shareholders held more than 20 per cent of the voting stock. Many of these companies may reasonably be seen as controlled through a constellation of interests and should be added to the total of owner-controlled companies.[5]

Table 13 brings out the fact that the proportion of shares held by the twenty largest shareholders was greater in England than in the USA, though Table 14 suggests that this is mainly due to the size of the largest single holding. Minority control in English companies involved relatively large minority holdings in comparison with the more 'diffused' American pattern. The evidence from both of these tables suggests that control through a constellation of interests was of less significance than minority control in the 1930s in both England and America.

In a study relating to 1942, Parkinson (1951) investigated the

Table 12 *Strategic control of top corporations in England
(1936) and the USA (1937)*

	England (1936)		USA (1937)	
Mode of control	*No. of companies*	*% of companies*	*No. of companies*	*% of companies*
Dominant ownership interest	48	(58)	73	58
Marginal	27	(33)	18	15
No dominant interest	7	(9)	34	27
Totals	82	(100)	125	100

SOURCE: Adapted from Florence (1953), 201–2. The US figures are Florence's calculations from Goldsmith and Parmelee (1940).

NOTE: The US classifications are based on the holdings of the two or three largest holders, and the 'dominant ownership interest' category involves a 10 per cent cut-off value. The English classifications are based on the holdings of the twenty largest holders, and a 20 per cent cut-off value is used. The percentage figures in brackets relate to fewer than 100 cases and are included merely to facilitate comparison.

Table 13 *Shareholdings by the top twenty shareholders in
England (1936) and the USA (1937)*

	England (1936)		USA (1937)	
Proportion held by top 20 holders	*No. of companies*	*% of companies*	*No. of companies*	*% of companies*
0–9·9	7	(9)	4	3
10–19·9	11	(13)	37	28
20–29·9	17	(21)	29	22
30–49·9	14	(17)	30	23
More than 50%	33	(40)	32	24
Totals	82	(100)	132	100

SOURCE: Florence (1953), 189, table Vc.

NOTE: See note to Table 12.

Table 14   *Relative significance of large shareholders in England (1936) and the USA (1937)*

	Median percentage held	
	England (1936)	*USA (1937)*
1st largest shareholder	10·3	6·0
2nd ,, ,,	3·0	2·6
3rd ,, ,,	1·9	1·8
4th ,, ,,	1·3	1·6
5th ,, ,,	1·1	1·3
10th ,, ,,	0·6	0·7
15th ,, ,,	0·3	0·5
20th ,, ,,	0·3	0·4
All top 20 shareholders	25·0	22·7

SOURCE: Florence (1953), 190.

pattern of shareholdings in thirty large British companies. He discovered that just under 90 per cent of shareholdings were very small, many being holdings of less than £100, and that these holdings represented only 29 per cent of the ordinary capital. The 0·2 per cent of holdings which were larger than £10000, however, accounted for about a third of the capital (ibid., 51, 125, 128–9). Table 15 shows that among the large holdings there was considerable inequality: out of a total of 1915 large shareholdings there were 131 holdings of more than £100000.

Table 15   *Top shareholders in thirty large British companies (1942)*

Shares held	*No. of holdings*	*% of large holdings*	*% of ordinary capital*
10 000–50 000	1608	83·9	10·7
50 001–100 000	176	9·2	3·7
100 001–500 000	113	5·9	6·5
500 001–1 000 000	13	0·7	2·5
More than 1m	5	0·3	6·3
Totals	1915	100·0	29·7

SOURCE: Adapted from Parkinson (1951), 41–2.

The proportion of a company's capital held in large holdings varied from 6 per cent upwards, though most companies had between 20 and 30 per cent of their capital held by the major interests. The larger the company, the larger the proportion of shares held by the large holders (ibid., 41). Table 16 shows that just over half of the large holders were 'persons' (bank accounts at this time represented mainly personal executor and trustee accounts), and that these personal interests held 14 per cent of the capital in the large companies studied. The corporate interests (including 'nominees' in this category) represented just under half of the large holders and held 19·4 per cent of the capital. Parkinson argues that the most likely controlling interests are the corporate holders, but he draws few direct conclusions about this (ibid., 46).

Table 16 *Identity of top shareholders in thirty large British companies* (*1942*)

Category of holder	No. of holders		% of large holders		% of all capital held	
Persons	815		42·6		12·3	
Trustees	85		4·4		0·8	
Banks	74		3·9		1·0	
Total personal		974		50·9		14·1
Insurance companies	197		10·3		1·9	
Investment trusts	153		7·9		1·8	
Other companies	70		3·7		6·9	
Nominees	521		27·2		8·8	
Total corporate		941		49·1		19·4
Totals		1915		100·0		33·5

SOURCE: Adapted from Parkinson (1951), 45–6.
NOTE: Parkinson calculates his figures on the basis of various samples and so his estimates for particular quantities do not always agree exactly with one another.

While the studies by Florence and Parkinson are not totally comparable, the importance of corporate shareholders is brought out by both writers. A study carried out by Florence in 1951 suggests that this trend has been associated with a greater diffusion of share-ownership. Florence argues that the level of concentration in share-ownership in England fell between 1936 and 1951 – just over half of the largest companies being owner-controlled in 1936, and just under a third in 1951. Table 17 shows that the proportion of shares held by the twenty largest shareholders fell quite markedly over twenty years. The average percentage held by the major shareholders fell from 30 per cent to 19 per cent, and personal holders gave way to corporate holders. As the figures suggest, majority ownership declined and minority control increased (Florence 1961, 192). Florence recognizes a certain degree of management control but claims that this is not a sign of a managerial 'revolution' but of managerial 'evolution' (ibid., 187).

Table 17   *Holdings by the top twenty shareholders in English companies (1936, 1951)*

Proportion held by top 20 holders	Number of companies	
	1936	*1951*
0–9%	10	17
10–19%	15	28
20–49%	45	40
More than 50%	24	13
Totals	94	98

SOURCE: Adapted from Florence (1961), 112–15, tables V*a* and V*b*.

Two related studies carried out in the 1950s and 1960s confirm and elaborate these conclusions. On the basis of representation on the board, Barratt Brown classifies companies into three categories: family or tycoon control, management control, and external control. He argues that from 1954 to 1966 there was a tendency for the number of family-, tycoon- and management-controlled companies among the top 120 to increase at the expense of companies which were externally controlled (see Table 18). The growth in the number of management-controlled companies was, he argues, due to the fact that many of them (nearly a quarter) were subsidiaries of foreign corporations (Barratt Brown 1968*a*, 48). Clearly, such companies are not 'management-controlled' in the strict sense, but are majority- or wholly-owned companies with local boards drawn from their operational managers.

Barratt Brown's study did not examine shareholdings and so must be treated with caution. However, it would seem that many of the externally controlled companies and some of those which he classifies as managerial may best be seen as controlled through a

Table 18 *Board representation in the top 120 British companies (1954, 1966)*

Dominant interest on board	1954	1966
Family or tycoon	36	38
External interests	53	47
Internal management	31	35
Totals	120	120

SOURCE: Adapted from Barratt Brown (1968a), 45, table 7.

constellation of interests. Barratt Brown argues that the externally controlled companies have their boards dominated by 'coordinating controllers' who sit on the boards of many industrial and financial companies, and it may be surmised that they represent the major corporate shareholders and creditors of the corporations. These 'coordinating controllers' are evidence of control through a constellation of interests and correspond to what Florence (1947) termed the situation of 'oligarchic minority owners control'. Hall *et al.* (1957), in a less systematic study, elaborate this point and present detailed shareholding data for 1957 on ICI, which Barratt Brown had classified as controlled by external coordinators. This company had fewer than fifty shareholders with 100000 or more in shares, most of these holders being financial companies and nominees which were connected through intercorporate shareholdings and interlocking directorships. The eleven top shareholders included an interconnected group of two commercial banks, four insurance companies, and a merchant bank which collectively held 9 per cent of ICI's shares and were represented on its board. The second largest shareholder, with 2 per cent, was the ICI pension fund, which shared directors with the main ICI board. Altogether, 10 per cent of the share capital was represented on the board. Hall *et al.* do not demonstrate that the major interests are able to form the kind of stable coalition required for the exercise of minority control, and so it may be presumed that ICI, like many of those classified by Barratt Brown as 'externally controlled', was in fact controlled through a constellation of interests (Hall *et al.* 1957, 27–8). The fragmentation of small and medium holdings among a large number of individuals gives effective possession to the major

c

shareholders. Hall *et al.* argue in relation to large companies that

The ownership and control of these concentrations of industrial property can now be exercised only through a series of loosely organized but tightly knit oligarchic groups. These groups may represent several interests . . . but, as in any true oligarchy, the 'natural competitiveness' of these elites of power has been subsumed into their greater interests – the mutual care of corporate property [ibid., 31].

During the 1960s and 1970s an important series of investigations into share-ownership demonstrated the changing balance between personal and corporate shareholders. As Table 19 shows, between 1963 and 1969 personal holdings in British companies fell from 54 per cent to 47 per cent, and by 1975 the proportion of personal holders of stock in large companies was as low as 42 per cent. Conversely, holdings by financial interests rose from 30 per cent in 1963 to 36 per cent in 1969, and financial holdings in large com-

Table 19   *Beneficial share-ownership in British companies (1963–75)*

	% of shares held		
Category of owner	1963 (all cos.)	1969 (all cos.)	1975 (large cos.)
Persons, executors, trustees	54·0	47·4	42·1
Insurance companies	10·0	12·2	14·9
Pension funds	6·4	9·0	15·2
Investment trusts	7·4	7·6	4·7
Unit trusts	1·3	2·9	2·0
Banks	1·3	1·7	2·1
Stock exchange	1·4	1·4	0·1
Other financial cos.	2·6	1·1	0·5
Non-financial cos.	5·1	5·4	2·2
Public sector	1·5	2·6	0·8
Charities	2·1	2·1	4·2
Overseas	7·0	6·6	3·5
Totals	100·0	100·0	92·3

SOURCE: Diamond Report (1975*b*), 9, 13.

NOTE: The figures for 1975 are based on the Royal Commission's 'Mini Survey' into shareholdings in thirty of the hundred largest companies. The total for 1975 is less than 100 per cent, since nominee holdings to a total of 7·7 per cent could not be allocated to their beneficiaries. Most of these nominee holdings will be on behalf of investment trusts and overseas interests. The Commission drew its data for 1963 and 1969 from Stone *et al.* (1966) and Moyle (1971).

panies in 1975 amounted to 40 per cent. According to the Royal Commission on the Distribution of Income and Wealth, nearly 40 per cent of the large shareholders in British companies were insurance companies, and more than half of these holdings were of more than 2 per cent of the stock of the company involved. While just under half of all large holdings were in the names of nominees, these were found to be acting on behalf of pension funds, insurance companies, unit trusts and investment trusts. A mere 4 per cent of large holdings were personal interests, though in each case these individual holdings were substantial (Diamond Report 1975*b*, 11–12; Westergaard and Resler 1975, 160). The most recent data on ownership and control in Britain suggest that large corporate shareholdings have resulted in a level of owner control which is not dissimilar to that which Florence discovered in 1936 (see Table 20).

Table 20 *Major shareholders in the largest British non-financial companies (1975)*

Proportion held by a single large interest or by directors	*No. of companies*	*% of companies*
No dominant interest	98	39·2
0–5%	15	6·0
5–10%	10	4·0
10–20%	32	12·8
20–30%	12	4·8
30–40%	11	4·4
40–50%	8	3·2
More than 50%	22	8·8
Unquoted	16	6·4
Unknown	26	10·4
Totals	250	100·0

SOURCE: Nyman and Silberston (1978), table 1; see also Francis (1977).

NOTE: In the 10–20 per cent category I have included six companies which had in excess of 10 per cent of their shares held by single interests but for which the authors could give no precise figures.

In 1975, almost half of the top 250 British companies were minority-controlled or majority-owned. In sixty-two companies directors and their families held more than 5 per cent, and in another fifteen they were a dominant influence. In twenty-three companies another industrial company held a controlling block, and in nine companies financial interests had control. An important group is the ninety-eight companies in which Nyman and Silberston found no large block holdings. The immediate presumption is that they are management-controlled, though there is no evidence on which to base this judgement. Some indication that these companies may actually be controlled through a constellation of interests comes from a study of Scottish companies. As Table 21 shows, the extent of owner control was greater in Scotland than in Britain as a whole,[6] more than three-quarters being either majority-owned or minority-controlled. A study of those companies in which there were no dominant interests suggests that they might best be seen as controlled through a constellation of interests. The top twenty Scottish companies included seven which had no dominant interest and which would conventionally be classified as subject to management control. However, in four of these companies the twenty-five largest shareholders held between 20 and 30 per cent of the stock, and in the other three companies the major interests held between 40 and 50 per cent. This is strong evidence for the view that large corporations without dominant shareholding interests may be controlled through a constellation of interests.

Table 21   *Major shareholders in the largest Scottish companies (1973)*

Proportion held by a single large interest or by directors	*No. of companies*	*% of companies*
No dominant interest	50	22·7
5–10%	8	3·6
10–20%	19	8·6
20–50%	69	31·5
More than 50%	74	33·6
Totals	220	100·0

SOURCE: Scott and Hughes (1976), 28, table 4.

The evidence from Britain suggests a similar picture to that from the USA. Personal possession is giving way to impersonal possession, and control through a constellation of interests is becoming the characteristic mode of strategic control. In Britain the transition may have been a little later and a little slower, but the movement is in the same direction.

Further evidence: Europe, Australia and Canada

While there are fewer studies of ownership and control in countries other than the USA and Britain, it is possible to extend this discussion to other countries. Within mainland Europe, the best-studied countries are France and Belgium, though less systematic information is available on Germany and Scandinavia. Outside Europe a certain amount of data have been produced in studies of Australia and Canada.

In his study of French industry, Bleton points to a trend which corresponds to that identified in the USA and Britain. While it is still the case that wealthy controlling families exist, their direct stake in the companies which they control is lower than in the past. Extremely wealthy families such as Rothschild and Dassault still exist, but the majority of business families hold controlling positions for reasons in addition to their immediate shareholdings. The controlling families of the nineteenth century have spread their interests from one industry to another and have been joined by new entrepreneurial families which came to prominence between 1870 and 1914, and after 1945. The old dynastic families are supplemented rather than displaced, but as they become established their interests are dispersed and their proportionate share in each enterprise declines (Bleton 1966, 135–42). A more recent study by Morin confirms this view, and Table 22 presents his findings.

Half of the largest French industrials were family-controlled, most families having majority ownership or exclusive minority control. Morin argues that the significant number of family firms in which there is 'relative minority control' indicates that direct family control is being challenged by industrial and financial interests. Family control remains the main feature of French industry, as Bleton argued, though the size of family holdings in particular companies declined as firms grew in size (Morin 1974, 66, 79). The companies with corporate controllers (which Morin terms 'techno-cratic') include twenty-five companies controlled by financial interests and ten controlled by industrial interests, in both cases minority control being more likely than majority ownership (Citoleux *et al.* 1977, 59). Morin discovered that two banking monopolies played an important part in the corporation-controlled companies. Paribas directly controls fourteen companies and influences four others, and the Suez group directly controls nine companies and influences one other. In addition, the Banque d'Indochine, which

Table 22   *Strategic control in the 200 largest French industrial companies (1971)*

Mode of control	Type of controller					Totals
	Family	Corporate	State	Foreign	Cooperative	
Majority ownership	38	6	7	41	1	93
Exclusive minority control	43	13	1	9	0	66
Relative minority control	19	11	0	6	0	36
Internal control	—	5	—	—	—	5
Totals	100	35	8	56	1	200

SOURCE: Adapted from Morin (1974), 65, table 9.

NOTE: 'Relative minority control' refers to the situation where a minority controller is subjected to influence from other groups and is therefore similar to 'control through a constellation of interests'. Morin misleadingly allocates the five 'internal' (i.e. management) controlled companies to the column for corporate controllers.

became part of the Suez group in 1972, directly controls two companies and influences five others. These banking interests control all twenty-five of the corporations subject to financial control and are influential in ten of the thirty-six companies in situations of relative minority control (Morin 1974, 1977).

As Table 23 shows, the situation in Belgium is very similar to that in France. De Vroey discovered that the main corporate shareholder was the Société Générale de Belgique, which was the principal shareholder in most of the corporation-controlled companies. The SGB, a financial holding company, controlled twenty-five of the top 115 Belgian companies in 1969 and was joint-controller in a further eight. Among the top forty-one companies all eight companies which were dominated by corporate interests were controlled by the SGB, which also had a minority stake in two family firms and many others (De Vroey 1973, 112 ff.; 1975b, 7–8). De Vroey found that all the controlling groups were involved in strategic control, and he found no examples of companies subject to 'management control' in the strict sense.

Table 23 *Strategic control in forty-one large Belgian non-financial companies (1972)*

Proportion of shares held by principal owners	Type of controller				
	Family	Corporate	Foreign	Mixed	Totals
0–25%	0	0	0	1·5	1·5
25–49%	0	4	1	1	6
50–74%	2	2	1	3	8
75–99%	5	2	3	2	12
100%	0	0	11	0·5	11·5
Not known					2
Totals	7	8	16	8	41

SOURCE: De Vroey (1973), 119–20.

NOTE: The firm of Agfa-Gevaert is a union of a minority-controlled company and a wholly owned company, and so De Vroey allocated half to each category.

In both France and Belgium, family interests are supplemented by corporate interests, and in both countries financial corporations are predominant. As I shall show in the following chapter, these financial corporations are controlled through a constellation of interests. In both countries, however, direct family interests seem to be of greater importance than in Britain or the USA. In Belgium, families such as Solvay, Launoit, Empain, Coppée, Boel, Hallet and Gilson remain in dominant positions (CRISP 1962), and Bleton argues that a similar situation holds in France, Italy and Germany. A study of German industry found that families such as Krupp, Siemens, Klöckner, Flick and Quandt were dominant in forty-seven of the top 115 companies, and that three banks (Deutsche Bank, Dresdner Bank and Commerzbank) were dominant minority influences in fifty-one of these large companies (Marcus 1970, cited in Krejci 1976).

The survival of family influence and control is even more marked in Sweden and Norway. In Sweden, fifteen families and two corporations have majority ownership in 200 large industrial companies employing almost half of those employed in private industry. The Wallenberg family controlled seventy companies, including Electrolux, Scania, Saab, Swedish Match, Alfa-Laval and SKF, employing 20 per cent of private employees (Tomasson 1970). An official investigation for 1963–4 discovered that the twenty largest shareholders in each of the top 282 companies held between 41 and

86 per cent of the stock. The study concluded that the degree of concentration was so high that 'In no company quoted on the stock exchange were more than ten shareholders required to obtain the majority of votes' (Commission on Concentration 1968, 37; Gustavsen 1976). In Norway in 1963, 80 per cent of companies in manufacturing and services, except shipping, were personally owned and employed two-fifths of the labour force in these sectors. Almost all companies in primary industries and shipping were personally owned (Higley *et al.* 1976, 131–2).[7] Even in corporations, family control was marked: in 1963, 85 per cent of corporations had a pattern of share distribution such that the twenty largest shareholders owned 50 per cent or more of the stock, and two-thirds of these large holders were individuals or personally owned companies. In a total of 22 per cent of the corporations, a majority of the shares were held by fewer than ten people (ibid., 132). Discussing studies by Hermansson and Maurseth, Seierstad argues that in both Norway and Sweden elite families control strategic decisions (Seierstad 1968, 100–1).

In Europe, it would seem, the extent of direct family control is greater than in the USA, though the extent varies considerably from country to country. France, Belgium and Germany would seem to be following the same line of development as Britain and the USA, but each country is at a different stage of development. Outside Europe, studies of Australia and Canada confirm the idea that the transition from personal to impersonal possession is a generic feature of the development of industrial capitalism. Table 24 gives basic ownership and control data for Australia and Canada.

Table 24   *Strategic control in Australian and Canadian companies* (*1955 and 1960*)

	Number of companies	
Mode of control	Australia (1955)	Canada (1960)
Private ownership	2	11
Majority ownership	6	16
Minority control	33	23
Management control	32	3
Not known	0	11
Totals	73	64

SOURCE: Wheelwright (1957) and Porter (1965), 589, table 12.

Porter's study shows that sixty-four large corporations accounted for most of the output of Canadian industry (Porter 1965, 233). Within these corporations, the extent of owner control would seem to be greater than in the USA and Britain and to be very similar to that in France. By contrast, the figures for the dominant Australian corporations are similar to those for US companies, although Wheelwright argues that the apparently 'managerial' corporations are in fact controlled by the original dynastic families. It may be suggested that many of these 'managerial' corporations are in fact controlled through a constellation of interests (Wheelwright 1957; 1974, 131; Connell 1976). In both Canada and Australia there is, furthermore, an extremely high degree of foreign ownership, and the complexities in which this results will be discussed in a later chapter.

The evidence presented in this chapter documents the continuing connection between 'ownership' and 'control'. The legal form of the joint-stock company has undoubtedly affected the modes and mechanisms through which strategic control is exercised, but it has not resulted in the dispossession of all shareholders. The major shareholding interests still have effective possession of corporate capital and are able to determine corporate strategy. What seems to have occurred is a transition from 'personal' to more 'impersonal' forms of possession and control. Direct family control through majority ownership has given way to control through a constellation of interests. This process of development is nowhere complete, but it is certainly most advanced in the USA. The various countries began the transition at different times and so have reached different stages, and it is for this reason that the balance between the various modes of control differs from one country to another.

The theory of industrial society recognizes the changing legal forms of ownership, but it fails to recognize the 'social function' of the law. The joint-stock company has created the conditions for social relations of effective possession which do not correspond to legal relations of ownership. But effective possession and strategic control are not merely matters of 'authority' relations at work, as Dahrendorf and Bendix have suggested. Nor does there seem to be any great evidence that internal operational managers have displaced the owners of capital as the controllers of corporate strategy. I have suggested that many of those corporations which have been classified as subject to management control, and which the theory of industrial society sees as the characteristic type of modern corporate enterprise, can best be seen as controlled through a constellation of interests. Effective possession is held by a loose grouping of major shareholders, who may nevertheless delegate some aspects of strategic control to professional managers or to the old controlling families. But these latter groups can achieve no real autonomy from those in effective possession. I would suggest that all the capitalist industrial societies are undergoing a transition from private family control to control through a constellation of interests. In the course of this transition, the board of each company will gradually come to reflect the balance of power among those in effective possession, though at any particular point in time it may appear that managers or families are in control.

The evidence presented here suggests that family ownership is still important, not merely as a 'survival' from the past but as an integral part of the modern economy. Furthermore, I have not yet said a great deal about the identity of the financial interests involved in the constellations of major shareholders. If it is the case that industrial corporations are controlled by financial interests, it is necessary to investigate the nature of control in financial corporations. If financial companies are controlled by families, then the transition identified in this chapter with respect to industrial companies is of secondary importance. If financial companies are management-controlled, then the theory of industrial society is back in the running. The next chapter asks: who controls the financial corporations?

4 Finance capital and strategic control

The development of industrial capitalism has involved a move away from personal possession to impersonal possession. Individual and family ownership of industrial and commercial companies has gradually been supplemented by the interweaving interests of financial companies, and the latter are becoming the most important bases of strategic control. 'Control through a constellation of interests' becomes the most characteristic mode of control in large industrial corporations in modern capitalism. This apparent dominance of financial interests over industrial interests is the origin of various notions of 'finance capital'. Marx (1894) emphasized the role of the 'credit system' in bringing about the separation of 'money capital' from 'productive capital'. Hilferding (1910) elaborated this argument and proposed that the monopolization of banking led to the fusion of 'bank capital' and 'industrial capital' into the new form of finance capital. Capitalist monopolies, argued Hilferding, had become financial complexes with both banking and industrial interests, though these monetary interests were almost completely dissociated from the actual production process. Capital without productive functions is pure money capital (*Geldkapital*). With the rise of the joint-stock company, a large number of companies can be possessed through mere majority ownership, and so the number of capitalists falls. There emerges a small circle of persons in whom the power of monopolized capital is concentrated. These finance capitalists control other people's capital and are united through interlocking directorships (*Personalunion*) between the industrial enterprises and the banks. The banks are the mechanisms through which the fusion of the various spheres of monopolized capital is brought about (Hilferding 1910, 132 ff.; Renner 1904, 144 ff.).

Hilferding's work was the basis of Lenin's (1917a) analysis of finance capital, and it is this version of the idea which is contained in the theory of capitalist society. It is held that large 'empires' of finance capital arise, and that these groupings are 'a method by which a handful of financial magnates can establish and extend their rule over a vast number of industrial, financial and other enterprises' (Ryndina and Chernikov 1974, 182). The nucleus of the financial empire is a closely interlinked group of monopolies which pursues a common policy and exerts control over a large number of operating companies in various branches of the economy (Aaronovitch 1955, 12, 54 ff.; Rochester 1936, 104). As capitalism develops, so these financial groupings are transformed 'from purely family groups into broad coalitions consisting of many families of financial magnates' (Ryndina and Chernikov 1974, 186; Rochester 1936, 104–6; Menshikov 1969, 216). The typical large corporation 'is run by a tiny clique of large shareholders and their banker-associates' (Perlo 1957, 37). A 'parasitic' financial oligarchy controls money capital, and thereby controls production in an indirect way by determining when and if capital will be available for further accumulation.

In this chapter I shall assess whether the concept of finance capital has any application to contemporary reality. I shall investigate whether those who exercise strategic control in large corporations do so as representatives of 'finance capital' centred in the banks and other financial companies. I shall examine the relation of the financial sector to the industrial sector and discuss whether this relation can be described in terms of the concept of finance capital.[1]

Who controls the controllers?

In the previous chapter I discussed the growing importance of 'institutional' shareholdings. In this section I shall discuss this in more detail and assess the patterns of strategic control in financial companies themselves. Table 25 shows that in the USA over 90 per cent of shareholdings have been held by individuals throughout the period 1922–59, though the value of these individual shareholdings has fallen from 65 to 53 per cent of total value. (See also: Goldsmith 1958; Baum and Stiles 1965, 31 ff., 54–5.)

Perlo argues that, while many institutional holders are concerned with insurance and pension benefits, 'the great bulk of financial institution stockholdings are of a character that cannot by any stretch of the imagination be regarded as representing ownership by masses of the population', and he adds that 'institutional holdings, in fact, reinforce the extreme concentration of stock-ownership in the hands of a small minority in the upper-income brackets' (Perlo 1958, 30). Though not going as far as Perlo, the Patman Committee

Table 25 *Ownership of US company shares (1922–59)*

| | 1922 | | 1952 | | 1959 | |
| | % of holdings | % of value | % of holdings | % of value | % of holdings | % of value |
Type of holder						
Individuals	92·1	65·0	92·1	57·6	91·8	53·4
Fiduciaries	3·4	10·4	4·5	6·9	4·5	7·2
Brokers and dealers	1·7	11·9	1·1	10·4	1·1	8·5
Nominees	—	—	0·6	9·9	0·8	12·6
Companies and institutions	2·8	12·7	1·7	15·2	1·8	18·3
Totals	100·0	100·0	100·0	100·0	100·0	100·0

SOURCE: Adapted from Cox (1963), 52, table 3.

felt obliged to point out that 'the trend of the last 30 or 40 years toward a separation of ownership from control because of the fragmentation of stock ownership has been radically changed towards a concentration of voting power in the hands of a relatively few financial institutions, while the fragmentation in the distribution of cash payments has been continued' (Patman Report 1968, 13). The report argues that this trend towards 'bank minority control' – or control through a constellation of interests – brings industry into a close relationship with the banks. The significance of this is brought out by Blumberg, who found that in 1969 financial companies held at least 10 per cent of the stock of the top ten US corporations, and that in eight of these companies financial interests held between 30 and 40 per cent. All except one of these ten companies had been classified by Larner (1970) as 'management controlled'. IBM, the largest US corporation at that time, had 10 per cent of its stock held by three financial companies, 15 per cent held by six, and 20 per cent held by ten (Blumberg 1975, 98–9).

Evidence on the proportion of shares held by individuals and institutions in Britain has already been given (Table 19), and I have suggested that this supports the view that control through a constellation of interests is becoming the predominant mode of control. The data in Table 26 show that the size of these holdings is so great that institutions are unable to sell the shares which they own without affecting their market price. The proportion of market value held by individuals has fallen from just over half in 1963 to just over a third in 1975. The main increase in non-personal holdings has been in holdings by pension funds and unit trusts.

Table 26   *Ownership of U K company shares (1963–75)*

Type of holder	Proportion of market value held		
	1963	*1969*	*1975*
Personal	54·0	47·4	37·5
Insurance companies	10·0	12·2	15.9
Pension funds	6·4	9·0	16·8
Unit trusts	1·3	2·9	4·1
Investment trusts	10·0	8·7	10·0
Banks	1·3	1·7	0·7
Totals	83·0	81·9	85·0

SOURCE: Erritt and Alexander (1977), cited in Wilson Report (1977). For similar estimates see Diamond Report (1975*b*), 16–17.

On the basis of evidence such as this, the Diamond Report remarks that 'individuals as a group have been turning away from direct investment in industry and placing their savings with pension funds, life insurance companies, unit trusts, etc., which in turn invest them in industry' (1975*b*, 79). However, the argument of the previous chapter suggests – as Perlo and the Patman Report claim for the USA – that 'indirect' investment in industry by individuals is not the same thing as participation in strategic control. Although the Prudential Assurance Company has a large minority holding in the Distillers Company, those who have their lives insured with 'the Pru' have no appreciable control over the strategy followed by Distillers.[2] Who, then, does own and control the financial 'institutions'?

In a study carried out in the 1960s, Vernon followed Larner's methods and analysed ownership and control in the major US commercial banks. As Table 27 shows, the majority of banks were classified as 'management-controlled', and Vernon found that the larger the bank, the more likely it was to be subject to management control (Vernon 1970, 654). The forty-four which were owner-controlled accounted for only 10 per cent of bank assets. By contrast, the 149 which were management-controlled accounted for 87·5 per cent of assets.

Table 27 *Strategic control in the 200 largest member banks, USA (1962)*

Mode of control	No. of banks	% of banks	% of assets
Private ownership	1	0·5	0·1
Majority control	4	2·0	0·6
Minority control:			
(a) 20–50%	22	11·0	6·2
(b) 10–20%	17	8·5	3·1
Management control	149	74·5	87·5
Not known	7	3·5	2·5
Totals	200	100·0	100·0

SOURCE: Adapted from Vernon (1970), 654, table 1.

NOTE: 'Member Banks' refers to those banks which are members of the Federal Reserve System, i.e. all the major commercial banks.

Vernon's study can, of course, be criticized in the same way as Larner's study. In particular, it is necessary to consider whether the banks classified as subject to management control are actually controlled through a constellation of interests. The main source of evidence on this is the series of reports produced by the Patman Committee. It was found that, in Chevalier's words, 'the most important shareholders of the banks are the banks themselves' (Chevalier 1970, 115). In 1966, almost all of the top 210 banks held some of their own shares, over half held more than 5 per cent, and over a quarter held more than 10 per cent of their own shares. As Table 28 shows, this was true even for the largest banks. Additionally, there were significant cross-holdings of bank shares: each of the top six New York banks had between 12 and 20 per cent of its shares held either by itself or by the other five banks. Each of these banks might appropriately be seen as controlled through a constellation of interests.

A high proportion of bank shares was held by other financials. Almost half of the top 275 banks had 5 per cent or more of their shares held by other financial companies with full voting rights, and a third of the banks had other commercial banks in a position of minority control. Furthermore, some banks had effective control over 'satellite banks' in their own region, even though they were not subsidiaries (Patman Report 1966, 833, 878). This pattern of cross-shareholding is reinforced by the fact that individual and family holdings link banks together: 'there appear to be situations where

Table 28   *Inter-bank shareholdings in the top ten US banks (1966)*

Bank	Proportion of shares held by top ten banks
1 Bank of America	2·23
2 Chase Manhattan	2·30
3 First National City Bank	4·26
4 Manufacturers Hanover	7·37
5 Morgan Guaranty Trust	7·75
6 Chemical Bank New York Trust	5·79
7 Bankers Trust	8·26
8 Continental Illinois National Bank	5·48
9 Security First National Bank	6·46
10 First National Bank	15·15

SOURCE: Patman Report (1966), 817, table VI.

the beneficial owners of large blocks of commercial bank stock are in fact holdings by a few families who have management connections with competitor banks in the same geographical area' (ibid., 879). An interesting discovery was the fact that subsidiary banks tend to hold shares in their own bank holding companies, and also in the holding companies of other banks (Patman Report 1967, 918 ff.). As Chevalier argues, 'the American banks are linked amongst themselves by an extremely dense network of financial participations' (1970, 117). Many banks are controlled through a constellation of interests and are themselves members of the constellations controlling other banks. If this is taken into account alongside the evidence on minority control and majority ownership which Vernon established, a complex picture emerges. Chevalier, for example, has argued that among the 26 banks which were important shareholders in the top 200 industrial companies, 3 were closely controlled by families, 8 were influenced or controlled by other banks and financials and the rest owned substantial amounts of their own shares, though also being subject to influence from other interests (ibid., 121).

A similar picture of the control of controlling financial interests comes in evidence from France and Belgium. Morin analysed the top banks in France and discovered that, apart from the five nationalized banks, there were eight family banks and ten which were controlled by other corporations. The two main banks are, it will be recalled, Paribas and Suez, both heading large industrial groups. In Suez, the board of directors is based upon reciprocal shareholdings between Suez, SGPM (Saint-Gobain – Pont-à-Mousson), and companies which they control. In Paribas, Morin found no dominant interests and a wide dispersal of shares (Morin 1974, 198). Each company had a large board, half the membership being external directors who had no executive functions but were present as representatives of other financial interests. Suez may certainly be classified as controlled through a constellation of interests, and Paribas is probably management-controlled. Morin argues that both companies are part of a complex network of interests and that an analysis which focuses merely on shareholdings is insufficient. 'Without doubt, the relative separation of property and power is the principal aspect of the functioning of these two companies, but there is no question of ignoring the interests which represent at one and the same time the largest shareholders and the most important allies of the two companies' (ibid., 203). In Belgium, the dominant controller is the Société Générale de Belgique, which operates, like Suez and Paribas, in many industrial sectors. De Vroey argues that the SGB group is an extensive network in which there is little centralization. Those who own the active 10 per cent of its shares are the very corporations which are controlled by the SGB itself – there is no principal owner as such (De Vroey 1973, 145–6; Cuyvers and Meeusen 1976, 1978; Daems 1975). The complex crossing of holdings means that, while the SGB has influence and minority control in a number of industrial concerns, it is itself controlled through a constellation of interests composed of these same industrial concerns. The SGB has achieved a certain autonomy from particular ownership interests, yet this is not the autonomy which Berle and Means (1932) believed to be characteristic of the management-controlled corporation. The constellation of interests in which the SGB is enmeshed comprises a specific set of interests to which it must adapt (De Vroey 1973, 157).

In the USA, Britain and elsewhere, an increasingly important part in the financial sector is played by 'mutual' companies. These companies have no share capital and are 'owned' by those who benefit from their operations – insurance policy holders, pension contributors, unit holders, and so on. Because of this, it is possible that the management of mutual companies can achieve a relative insulation from control by their beneficiaries. That is, they can be regarded as subject to 'management control'. Morin has shown that even a company like Paribas, which is management-controlled, is constrained by a constellation of financial interests which do not have direct ownership-based control over the company but exercise a dominant influence over its activities.

A major investigation into mutual life insurance companies carried out by the US Temporary National Economic Committee in the 1930s confirms this view of management-controlled companies. Gessell and Howe (1941, 13) found that in 1938 there were 297 life insurance companies operating in the USA, seventy-four being mutual companies. These seventy-four accounted for 80 per cent of all life insurance assets. Only one of the ten largest insurance companies was a stock company. Perlo claims that mutualization of a stock company involves an attempt to reinforce the position of the dominant group: 'The group in control at the time of mutualization of the stock company maintains its position through a self-perpetuating board of directors' (Perlo 1957, 82). The study by Gessell and Howe shows that this is true for all mutual companies. They argue that 'the putative rights of the policyholders to select and elect directors are of no practical value. The directors are completely self-perpetuating' (Gessell and Howe 1941, 14). The directors have control over nominations and elections, and it is extremely difficult for a rival candidate to enter the lists. Companies were found to give inadequate information about voting. In the 1937 elections, the proportion of policy holders voting on the largest companies ranged from 0·01 to 2·51 per cent, most of the votes cast being those of employees who were also policy holders (ibid., 16). In the companies with the highest vote there was considerable evidence of forgery of signatures, even though the elections were uncontested and only one affirmative vote was needed for the re-election of all those nominated (ibid., 18–20). All these features of the voting and proxy systems preclude effective policy-holder participation. Gessell and Howe give an example of a typical case where only a portion of the directors stand for re-election each year. In such cases, an opposition group must win at two or three successive elections in order to gain a majority on the board. In the same way as the small shareholders in joint-stock companies, the policy holders in mutual companies are effectively disenfranchised.

Who, then, does control the mutual companies? Gessell and Howe show that the top five companies had 135 directors who sat on the boards of 100 other insurance companies, 145 other financial companies and 534 non-financial companies (ibid., 29). The most important multiple directors were those from the major New York commercial banks, who had a considerable influence over the investment of insurance company funds. Gessell and Howe argue that 'the relationship is so close that it may be said that a single group of directors has a substantial voice in determining the policies of the two most powerful financial enterprises in this country, insurance and banking' (ibid., 34). That is, the management-controlled mutual companies had their management drawn from the management of the large commercial banks. Mutual companies participate in the constellations and coalitions which control other companies, and they are themselves controlled by these same constellations of interests.

The evidence presented in this section shows that the trend towards 'impersonal' forms of possession and control is as characteristic of financial companies as it is of industrials. The question now to be answered is whether there is evidence to support the idea that bank-centred finance capital dominates the economy.

From financial empires to spheres of influence

The formative period for relations between the financial and industrial sectors in the USA was the late nineteenth and early twentieth century. The period from 1896 to 1905 was marked by the social and economic power of the business 'tycoon' and the financial 'magnate' (Veblen 1904). At the end of the nineteenth century the main growth area was railway development. The promotion and expansion of railways was the preserve of the investment bankers and served as the basis of the financial empires which they headed (Chandler 1962). After the depression of the 1890s manufacturing industry began to expand on a large scale, and this industrial growth took place under the aegis of the established Wall Street banking groups (Sweezy 1940, 1941). Investment bankers were important throughout the phase of company formation, mergers and expansion because of the specific services they could offer and, above all, because of their ability to mobilize the savings of individuals and make them available to industry. Between 1896 and 1905 many 'cartels' and 'trusts' were formed – associations and alliances between formally independent corporations which were intended to maximize the advantages to be gained from the expanding economy. During the early years of the century considerable public disquiet was expressed about the emerging 'money trust' or 'financial oligarchy', which many of a liberal persuasion saw as a threat to the competitive market economy (Pratt 1905; Brandeis 1914; Pujo Report 1913).

This concern stimulated both anti-trust legislation and also official and academic investigation of the powers of the banks in relation to industry.

Bunting and Barbour (1971) argue that between 1896 and 1905 many large corporations were drawn together through the device of the 'interlocking directorship'.[3] Relations of strategic control between companies were expressed in the sharing of a director. In 1905, as Table 29 shows, almost 18 per cent of the directors of the top 200 companies were multiple directors sitting on two or more boards, and a significant number sat on more than five boards.

Table 29   *Interlocking directorships in the top 200 US corporations (1905–64)*

No. of director-ships per person	1905		1935		1964	
	No. of people	No. of director-ships	No. of director-ships	No. of people	No. of director-ships	No. of director-ships
1	1838	1838	2347	2347	2998	2998
2	224	448	250	500	288	576
3	93	279	76	228	80	240
4	32	128	28	112	18	72
5	15	75	11	55	11	55
6 or more	30	229	6	43	2	13
Totals	2232	2997	2718	3285	3397	3954

SOURCE: Adapted from Bunting and Barbour (1971), 324, table 2.

The degree of interlocking increased from 1896 to 1905 and probably remained fairly high for some years. Writing in 1914, Brandeis argued that 'The practice of interlocking directorates is the root of many evils. It offends laws human and divine' (1914, 35). Brandeis showed that such interlocks expressed the dominance of a New York-based money trust, involving the financial empires of J. P. Morgan, the First National Bank, the National City Bank, and their satellites (ibid., 28–9; Pujo Report 1913, II, 1102–3). Interlocking within financial empires was complemented by interlocks between empires, and Brandeis argued that interlocks create a 'vicious circle of control': 'The chain is indeed endless; for each controlled corporation is entwined with many others' (Brandeis 1914, 38).

Investment bankers remained dominant until the depression years of the 1930s. Their power declined rapidly after 1929 owing to the decline in the pace of economic expansion. But there were also deeper causes in operation. The established industrial companies were able to exploit their advantageous market positions so as to secure internal resources for expansion and were able, in a period of restricted expansion, to dispense with the services of the investment bankers. At the same time, the growth of institutional investment and the associated 'private placement' of company shares bypassed the role of the banker as dealer in corporate stock (Gordon 1945, 214–16; Sweezy 1941, 190–3; 1942, 267). By the 1930s, as shown in Table 29, the proportion of multiple directors had fallen to 14 per cent, and Bunting and Barbour see this as evidence that the power of the financial magnates had begun to decline. Sweezy's study for the National Resources Committee analysed data for 1935 and found that there were at least eight 'interest groups' among the top 200 corporations, those associated with Morgan, Rockefeller and Mellon being particularly prominent (Sweezy 1939, 168; Rochester 1936, chapters 2–5; Anderson *et al.* 1941, 25; Goldsmith and Parmelee 1940, 129–30). In these interest groups, strategic control was exercised through a complex mix of family majority interests, minority holdings and bank credit. Sweezy argues that the period of banker dominance from 1890 to 1929 was a period of transition from 'competitive' to 'oligopolistic' markets, and he claims that Hilferding mistook a transitional phase of capitalist development for a lasting trend (Sweezy 1942, 267–8; Means *et al.* 1939; Poland 1939).

By the 1960s the power of the banks had declined even further. Villarejo found that 11 per cent of the directors of top US corporations were multiple directors (1961*b*, 54–5), and he argued that the data suggested that interest groups of some kind still existed. A study by Warner and Unwalla confirms this view, arguing that the interest groups showed a territorial pattern of 'a giant national wheel of interlocking directorates with the New York hub dominating the many spokes that spread out from and back to it' (1967, 146). Villarejo (1961*b*, 60) argues that the centres of power were not financial empires but 'communities of interest': 'Many of the corporations here considered were launched by a single family, and yet, over the years through mergers and acquisitions these enterprises have had to reach an understanding with other enterprises, as well as with financial interests'. There were 'communities' with 'centres', but there were few if any 'empires'. Dooley compared the pattern in 1965 with that of 1935 (see Table 30) and found that among the top 250 companies there was little evidence that the overall extent of interlocking had decreased. The fifteen regional interest groups, which included the eight identified by Sweezy, still exhibited the characteristic structure of a financial core surrounded by industrial and utility companies, though these groupings were less compact than they had been thirty years before (Dooley 1969, 320–1).

Table 30 *Interlocking directorships in the top 250 US Corporations (1935–65)*

No of directorships per person	No. of people	
	1935	1965
1	2234	2603
2	303	372
3	102	123
4	48	49
5	19	13
6 or more	16	5
Totals	2722	3165

SOURCE: Dooley (1969), 315, table 1.

Comparison of Table 30 with Table 29 shows an apparent disagreement about the trend from 1935 to the mid-1960s. Bunting and Barbour show that the proportion of multiple directors fell from 14 to 12 per cent, while Dooley finds that it is fairly constant at 18 per cent. The difference in the size of the figures can be attributed to differences in the selection of companies, but Bunting and Barbour make great play of the fact that their data show a downward trend, while Dooley's suggest a constant level of interlocking. However, a 2 point fall in thirty years, measured in terms of cross-sectional data, can hardly be regarded as a significant trend. Both studies agree that the number of people with more than six directorships fell, and both agree that the actual number of people involved in the interlocking directorate increased substantially. According to Dooley, the number of industrial companies with connections to financial companies increased over the period: more industrial companies were drawn into the existing corporate network

(Dooley 1969, 315, table 2). A related study by Allen also suggested that the overall density of the corporate network had remained fairly constant from 1935 to 1970 and that interlocking between financial and industrial companies had increased (1974, 404). Bunting and Barbour (1971, 330–4) suggest that the increase in financial-industrial interlocks is associated with a decrease in the total number of interlocks for each company. On the one hand, the 'endless chain' identified by Brandeis has grown to encompass more and more companies; and, on the other hand, the interlocked companies have a less intense relationship with one another (Fennema and Schijf 1978, 11–12; Baran and Sweezy 1966, 31). Menshikov attempts to show that financial groups are still an important feature of the economy, though he also recognizes that the groups are more diffuse (Menshikov 1969, 229; Chevalier 1970, 123 ff.). Financial groups are seen as alliances which do not eliminate the differing interests of the various corporations, and their changing composition over time and cross-cutting joint ventures generate a 'condominium system' of groupings with relatively open boundaries:

The evolution of control . . . signifies that family financial groups must gradually either vanish or become dissolved in broader financial associations, in which there is no domination of one family, nor can there be any. Joint control, whatever its form, implies a more or less solidly formed alliance, association or co-operation of several families, banks, and corporations [Menshikov 1969, 216–21].

A diffuse network of companies had evolved, within which more intense, bank-centred groupings could be identified. In this network, commercial banks and corporate law firms play an important role (Smith 1970, 48–9; Smith and Desfosses 1972, 66; Patman Report 1967, 965; Antitrust Committee 1965). The problem thrown up by the studies discussed is stated by Bearden *et al.* (1975, 14): 'while past research indicates that banks play a particular role within the corporate structure, the nature of that role is not understood'.

Bearden and his co-workers on a number of related projects in the USA have studied interlocking directorships over the period 1962–73. They argue that when all interlocks among top companies are investigated an extensive network of companies with little sign of grouping is discovered. If, however, only those interlocks involving individuals who hold office in a corporation are examined, regional groupings become apparent. There seems to be an overall national network which is extensive but loosely connected, together with dense regional groupings associated with intercorporate shareholdings, common ownership, indebtedness, economic interdependence, etc. (ibid., 50). In a study of the national network in 1970, Mariolis found that 94 per cent of the 797 corporations studied were linked into an extensive corporate network. While financial companies were the most heavily interlocked, banks were more central than insurance companies (Mariolis 1975, 433–5) The 1969 data analysed by Sonquist *et al.* confirm the existence of regional groupings. Evidence was found for thirty-two region-based groupings ranging in size from three to fifteen corporations and having a structure comprising a financial core and an industrial periphery. Most of the groups overlapped one another, and a large New York group overlapped eleven others. More than half of the central corporations were banks, and in almost half of the groups a single bank was central. Most groups had at least one bank and one insurance company at their core (Sonquist *et al.* 1976, 70; 1975). These studies suggest the coexistence of national and regional linking. As Bearden *et al.* put it,

. . . the integration of New York, Boston, Philadelphia and California centers of business into a national and even international network of corporations has occurred simultaneously with the maintenance and further development of interest groups which continue to organize and coordinate intercorporate cooperation and control [Bearden *et al.* 1975, 50; Mintz and Schwartz 1978].

The three most central corporations in the national network are banks (Morgan Guaranty, Chase Manhattan, First National City Bank), and seven of the ten most central corporations are banks. The twenty most central corporations include eight banks and three insurance companies (Bearden *et al.* 1975, 54). The basic structure of the national network is due to the continuing centrality of banks: while the central industrial companies varied from year to year, four-fifths of the central banks in 1962 were still central in 1969. Bearden *et al.* conclude that 'banks are the foundation of intercorporate networks. While other firms may rise into momentary prominence and a few remain there for some years, the major commercial banks persist from year to year' (ibid., 59). In the regional groups, four of the five most central, and seven of the twenty most central corporations were banks. The five major groups all had banks at their core, being centred around Continental Illinois National Bank, Mellon National Bank, Morgan Guaranty Trust, Bankers Trust and United Californian Bank (ibid., 66; Levine 1972; Knowles 1973).

Examining the US economy from the 1890s to the present shows clear evidence of a changing relationship between the financial and industrial sectors. The huge financial empires have declined rapidly since the 1930s, yet banks, insurance companies and industrials are still grouped into 'communities of interest' or spheres of influence. Financial-industrial relations are no longer characterized by the dominance of an all-powerful banking oligarchy. Is this development unique to the USA, or is it a generic feature of industrial capitalism?

In Britain, the nineteenth century was marked by a sharp division between the financial interests of the City of London, who concentrated their activities on government loans and foreign stock (including the American railways), and the industrial concerns of the Midlands and the North. Manufacturing industry was, by and large, self-financing from the personal wealth of the owners. The individual entrepreneur and his family and associates provided capital for accumulation, and local banks supplied short-term working capital (Rubinstein 1976; Mathias 1969; Longstreth 1977*b*; Payne 1967, 1974). The financial interests, particularly the merchant bankers, had developed in relation to agrarian and mercantile capitalism and were particularly involved in state finances and trade with the British Empire. For this reason, landowners were an important element in the financial sector (Moore 1966; Anderson 1964; Nairn 1972; Hobsbawm 1968). Towards the end of the nineteenth century the merchant bankers became a little more interested in the expanding industrial sector, and from 1887 to 1917 the many localized commercial banks crystallized into a system of eleven major banks, this system remaining stable until the 1960s (Stanworth and Giddens 1975, 7). During the 1920s and 1930s the diminishing empire and the declining opportunities for profitable foreign investment led merchant banks to be more concerned with domestic industrial investment and the boom in company formations and mergers following the First World War cemented this relationship (Clarke 1967; Pollard 1962; Rubinstein 1976). Table 31 shows that the proportion of multiple directors in the largest companies in the USA and the UK was similar in the 1930s. Three-quarters of the directors of large companies in Britain were multiple directors, and these men connected 56 of the 98 large companies studied by Florence (1961, 88). Interlocked companies most commonly had one multiple director on their boards, though a significant number had two or three.

Although the level of interlocking in the largest companies was

Table 31   *Multiple directors in large
companies: USA and UK (1936–7)*

No. of directorships	% of people	
per person	USA	UK
1–5	72·5	70
6–10	17·5	17
More than 10	10·0	13
Totals	100·0	100

SOURCE: Florence (1953).
NOTE: The US data come from the TNEC study.

comparable with that for the USA it is almost certain that the general
degree of interlocking was far less. The merchant and commercial
banks were certainly acquiring an important role in relation to
industrial development, and much concern has since been expressed
about the 'hold' of the City over industry (Radcliffe Report 1959;
Simon 1962). However, there is little evidence that banks were forming large financial empires on the American model. After the Second
World War, the financial-industrial relationship grew closer as
concentration and mergers in each sector, and between sectors,
brought about a greater overall economic concentration. Studies
carried out in the 1950s and 1960s suggest that 10 or more 'interest
groups' had formed around major banks and insurance companies
(Barratt Brown 1968a, 58–60; Aaronovitch 1961, 78 ff.). Aaronovitch argues that groupings such as those centred around Morgan
Grenfell (itself a subsidiary of Morgan Guaranty Trust), Rothschilds,
Lazards, Barclays, Lloyds and Jardine Matheson are alliances which
are occasionally subject to a common policy but which at least try
to avoid competition within groups (Aaronovitch 1961, 79;
Stanworth and Giddens 1975). In 1971, Whitley found that the
financial companies of the City of London formed a highly connected network which had close links to the top industrial companies,
although the network of industrial companies was not itself so
tightly connected as the financial network (1973, 623–4). The
industrial companies which were relatively isolated from the network
tended to be the 'tycoon'- or 'family'-dominated companies, although
these companies were linked into the network through indirect
interlocks. Family-owned companies were less interlocked than those
subject to 'external' or management control (Whitley 1974).[4]

In Britain, as in the USA, a close relationship exists between finance and industry. The integration of the two sectors has in each country been accelerated during periods of industrial expansion and company formation. In the USA industrial empires centred around particular banking interests were formed early on and have gradually given way to more diffuse spheres of influence. Britain shows little evidence of such empires, although the financial sector has come to play a more and more important part in relation to industry. In both countries, formative periods for financial-industrial relations were at the turn of the century and during the 1920s, although the relationship was not particularly close in Britain until the later period and was not consolidated until after the Second World War. The early intense relationship between the two sectors in the USA was probably a major reason for the rapid decline of the investment banker in the 1930s. Both countries show a movement away from small-scale businesses providing their own investment funds, towards large-scale businesses which are provided with funds from outside. Whereas investment funds in the small firm derive from the entrepreneur himself and from his family and associates, the large corporation acquires its investment funds as an 'advance' as 'finance', in the form of share capital, loan stock or bank credit. In this sense, and to this extent, the concept of 'finance capital' captures an important dimension of the transformation which industrial capitalism is experiencing. The growth of the whole 'credit system' leads to fundamental changes in investment funding (Edwards 1938; Hussain 1976). Both Britain and the USA are moving from entrepreneurial capital to finance capital, though they are moving at different rates and have followed different routes.

Germany, like much of mainland Europe, shows evidence of yet another route and another tempo. The banks in Germany sponsored industrial development from the very beginning, and the extremely close relationship, first pointed out by Jeidels (1905), was the exemplar for Hilferding's discussion of finance capital. The very close relationship between banks and industry intensified continually from 1900 to the late 1920s, though the direct power of the bankers declined after 1918 (Fennema and Schijf 1978). A study of 365 German firms in 1970 analysed company groupings in terms of intercorporate shareholdings and found that there were thirteen interrelated groups. The links between groups were banks such as Commerzbank and Dresdner Bank, and also industrials such as Mannesman Röhren and Thyssen. While one group was purely financial, being concerned with insurance and investment, most groups spread across both financial and industrial concerns (Farace and Wigand 1975, 10). A similar pattern was found by Mokken and Stokman in their study of Dutch companies in 1969. These researchers found a highly connected network in which financial companies were central. In a detailed investigation of the financial sector they found that the commercial banks were a group which created more links with other companies than did any other group (Mokken and Stokman 1974, 12). Among the twelve most central financial companies, four appeared as high points – two commercial banks (ABN, Mees and Hope), one insurance company (Delta Lloyd) and one mortgage bank (Westland-Utrecht).[5]

In Japan also an early and very close relationship existed between financial and industrial operations. From the Meiji period to the Second World War the Japanese economy was characterized by dynastic financial-industrial complexes (the *zaibatsu*), together with less dynastic industrial combines. These extensive and diverse business empires were family-owned and family-controlled, although state involvement was always important (Halliday 1975, 53–60; Hadley 1970, 20–4; Noguchi 1973, 85). Predominant were the four great *zaibatsu* – Mitsui, Mitsubishi, Sumitomo and Yasuda. During the 1920s and 1930s the controlling families moved away from private and majority ownership to minority control and so were able to draw on outside capital without giving up control (Hadley 1970, 66–7, 255; W. W. Lockwood 1964). Hadley (1970, 23) argues that 'Companies of a combine or *zaibatsu* were not operated for their individual advantage but collectively for the advantage of the top holding company'. The holding company was invariably a bank, and the companies comprising the combine were linked through ownership, interlocking directorships, intra-combine credit relations and centralized trading relations. Following the Second World War and the US attempt to break up the old *zaibatsu*, various changes occurred, though all four major groups and many of the smaller ones remain important today. In 1946 the big four accounted for 25 per cent of capital in Japanese companies, with a further 16 per cent of industrial capital held by the next six largest groups. Today, the thirteen largest combines account for 75 per cent of the sales of the top 170 firms (Halliday 1975, 180, 275). However, the degree of coordination within combines is far less, and the old family holdings are often matched by the holdings of outsiders (Hadley 1970, 215; 1975, 180; Noguchi 1973, 88 ff.). The banks remain the foci of the groups though they are not dominated by particular families and their relationships to other financial and industrial companies within the combines are neither so close nor so exclusive as in the past. Lockwood (1965*a*, 495–7) suggests a move away from the old *zaibatsu* towards 'communities of interest'. Combines take the form of *keiretsu*, groups with multiple ties and a low degree of internal coordination (Hadley 1970, 299; Allen 1940).

The movement from entrepreneurial capital to finance capital is also evident in Canada and Australia. It can be seen from Table 32 that there was an apparent increase in the level of interlocking in Canada between 1951 and 1972. In 1951, 22 per cent of directors were multiple directors, while by 1972 the number had risen to almost 30 per cent. The number of people with nine or ten directorships in top companies decreased over the period. In 1951, 16 per cent of all directors in Canadian companies were US citizens, and 3 per cent were British (Porter 1965, 578), although those people were excluded from the data in Table 32, resulting in an underestimation of the level of interlocking. In the 1960s, Safarian found that in the 280 foreign-owned companies in Canada, 42 per cent of directors were associated with the foreign parent. Of the total number of directors in foreign-owned companies, 14 per cent were 'outsiders', although a number of these represented significant owners who were not themselves parent or affiliate companies (Safarian 1966, 64; Gonick 1970, 51).

Porter shows that directors of the top banks held nearly a quarter of the top Canadian industrial directorships, and that over half of the top banking directorships were held by directors of the top industrials. Similarly, insurance company directors held 14 per cent of top industrial directorships, over half of insurance company directorships were held by top industrial directors and almost half by top bank directors. The 907 top industrial directors held 58 per cent of bank directorships and the same proportion of insurance directorships (Porter 1965, 579, 234). Although Porter claims that the nucleii of economic power are the large holding and investment companies which head 'interest groups', he gives no systematic information on this (ibid., 255 ff.). Clement agrees with this view of financial-industrial relations and argues that it is only recently that the dominant financial group has become involved in domestic industry, moving into industries which have been stabilized and made profitable by foreign capital (Clement 1975, 159). A similar picture emerges for Australia, although family interests remain

Table 32   *Interlocking directorships in Canadian industrial companies (1951, 1972)*

	1951		1972	
No. of directorships per person	*No. of people*	*No. of director-ships*	*No. of people*	*No. of director-ships*
1	704	704	672	672
2	112	224	155	310
3	43	129	58	174
4	21	84	28	112
5	13	65	20	100
6	7	42	6	36
7	3	21	6	42
8	2	16	1	8
9	1	9		
10	1	10		
Totals	907	1304	946	1454
No. of companies		170		113

SOURCE: Adapted from Porter (1965), 589, table 12; Clement (1975), 166, table 18.

strong. A study by Rolfe showed that 12 per cent of the directors of the top fifty Australian companies in 1962 held a quarter of all directorships. Two-fifths of the multiple directors also had financial directorships and were members of the dominant families (Rolfe 1967, cited in Encel 1970, 396). Encel argues that Australian companies are characterized by a solid core of private holdings by the dynastic families. Family control remains important, although it is being progressively replaced by 'institutional' and foreign capital (Encel 1970, 338–9, 376 ff.).[6]

The evidence which I have presented suggests that the development from personal to impersonal possession is associated with an integration and interdependence between the financial and industrial sectors of the economy. Each of the countries discussed has a unique history, yet each is undergoing a transition from entrepreneurial capital to finance capital. In Britain, as in Canada and Australia, the integration of financial and industrial interests developed slowly, the two sectors gradually coming together. In Germany and Japan, family-controlled banks forged an alliance between the state and entrepreneurial capital as the basis for rapid economic development. The close relationship between banks and industry in these two countries has gradually given way to the looser articulation which is developing in Britain. In the USA, banks were a dominant force in the immediate period of transition from entrepreneurial capital to finance capital, but the economy has since moved away from a structure of 'financial empires' to one of 'spheres of influence'. Indeed, the relationship between 'finance capital', as the predominant form of investment funding, and bank-centred 'spheres of influence' leads directly to the question of bank power, which is frequently seen as an element in the concept of finance capital itself.

Corporate interlocking and bank power

Fitch has argued that the close relationship between financial and industrial corporations is evidence that 'corporations are controlled by capitalists working through financial institutions' (1972, 126). Interlocking directorships, he claims, express 'the exercise of raw economic power by giant conglomerate corporations, especially against smaller rivals and suppliers' (ibid., 107). Bank control forces corporations to engage in 'buying and selling goods on the basis of considerations other than price, quality, and service' (ibid.). Numerous writers have pointed to the bases on which banks, and other financial companies, might be able to exercise this kind of power: the ability to grant or withhold credit and to vary the rate of interest, the possession of company shares and the voting rights attached to them, the extensive knowledge and information which banks acquire, and the various service relations which banks are able to offer their clients (Baum and Stiles 1965, 36; Patman Report 1968, 19, 23 ff.; Aaronovitch 1961, 49). Of these bases, two have been particularly emphasized – credit and shareholdings.

The ability of large industrial concerns to fund their investments from internally generated resources has often been taken as evidence against the notion of bank control. For example, Bell claims that 'only a minor proportion of corporate capital today is raised through the sale of equity capital. A more significant portion of capital comes through self-financing' (Bell 1974, 294). There is certainly considerable evidence that the decline of the investment banker in the USA during the 1930s was associated with a high level of internal funding from retained earnings and reserves (Sweezy 1941).[7] But Perlo has argued that a high level of internal funding is hardly significant when the economy is stagnant and there is little enough investment at all (1957, 26). This view is confirmed by the fact that, in the more prosperous years following the Second World War, the level of internal funding decreased. From 1946 to 1953, 64 per cent of capital expenditure in the USA was from internal sources. Of the 36 per cent raised externally, 18 per cent was bank credit, 12 per cent was raised through loan stock sold by private placement to insurance companies, pension funds, etc., and 6 per cent was raised on the stock exchange (Berle 1960, 25–6). Much of this investment was made in order to replace outdated machinery, and, when finance for expansion is examined over the same period, external funding accounts for nearly three-quarters of the total (Perlo 1957, 26). Kuznets (1961) shows that the level of internal funding between 1900 and 1929 was comparable with that for 1946–53, the annual figures varying from 55 to 65 per cent. Similarly, Menshikov produces figures for the period 1955–65 which show an average of 62 per cent for 1956–60 and 51 per cent for 1961–5. By 1966, the figure was 64 per cent (Menshikov 1969, 191). Fitch and Oppenheimer calculate a 61 per cent rate of internal funding for 1966, and they show that the level has declined from 70 per cent in 1964 to 57 per cent in 1968 (Fitch and Oppenheimer, 1970b, 74, table 1). Fitch (1971, 156) claims that this figure decreased further from 1968 to 1971. Clearly, the level of internal funding varies over time, but the variation is within fairly narrow limits. Fitch and Oppenheimer suggest the plausible explanation that, since the availability of internally generated resources depends on the profitability of corporations, the level of internal funding will vary inversely with the profit rate. When there are cash flow problems, corporations will be forced to borrow from the capital market (Fitch and Oppenheimer 1970b, 75). It might, therefore, be expected that internal funding will vary with the phases of the business cycle.

In Britain, the rate of internal funding since 1950 has averaged about 70 per cent. Thompson (1977, 254–5) has shown that the rate fell from 77 per cent in 1950 to 69 per cent in 1965, though it subsequently rose to 70 per cent in 1970. A study by Barratt Brown shows that there are fluctuations around this trend and that these fluctuations are associated with the business cycle. Internal funding is high at the low point of the cycle, when there is little investment, and it is low at the high point of the cycle, when expansion takes place. Growth is, therefore, funded externally. Barratt Brown suggests that in the early 1950s the fastest-growing companies obtained half of their funds externally (Barratt Brown 1968*b*; Williams *et al.* 1968, 111–12). The level of internal funding seems to be dependent upon both the scale of investment and the profitability of companies. This interpretation is confirmed by a study showing that from 1970 to 1976 there were considerable fluctuations in the level of internal funding, the highest figure of 98 per cent being found in 1975 when the proportion of funds allocated for expansion was at a low of 15 per cent. By contrast, the level in 1970 had been 66 per cent and the proportion of funds allocated for expansion had been 40 per cent (Stock Exchange 1977, 14, table 3) [8]

Thompson presents some useful comparative data on internal funding. His study shows that, in economies with a high level of internal funding, a higher proportion of the external funds comes from shares and loan stock than from bank loans. This is the case for both Britain and the USA. In France and Japan, the rate of internal funding is only 40–50 per cent, and these countries show a greater proportional reliance on bank loans for their external funds. Germany, however, is in an anomalous position: the level of internal funding is similar to that of the USA, though there is a high dependence on banks (Thompson 1977, 60, table 2; Halliday 1975, 273).

Does the evidence on internal funding show that banks are able to use the dependence of corporations on external resources as a way of controlling their strategies? Fitch and Oppenheimer suggest that this is the case and that the extent of bank power increases as external funding increases (1970*a*; 1970*b*; 1970*c*). As I have shown, there is no evidence of a long-term trend towards increasing reliance on external funds. It can further be argued that, where banks do control other corporations, they are not interested merely in increasing their indebtedness (Menshikov 1969, 196; Beed 1966, 39; Ryndina and Chernikov 1974, 181). Sweezy argues that much of the debate on internal funding fails to take sufficient account of corporate cash flow. While a low level of retained earnings means that investment funds must come from financial companies, it is not the case that this always involves 'dependence' on banks. A company with a good cash flow is regarded as an excellent customer by the banks. If it chooses to use a high proportion of external funds, such a company is able to choose to which bank to give its business. To the extent that cash flow is good, industrial corporations can retain their autonomy from banks (Sweezy 1971, 13). Banks and industry are involved in a relationship in which 'both sides hold strong cards and . . . their mutual lending and borrowing operations provide

D

no basis for assuming that either controls the other' (ibid., 14). Cash flow depends upon profitability, and a lack of profitability may lead to increased bank control (Herman 1973, 26), but the evidence on internal funding itself must be regarded as inconclusive. Dispute has also arisen as to whether banks and other 'institutional' shareholders actually use the power inherent in their shareholdings. In Chapter 2 it was suggested that the size of institutional holdings is such that financial interests are 'locked-in' to corporations and cannot readily sell their holdings if they are dissatisfied (Baum and Stiles 1965, 11). For this reason, argue Fitch and Oppenheimer (1970*b*, 62–3), there is the possibility of direct intervention. Similarly, Chevalier claims that 'In spite of the banks' apparent reluctance to intervene in the administration of corporations, it appears likely that they will be progressively impelled to give up their neutrality, in so far as the volume of stock they hold obliges them to shed the simple role of institutional investor' (Chevalier 1969, 168).[9] Against this, it has been argued that intervention is rare (Herman 1973, 20–1; O'Connor 1971, 139, 143). Parry has argued that 'It seems a reasonable surmise that many of the professional bankers who sit on the boards of industry are there to keep a watching brief for the shareholders they represent as nominees or to offer counsel on financial matters' (Parry 1969, 79; Allen 1976, 889–90; Blumberg 1975, 168). However, my discussion of the mechanisms of strategic control suggested that direct intervention is rare because it indicates a *failure* of the continuing and persistent exercise of pressure. The Wilson Report, for example, found that covert intervention was increasing:

There is occasionally therefore some intervention by the institutions, normally on a collective basis through Investment Protection Committees, when a company gets into difficulties. It takes place in an informal and confidential manner, since publicity about a company's problems can easily precipitate the crisis which it is the purpose of intervening to avoid [Wilson Report 1977, 26].

Institutions attempt to intervene in a covert way if necessary, but will often wish to avoid even this. It is necessary, therefore, to examine the mechanisms through which continuing pressure can be exercised in order to assess whether this constitutes 'bank control'. I shall approach this question by returning to the issue of interlocking directorships.

Interlocking directorships are a persistent feature of industrial capitalist economies, and the structures of interlocks in various countries seem to exhibit specific trends over time. Discussing the US evidence, Levine and Roy (1977) argue that the stability of the structure at any particular time does not depend upon the power of particular people or companies: the structure of the network is irreducible to the actions of its units. Some years earlier, Warner and Unwalla discussed their own study of interlocks and argued that 'the social system that continues through the generations is only momentarily concerned with any given individual. The personnel varies, individuals disappear, but the system persists or, modified, continues in a new form' (1967, 124–5). How, then, are interlocks to be explained? People are recruited as directors for a variety of reasons: as large individual shareholders, as representatives of corporate holdings, as providers of financial and legal services, as 'figureheads', to maintain contacts, as representatives of related firms, and so on (Kolko 1962, 58–9; Crosland 1962, 79–80; Baran and Sweezy 1966, 28; Blumberg 1975, 168; Blackburn 1965, 174). Abell (1974) has made the important point that structural analysis must move away from the 'local' details of particular parts of a system in order to grasp the 'global' properties of the system. All the specific relationships in a system are subject to a complex set of local determinants – each interlock has a specific history and meaning – but these are not necessarily the most important determinants of the overall structure of the system. One conclusion that can be drawn is that the structure of the network of interlocking directorships is not a consciously intended product of the actions of those who recruit directors. And, if this is the case, it cannot be held that the centrality of banks in the network is a result of self-interested bankers seeking to consolidate their power over industry. While conspiracies no doubt occur, complex structures and their historical development are never intentional consequences of such conspiracies. Interlocking director-ships must be explained in other terms, and to do this it is necessary to understand the real significance of interlocks.

The position adopted here follows the 'minimum inference' made by Mills and by Stanworth and Giddens:

... patterns of interlocking directorships indicate channels of communica-tion that are established within the corporate world. And channels which facilitate flows of information do also offer a *possible* means of using influence or power [Stanworth and Giddens 1975, 22; Mills 1956, 122–3].[10]

As Domhoff has argued, 'Bankers are the most important carriers of information and opinion from one sector of the business establishment to another' (1967, 53; Smith 1970, 49). Baum and Stiles have shown that the large institutional shareholders have access to business information on plans, markets, etc., and have the expertise and means to make the best use of this (Baum and Stiles 1965, 34–6; Wilson Report 1977, 26):

... institutional investors are in a position to obtain corporate information not available to other shareholders. This position springs from the power of large holdings and from the ability as a day-to-day matter to send competent men into the field to question management, not to mention the fact that institutions are themselves big business and, thus, their executives are the natural associates of industrial executives [Baum and Stiles, 1965, 65, 162–3; Chevalier 1970, 202].

The financial companies involved in the constellations of interests controlling the major companies have access to essential business information. Not only are they able to put their representatives on company boards, but these companies will actually seek out such people to serve as their directors. The result is an extensive network of communication through which business information can flow. Information flow is a possible basis of power over and above the power involved in capital flows such as shareholdings and bank loans. As Mokken and Stokman argue, 'Whatever the reasons underlying the structure, the consequence is that companies and institutions at the nerve centres of the communication network possess power by virtue of their position' (1974, 30). The large financial companies at the centres of the network are the foci through which information is 'switched' from one part of the network to another, and this ability to control the flow of information, whether used intentionally or unintentionally, is a way of influencing corporate strategy. Thus, banks may influence corporate strategy even where they have no direct control. Where there are direct control relations, this can be reinforced through access to information: 'The financial institutions represent an aggregate of well-informed and frequently aggressive investors in a position to judge management's performance' (Baum and Stiles 1965, 68–9).

The consequence of establishing director links between companies is to produce a system of communication with a definite structure. The flow of information through the system is determined by its structure, and the construction of corporate strategy is influenced by the information available to corporate management. The structure of the system of directorships is a determinant of the limits and possibilities of corporate behaviour. This influence on corporate strategy is not intended by financiers and company managers, and they are perhaps not aware that strategy is structurally determined in this way. Even when director links are made with the specific intention of exercising strategic control over another corporation, the unintended consequence is to contribute to a system of interlocks which constrains the strategies pursued by all corporations in the system. The structure of the system of interlocks and its development over time are not results of conscious design, but are the unintended consequences of actions which themselves take place within the constraints set by the very structure which these actions produce (Merton 1936; Elias 1939*b*, 313 ff.; Mennell 1977). Recruitment of company directors is constrained by the system of interlocks which that recruitment generates.

Relations of strategic control are cemented through shared directorships and so generate an extensive network of interlocks. The unintended consequence of those forms of strategic control which are based upon impersonal possession is the production of a system of communication in which the major financial companies function as 'nerve centres' and are therefore able to exert an influence over corporate strategies. The financial empires which figure in the theory of capitalist society were products of specific historical conditions and have given way to bank-centred 'spheres of influence' located in an extensive communication system.

A basic principle of sociological analysis, and not specifically of 'functionalism', is that persistent practices persist by virtue of their functions. Allen has argued that 'the coherent structure of corporate interlocking and its stability over time suggest . . . that interlocking directorates are an important and significant feature of the corporate economy' (1974, 404). According to Allen, interlocks enable corporations to 'anticipate environmental contingencies' and so control their relations with other corporations on which they are dependent. Numerous models of organization-environment relations have attempted to explore this notion in general terms (Lawrence and Lorsch 1967; Warmington *et al.* 1977; Perrow 1970; Aldrich 1978). Gustavsen has applied this specifically to interlocks and argues that

Investment decisions – decisions about where to allocate the capital – must be made on the basis of environmental conditions like market and raw materials development. This calls for information about various external issues, which again calls for contacts to people who might know something about the relevant issues [Gustavsen 1976, 277].

The provision of information is a way of 'reducing the complexity' of the environment. Aaronovitch and Sawyer have written that 'the deterioration of the environment for any firm or group of firms leads them to seek some increase in their control over the market so as to overcome any increase in uncertainty or instability which they experience' (1975, 261).[11] The relationships which bring credit, partners for mergers, and access to expertise, etc., also bring information and so permit a more planned strategy (Herman 1973, 25–6). In general, the system of interlocks as a whole will be at a level of organization which 'matches' the complexity of the environment and which enables corporations to adapt to changes generated in their environment (Gustavsen 1976, 279; Hughes *et al.* 1977). From this perspective, the composition of the board of directors can be seen as 'reflecting the organisation's perceived need to deal differentially with various important sectors or organisations in the environment' (Pfeffer 1972, 220). Recruitment through cooptation ensures that the board is adapted to the interests of its constellation of major shareholders, its sources of credit, its suppliers and competitors, and agencies such as the unions and the state which are able to influence its activities. Such processes *within* each corporation generate a system of relations *between* corporations which is itself adapted to the environment of the system as a whole. That is, interlocks are able to ensure a certain degree of integration and coordination (Williams 1960, 169). As Banks puts it, 'the device of interlocking directorships succeeds in creating a form of unity in a situation of diversity, without going all the way to monopoly in a single organisation' (1970, 223). The clearest statement of this point is perhaps that of Porter, who argues that

It is not . . . the role of directors as the overseers of individual corporations taken separately that makes them an economic élite. Rather it is the fact that collectively they preside over all major segments of the corporate world in an extensive interlocking network. They are the ultimate decision-makers and co-ordinators within the private sector of the economy. It is they who at the frontiers of the economic and political systems represent the interests of corporate power. They are the real planners of the economy. . . . Planning, co-ordination, developing, taking up options, giving the shape to the economy and setting its pace, and creating the general climate within which economic decisions are made constitute economic power in the broad sense [Porter 1965, 255].

It is not the case that the presence of a multiple director on the board always indicates a relation of strategic control, though this may be the case. Interlocking directorships involve not 'control' but 'constraint'. The constraint or 'regulation' involved is not that of company A *over* company B. Rather, it is the constraint inherent in the structure of the corporate system: control by the system as a whole over *both* A *and* B (Buckley 1967; Giddens 1976*b*, 121). The intercorporate configuration is a system which is based upon the power relations among its constituent elements, but in which the overall structure is so complex that it is unrealistic to depict a particular group as having the ability to form an 'empire' subordinate to its wishes. Owing to the complexity of the power relations, no corporation or group of associates will have the capacity to foresee all contingencies or to carry through its wishes without constraint.

Corporations enter into specific relations of strategic control, the controlling corporations being interlinked. The resulting pattern of power and dependence relations is such that particular corporations and groups are 'powerful' by virtue of their position in the power structure. That is, the direct power relations have the unintended consequence of systematically generating a distribution of power between the various positions (Cook 1977, 70–1; Hoerning 1971, 10–11; Benson 1977, 13; Perrucci and Pilisuk 1970, 1042–35; Baumgartner *et al.* 1978, chapters 4 and 5). These power relations are overlaid by the communication network of interlocking directorships in which the most central companies are the most influential (Mokken and Stokman 1976). Those who are most powerful in the system of strategic control are not necessarily those who are most influential in the system of communication. More specifically, the sphere in which a bank is able to exercise its direct power of strategic control may be far smaller than the sphere in which it is influential (Allen 1976, 889–90).

Relations of effective possession and strategic control involving constellations of financial interests generate a structure of interlocks, the main significance of which is the communication of business information. The consequence of the flow of information is to reduce uncertainty deriving from the 'complexity' of the environment. The centrality of banks and other financial companies is an index of their influence but not of their dominance. The notion of 'bank control' has limited application to contemporary conditions. How, then, is the concept of finance capital to be assessed? If the concept involves 'bank control', as Hilferding seemed to suggest, then it is clearly of limited value. However, I have argued that a more useful concept of finance capital can be identified. Both Hussain and Thompson see 'finance capital' in terms of the circuit of capital in its money form (Hussain 1976, 11 ff.). In the stage of finance capital, the movement of monetary advances determines when and where production will take place (Thompson 1977, 247). From this point of view, both shares and bank loans are forms of 'loan capital'. Production and commercial activity are now dependent upon the availability of such loan capital and, therefore, investment funding takes the form of finance capital. Even where companies rely upon internal funding they are dependent upon stockmarket valuations and the necessity of maintaining a satisfactory cash flow. The concept of finance capital refers to the situation where investment funds are advanced as 'finance', and internal funding does not necessarily count against the concept. Under a system of entrepreneurial capital, internal funding is a deduction from the personal income of the entrepreneur. Under a system of finance capital, internal funding is a deduction from the income of shareholders, banks and others who advance capital to the concern. Thus the meaning of internal funding varies between the two systems. Finance capital does not refer to the dominance of banks as 'financial' units, since large industrial corporations are in many ways 'essentially financial, not production, units' (Sweezy 1971, 31; O'Connor 1971, 125–6; De Vroey 1975a, 8–9). The nature of finance capital as the 'fusion' of banking and industry is expressed in the system of effective possession, the mode of investment funding, and the integration of large corporations into an extensive network of communication.

5 The corporation and the class structure

One of the major arguments derived from the supposed 'separation of ownership from control' and the 'managerial revolution' is the view that wealth and power have become dissociated. The capitalist propertied class has been replaced by a managerial class, which is 'broad and diffuse . . . with several loosely integrated components', and which is based not on property ownership but on 'occupational status and occupational earnings' (Parsons 1954*a*, 431; Lenski 1966, 352). On the basis of his analysis of ownership and control, Berle drew very radical conclusions about the future of the propertied class: 'the transformation of property from an active role to passive wealth has so operated that the wealthy stratum no longer has power' (Berle 1963, 53). The most sophisticated statement of this view from within the theory of industrial society is that of Bell in his paper 'The Breakup of Family Capitalism' (1957). Bell argues that the series of economic crises at the beginning of the century led to the reconstruction of family enterprises by investment bankers, and that the consequence of this was the establishment of 'finance capitalism'. Gradually the power of the bankers declined, and the professional managers that they had installed in the major corporations became the new 'corporate organizers' (Bell 1957, 40–1). As inheritance through the family became less important and technical skill became more important, there was a 'break-up' of the old ruling class: the mere possession of wealth did not give access to economic power (Bell 1958, 50 ff.).

Very similar conclusions to those of Bell have been arrived at by Burnham, who originated the notion of the 'managerial revolution'. Burnham begins from the position of the theory of capitalist society that economic power in the period after the First World War rested with the finance capitalists. In the 1930s Lundberg, for example, held that

The United States is owned and dominated today by a hierarchy of its sixty richest families, buttressed by no more than ninety families of lesser wealth. Outside this plutocratic circle there are perhaps three hundred and fifty other families, less defined in development and in wealth, but accounting for most of the incomes of $100,000 or more that do not accrue to members of the inner circle [Lundberg 1937, 3].

Burnham claimed, however, that the dominance of the financial oligarchy was a feature of the transition from capitalist society to managerial society. The managers are those who carry out the 'technical direction and coordination of the process of production and they are distinct from the finance executives and finance capitalists who are interested in the profitability of a company or group of companies' (Burnham 1941, 70). Owing to their technical indispensability, the managers are destined to become the dominant class in the place of the finance capitalists. The managers are not dependent on private property and will base their dominance on their *de facto* access to the means of production: 'The position, role, and function of the managers are in no way dependent upon the maintenance of capitalist property and economic relations; . . . they depend upon the technical nature of the process of modern production' (ibid., 80).

This view of the rise of the managers has not gone unchallenged: proponents of the theory of capitalist society hold that ultimate economic power is still vested in a financial oligarchy, and Zeitlin (1974, 46) has recently claimed that 'News of the demise of the capitalist classes . . . is, I suspect, somewhat premature'. The aim of this chapter is to assess these rival viewpoints in the light of the available evidence.

Relations of possession and social classes

In order to investigate the position of the propertied class it is first necessary to digress into a discussion of the concept of class itself. The most widely used notion of class is that of Weber, who defines class situation as the life chances which follow from effective disposition (*Verfügungsgewalt*) over goods and services within a given economic order (Weber 1921). Classes are differentiated by the income or revenue which they are able to acquire on the basis of their economic situation. Johnson has countered this concept by arguing that an analysis of class in terms of economic relations of distribution merely identifies 'certain of the mechanisms of class reproduction without seeing how these are determined within the production process' (Johnson 1977*b*, 102; 1977*a*; Crompton and Gubbay 1977, chapters 2 and 3; Bertaux 1977, 45). That is, relations of production are to be seen as determinants of relations of distribution. I wish to suggest that, while Johnson is correct to emphasize the importance of 'production', he is wrong to assign a determining role to it.

In Chapter 2 I argued that the conjunction of various social forms establishes the conditions of existence for relations of effective possession. The relations of possession characteristic of industrial capitalism, abstracting from historical variations, comprise a separation of possessors from non-possessors and the existence of autonomous units of capital. The conditions of existence for these relations of possession, i.e. relations of production, exist only because these social forms are articulated in a particular way. This articulation is the result of definite social practices and is in no way determined by the relations of production themselves. There is no way in which the relations of production can secure their own conditions of existence (Cutler *et al.* 1977, 227; Rey 1976, 93 ff.). But precisely because the social forms are structured so as to constitute definite relations of production, actions are constrained by this structure in such a way that they will tend to reproduce these relations of production (D. Lockwood 1964). To say that the relations of production determine the social forms is to be the victim of a sort of optical illusion. While it may be true that certain distributive patterns of inequality 'correspond' to particular relations of production, the latter do not determine the former. Patterns of inequality are generated in the very social forms which are conditions of existence for the relations of production. None of this is to imply that social structures are self-maintaining. Whether structures are reproduced or transformed depends on the concrete historical practices in which individuals and groups engage. As I argued in Chapter 4 with reference to structures of interlocking directorships, the 'bias' inherent in a structure tends to ensure its reproduction, but this is by no means inevitable.

'Class' can be conceptualized in Weber's terms, provided that classes are further analysed in relation to the relations of production. Weber recognized two main dimensions of class situation: property and commerce. A property class (*Besitzklasse*) depends upon ownership as such and is distinguished from those who buy and sell property (*Eigentum*) on the market. The latter, along with all others who earn their living through the market, are members of a commercial class (*Erwerbsklasse*). While positively privileged property classes are typically *rentiers*, positively privileged commercial classes are typically entrepreneurs (Weber 1921). Thus, Weber's analysis of class identifies the two main categories with which this chapter began: 'owners' and 'managers'. Weber recognizes that the classes identified in these terms may be indistinguishable from one another in terms of life chances and life style and that they may comprise parts of a broader 'social class' (*sozial Klasse*). A social class comprises a totality of specific class situations between which personal or intergenerational mobility is typical. *Rentiers* and entrepreneurs, that is, may not be distinct social groups but different positions within the same social class (Boltanski 1973).[1]

Westergaard argues that the patterns of inequality found in capitalist industrial societies correspond to capitalist relations of production because distribution is in accord with certain 'principles': income derives from the use of property for productive purposes and from the exercise of labour power for production (Westergaard 1977, 183 ff.; Castells 1976, 117–18). The bias of the structure is such that the division of revenue into wages and profits and its distribution according to 'market capacities' conforms to those very principles which are conditions for the relations of production. This pattern of distribution reproduces the separation of possessor from non-possessor and reinforces the legitimation of work motivations in terms of the 'achievement principle' (Offe 1970).

In much recent work the relations of production are seen as the 'economic' aspect of society. For Cutler *et al.*, for example, relations of production are 'economic class relations' (1977, 239, 243, 249), and for Carchedi (1975) classes are 'economically defined' at the level of the relations of production. As Laclau has argued, this position follows from the dual meaning of 'economic' in Marx: 'economic' is used to refer both to the process of material production in its broadest sense and to historically specific commodity and market relations (Laclau 1975, 106). Economic relations, in the sense of relations of distribution, circulation and consumption, are among the conditions of existence of the 'deeper' relations of production (Holloway and Picciotto 1977, 84; Clarke 1977, 10; Wirth 1973; Corrigan *et al.* 1977). This is not to imply that relations of production are different 'things' from the other social relations. As Sayer argues, the deeper relations do not lie behind social forms in any physical sense: the abstract relations of production are the structure described by a specific articulation of the social forms and can be discovered only through analysis (Sayer 1975, 794; Ollman 1971, 207; Hall 1977, 63).

It is now possible to investigate the connection between relations of production and social classes. According to the position adopted here, social classes are structures of social positions (occupations, income levels, education levels, etc.) which are filled by individuals and which are reproduced over time. The hierarchical relations between social classes derive from the unequal distribution of the various privileges which define the social positions. The 'economic' aspect of social class, Weber's 'market situation', is certainly a crucial determinant of the overall character of social class relations, but social classes are more than just economic phenomena. In Carchedi's terms, social classes are 'identified' as economic, cultural and political entities, although they are 'defined' at the level of the relations of production (Carchedi 1975). Social classes are the result of a complex process of structuration and are not, therefore, to be seen as clearly bounded categories. Each class consists of a 'core' and a 'fringe', the fringes of adjacent classes overlapping and producing indeterminate boundaries. As Cole has argued, social classes

. . . are not sharply definable groups whose precise numbers can be determined by gathering in enough information about every individual. They are rather aggregates of persons round a number of central nuclei, in such a way that it can be said with confidence of those nearer each centre that they are members of a particular class, but that those further from a centre can be assigned to the class it represents only with increasing uncertainty [Cole 1955, 1; Sweezy 1951].

The structural continuity of social classes depends upon the achievement of a certain amount of closure. This involves monopolization of access to privileged social positions in such a way that a stable structure of class relations is reproduced over time. Restriction of opportunities for mobility is a condition for the crystallization of social classes and so facilitates their reproduction (Giddens 1973, 107). As Dahrendorf has argued, while the structure of positions which constitutes a system of classes exists independently of the movement of persons through that structure, the crystallization of social classes depends on the restriction of recruitment and mobility (Dahrendorf 1959, 108, 145; Schumpeter 1927; Parkin 1974a). Closure is achieved through the strategies which people are able to use in order to monopolize and accumulate privileges. Bourdieu has demonstrated that economic, social and cultural assets are mutually convertible and reconvertible in such a way that a person's total resources increase (Bourdieu et al. 1973; Bourdieu 1971). The key to understanding such 'reconversion strategies' is the system of inheritance which is embodied in the family. Inheritance of economic assets (shares, money, goods), social assets (networks of kinship and friendship relations) and cultural assets (knowledge, life style, etc.)[2] in and through the family determines the opportunities available to a person for the accumulation of privilege (Bertaux 1977, 49–51; Marceau 1977; Touraine 1969, 28–9). Owing to the centrality of the family in class structuration, it is not surprising that marriage is one of the most important mechanisms of class reproduction. The choice of a marital partner is a strategy, intended or unintended, for ensuring the maintenance and accumulation of privilege. But other social relations are also important means of class structuration: friendship, visiting, receptions, the more organized unity of clubs and associations, and the diffuse unity engendered by a particular type of schooling. All these practices bring about a commonality of background and attitudes which crystallizes a social class into a collectivity whose members possess not merely equivalent life chances, but also a similarity of life style (Baltzell 1958; Domhoff 1967, 3–4; Domhoff 1971, 21–6, 77, 84; Tawney 1931, 53; Wesolowski 1967, 124).

Since they are more than just economic phenomena, social classes are not merely market situations but also 'status situations'. Weber argued that the status dimension of stratification derived from social estimation based upon such factors as mode of life, form of education, descent, and occupation, all of which can lead to the monopolization of privileges. Societies will be divided not only into economically determined classes but also into 'statuses' (*Stände*).[3] Such statuses will normally correspond to economic classes, though mere property and skills are not always sufficient as status qualifications. Market factors and status factors interrelate with one another to produce the overall pattern of monopolistic appropriation which defines social classes. Thus, in a class-like society (*klassenmässig*) the two dimensions are related, and social classification is based pre-eminently on market distinctions (Weber 1921).

Social classes are not themselves capable of action (Hindess 1977, 99 ff.; Hirst 1977, 125–6). Social classes are what Dahrendorf, following Ginsberg, terms 'quasi-groups'. They are not themselves 'groups' in the strict sense, but 'Being united by a common, potentially permanent, characteristic, they are more than mere masses or incoherent quantities' (Dahrendorf 1959, 179; Ginsberg 1953, 41; Aron 1964). Social classes are loose configurations of persons with common, though frequently latent, interests, who may form themselves into definite groups. The conscious and purposive interest groups and social movements which act in relation to one another are *not* classes, though they may engage in 'class action'. That is, 'they can and do become in varying degrees the representatives of class aspirations and points of view' (Cole 1934, 32). Dahrendorf argues that the degree of closure through restriction of mobility which a social class is able to achieve is a determinant of the solidarity and consciousness of class members, and is, therefore, a determinant of the intensity of conflict and of whether this takes an individual or a group form. A social class with a high degree of closure – other things being equal – is more likely to become conscious of itself as a social class and so to organize itself into associations aimed at the conscious pursuit of common interests (Dahrendorf 1959, 222; 1967, 19–20).

Social classes, I have argued, are clusters of positions which are filled by individuals and which are associated with definite relations of production. For Marx, the principal classes in a society were defined by their 'reciprocal dependence' within its mode of production: the identity of each class depends upon the relations of production within which it meets the other (Giddens 1973, 28–9; Miliband 1977, 22–3; Ossowski 1956, 80–2). These relations generate a dichotomous structure separating capital from labour. Numerous recent works on class structure have followed this point of view and have attempted to clarify the connection between the capital function and the structuration of a propertied class. Poulantzas has defined the 'bourgeoisie' as that social class which occupies the 'place' of capital in the relations of production and which therefore performs the function of capital. Since managers in positions of operational administration perform a part of the capital function, they are held to be members of the bourgeoisie, even if they do not participate in strategic control (Poulantzas 1974, 14). Carchedi argues that the capitalist class is 'defined' as the category of persons performing the function of capital, but that the bourgeoisie is 'identified' as those members of the capitalist class who perform *only* the capital function. That is, operational managers who coordinate the labour process itself, and therefore perform part of the 'labour function', are not a part of the bourgeoisie (Carchedi 1975, 47–8). Such managers are either part of the 'new middle class' or of the working class (Johnson 1977*b*, 104; Becker 1971; 1973; Cutler *et al.* 1977, 304). Carchedi's position is certainly an improvement on that of

Poulantzas, since it recognizes the importance of the delegation of day-to-day operations to a managerial 'technostructure'. The 'bourgeoisie' retain strategic control in relation to investment and resource allocation, while the immediate administration of production is delegated (Wright 1976, 29; Crompton and Gubbay 1977, 69 ff.). These analyses suggest a transition from the performance of the capital function by a person to its performance by a differentiated role structure, and this seems to be associated with the transition from personal to impersonal possession. It is in these terms that I would like to define the propertied class in industrial capitalism. It is that class of individuals occupying privileged positions in the system of inequality by virtue of their participation in the possession of units of capital. The leading members of this propertied class are those who are involved directly in the exercise of strategic control, and its internal constitution will vary with developments in the structure of possession and strategic control.

I have defined what is meant by 'social class' and have indicated what a capitalist propertied class would look like. It is now possible to turn to the all-important empirical question of whether such a class still exists. In the following sections I shall argue that there is evidence to suggest that industrial capitalist societies do still have such propertied classes but that the structure and the mechanisms of reproduction of the propertied class have been transformed.

The managerial reorganization of the propertied class

Studies of the distribution of income and wealth in the USA and in Britain have shown that both societies are highly inegalitarian. There is clear evidence for the existence of a privileged social class. A study by Kuznets (1953) has been used by Kolko (1962, 15, 24, 37) and others to show that before-tax income in the USA was distributed in such a way that the top 10 per cent of income recipients received a more or less constant share of 30 per cent of all income throughout the first half of this century. The share of the top 1 per cent declined from 14 per cent of income to 10 per cent during the 1930s and 1940s (Birnbaum 1971; Bottomore 1965, 44). Domhoff shows that by the late 1950s the share of the top 1 per cent of families in total income stood at 8 per cent (1967, 41). It would appear that the share of top income groups increased until 1969, decreased during the Depression and the Second World War, and has remained constant since then. This view is confirmed by Miller's

findings that the 30 per cent share of the top 5 per cent of families
in 1929 had fallen to 21 per cent in 1944 and stood at 20 per cent in
1962 (Miller 1966, 113). Kolko has argued that the effect of taxation
on this pattern has not been very great, and the work of Lydall and
Lansing (1959, 141) shows that during the 1950s taxation reduced
the share of the top 10 per cent from 30 per cent to 26 per cent. The
picture in Britain is remarkably similar. While the share of the
top 10 per cent of income recipients in before-tax income seems to
have remained in the region of one-third, the proportion received by
the top 1 per cent has fallen in the post-war period from 11 per cent
to between 6 and 8 per cent (Nicholson 1967, 42; Lydall 1959;
Soltow 1968; Blackburn 1967). On the basis of their criticisms of
the official statistics on income, various writers have suggested that
concentration may be somewhat higher than this (Titmuss 1962;
Meade 1964; Atkinson 1975). The reduction in the share of the top
1 per cent occurred primarily between 1949 and 1957, the proportion
remaining constant since then.[4] The major cause of the reduction
was the fact that from 1949 to 1957 earned incomes rose faster than
income from other sources, while after 1957 the most rapidly growing
sources of income were rent, dividends and interest (Nicholson 1967,
49). The trend in after-tax income has been slightly less marked, the
share of the top 1 per cent being 6 per cent in the 1940s and 5 per
cent in the 1950s and 1960s. Even the conservative estimates of
Polanyi and Wood suggest that in 1970 the share of the top 1 per
cent in after-tax income was 5 per cent (Polanyi and Wood 1974, 64).
Noble (1975, 178, 199) shows that, while the share of the top 1 per
cent before tax fell from 9 per cent to 7 per cent, their share after
tax fell from 5 per cent to 4 per cent. Allowing for minor variations
in techniques, units and data, the basic pattern is clear. In Britain
and in the USA as well as in France and Germany (Atkinson 1973*a*;
Babeau and Strauss-Kahn 1977, 41 ff.), one-tenth of the population
receives about one-third of total income, and has done for most of
the century. One per cent of the population, about half a million
families in the USA, receive between 5 and 8 per cent of total income
and have received this proportion since the 1950s, having declined
from an earlier position of greater concentration.

   With respect to wealth distribution, a major study of the USA by
Lampman (1959; 1962) shows that the share of the top 1 per cent
in personal wealth fell over the period 1922–49 and then rose again
through the 1950s to stand at between 25 and 30 per cent. It has
since been suggested that this proportion continued to rise through

the 1960s (Smith and Calvert 1965; Domhoff 1967; Lundberg 1969). Lampman argues that much of the reduction in concentration in the period between the wars can be explained in terms of the redistribution of wealth *within* families and so does not represent a significant change in the social distribution of wealth. Nearly half of the wealth held by the top 1 per cent in 1953 was held by the top 0·11 per cent of the population, about 113 300 people, and there is no evidence to suggest that the situation is different today. Data for Britain suggest a higher degree of inequality than in the USA, though wealth has gradually become more equally distributed. The share of the top 1 per cent fell from 69 per cent in 1911 to 56 per cent in 1936, 45 per cent in 1946, 42 per cent in the 1950s and 1960s, and to about 30 per cent in the 1970s (Lydall and Tipping 1961, 253; Noble 1975, 175; Atkinson 1972, 21; Revell 1965; Blackburn 1967; Atkinson 1975, 134). The proportion of wealth held by the top 5 per cent declined from 86 per cent to 55 per cent over the same period, and Atkinson shows that, while the share of the top 1 per cent has declined by a half, the proportion of wealth held by the next 4 per cent remained constant or actually increased over the period. Atkinson draws the conclusion that this reflects redistribution within families in order to avoid estate duty (Atkinson 1972, 22–3; Polanyi and Wood 1974, 17). This view is confirmed by numerous studies pointing to the continued importance of inheritance in the accumulation of wealth (Harbury 1962; Revell 1960; Harbury and McMahon 1974; Rubinstein 1974). As in the USA, almost half of the wealth held by the top 1 per cent is held by the top 0·1 per cent, about 55 000–60 000 people today (Atkinson 1975, 134).

It can be demonstrated not only that the top income recipients and the top wealth holders are the same people, but also that the major source of their income is that portion of their wealth which is held as company shares. The number of individual shareholders in US corporations increased rapidly from 1916 to 1921 and from 1927 to 1933, and by the early 1930s about 8 million people held company shares (Cox 1963, 33; Means 1930; Goldsmith and Parmelee 1940, 16–18; Perlo 1958, 26). These people represented about 7 per cent of the population and held just over 60 per cent of all company shares, the remaining 40 per cent being held by other companies. This same group represented the top 20 per cent of income recipients, and it was found that the importance of stockholding increased with income. The higher the income within this group, the greater the contribution made by dividend income. Dividends accounted for

60 per cent of the income of individuals with incomes over $100000 (Goldsmith and Parmelee 1940, 10–13). Half of the 1937 shareholders held shares in one company only, but those with incomes over $100000 held shares in an average of twenty-five companies. The concentration was such that 0·1 per cent of shareholders, representing 0·02 per cent of income recipients, received a quarter of the dividend income accruing to individuals. Goldsmith and Parmelee claim that 'notwithstanding the wide dispersion of ownership indicated by the large number of stockholders, ownership of stock was highly concentrated in the hands of a relatively few persons' (ibid., 13). This is confirmed by the fact that only a third of shareholders held shares in the 200 largest companies. While the number of shareholders declined somewhat through the Depression and the Second World War, it began to rise again during the 1950s and had reached its 1937 level by 1959, although in proportional terms individual shareholdings were being overshadowed by 'institutional' holdings. However, the continuing concentration of individual shareholdings is shown in Lundberg's finding that 1·4 million families held 65 per cent of all investment assets in 1962, under a quarter of a million families holding 32 per cent (Lundberg 1969, 28).

Atkinson has shown that the wealthiest groups in Britain have the highest rate of shareholding, the top 5 per cent of wealth holders in 1961 holding 96 per cent of all personally owned shares (Atkinson 1972, 30; Atkinson 1975, 135; Westergaard and Resler 1975, 107 ff.). Shareholdings make an important contribution to income: the top 10 per cent of those in receipt of investment income in 1960 received 99 per cent of all income from this source (Blackburn 1967), and the top 1 per cent of income recipients in 1970 received 7 per cent of all income but 17 per cent of investment income (Noble 1975, 180). Noble argues that 'About 500000 people, one per cent of the population, own just over a third of all private wealth in contemporary Britain and receive just over half of all the personal income derived from possession of wealth'. Within this stratum the very rich 50000, 0·1 per cent of the population, are the most important group (ibid., 182; Westergaard and Resler 1975, 119).

The evidence which has been briefly reviewed here gives substantial support for the view that the class which is most privileged in relation to the distribution of income and wealth derives this privilege from property ownership. The propertied class remains a reality. But Berle and Bell have both argued that wealth has become dissociated from 'power' – that is, that the propertied class no longer monopolizes the control of business. In order to examine this claim it is necessary to analyse the composition of the propertied class in more detail. Considerable evidence has been amassed to show that the most important categories within the propertied class are company directors and executives. In the 1930s, Goldsmith and Parmelee showed that officers and directors in the top 200 US corporations held 38 million shares, representing 5·5 per cent of the value of all corporate stock. Of the 2500 people involved, 367 held positions in more than one of the companies, 65 held positions in more than 3, 10 in more than 4, and 9 in more than 5. As Table 33 shows, those who were directors only were most important and those who were executives only were least important (Goldsmith and Parmelee 1940, 56–9).

Table 33   *Management holdings in the top 200 US corporations (1939)*

	% of holdings	% of value	% of total value
Directors	52·0	63·6	3·5
Officer-directors	28·1	34·8	1·9
Officers	19·9	1·6	0·1
Totals	100·0	100·0	5·5

SOURCE: Goldsmith and Parmelee (1940), 60, table 2.

NOTE: The total number of holdings was 3511, and the total number of individuals was 2500. The column headed '% of value' refers to the value of management holdings in the top 200 companies. This value was $2163m.

In 1939, the most common management holding in one of the largest corporations was less than 1 per cent, though a quarter of all companies had management holdings of 5 per cent or more (ibid., 64–5; Gordon 1936; 1938). According to Kolko, the board of directors owned or represented an average of 9·9 per cent of the shares in each of the top industrials in 1957, and the personal share of management remained considerable. The managers were 'the largest single group in the stockholding class' (Kolko, 1962, 67; Domhoff 1967, 58). A number of writers have made the point that, even when management do not own a large proportion of the shares in their own company, they nevertheless have a large absolute stake. Larner, for example, shows that the median value of stocks held by executives in 94 top companies was $658359 and that this resulted in a median dividend income of $23605. Executives obtained a considerable portion of their income in the form of dividends. Executives therefore have a substantial personal stake in the success of their company as well as in the success of the company sector as a whole (Larner 1970, 36–7, 66). For example, in 1967 the chairman of General Motors owned a mere 0·017 per cent of its stock, but this holding had a market value of nearly $4m. (Miliband 1968, 52; Villarejo 1961*b*, 53). Table 34 shows the actual percentage distribution of directors' shareholdings in their own companies. Table 35 gives comparable data for Britain.

Table 34 *Directors' holdings in 250 large US industrials (1960)*

% of shares held by directors	No. of corporattons in each category					
	Top 50	51–100	101–150	151–200	201–250	Totals
Less than 1%	27	22	5	7	7	68
1–2%	8	9	13	6	9	45
2–3%	1	5	2	1	5	14
3–4%	3	1	5	6	2	17
4–5%	3	2	5	2	0	12
5–10%	3	3	10	14	9	39
More than 10%	3	5	8	7	14	37
Totals	48	47	48	43	46	232

SOURCE: Villarejo (1961*a*), 51, table X.

NOTE: No information was available on eighteen companies. The figures do not include trustee holdings by directors.

Table 35 *Directors' holdings in 233 large British companies (1951)*

% of shares held by directors	No. of companies in each category			
	Very large	Medium-large	Small-large	Totals
Less than 1%	44	16	19	79
1–5%	32	17	38	87
5–10%	4	8	13	25
10–20%	5	0	11	16
More than 20%	13	6	7	26
Totals	98	47	88	233

SOURCE: Florence (1961), 90–1, table IV*c*.

On the basis of the British figures, Florence has argued that those who own company shares are a 'pool' from which directors are drawn, although holding a directorship in a particular company is not directly associated with holding shares in that company (Florence 1961, 93, 137; 1953, 200). That is, directors and major shareholders were one and the same people, though individual shareholdings were rarely large enough to ensure board representation in a specific company (Beed 1966, 35; Klein *et al.* 1956). Stanworth has analysed holdings by directors in the companies on which they sit and, as shown in Table 36, has documented the substantial monetary value which these holdings represent.

Table 36   *Directors' holdings in the top seventy-five British companies (1971)*

Market value of shares (£000)	% of directors
Less than 1	18·9
1–3	19·8
3–5	9·8
5–10	13·9
10–25	11·7
25–100	12·4
More than 100	13·5
Total	100·0

SOURCE: Stanworth (1974), 255.

NOTE: Where a person sits on more than two boards, he will be counted twice in this table. The actual concentration of shares is, therefore, somewhat greater than the table suggests.

It seems that directors in Britain and the USA comprise that very small proportion of the population who monopolize the ownership of company shares and derive a substantial part of their income from this source. They not only hold shares in the companies for which they work, but they own stock in other companies as well. They are not only the largest single shareholding group; they are the holders of the remaining large blocks of personally owned shares. The heart of the propertied class is the 'corporate rich'. The form taken by managerial remuneration is not a direct indication of changes in the relations of production. Banks has argued that the increasing number of salaried directors (Erickson 1959, 50) indicates a move towards a 'collective mode of production' within which management is able to benefit itself through fees, salaries, bonuses, expense accounts and pensions at the expense of dividend payments (Banks 1970, 168). However, if 'managers' and 'shareholders' are not distinct social categories, then the precise form in which managers are able to remunerate themselves becomes a reflection of such factors as the relative taxation advantages to be gained from 'earned' rather than 'unearned' income (Westergaard and Resler 1975, 162; Baran and Sweezy 1966, 47). The facts adduced here do suggest that important changes have occurred, but these changes are not those to which Banks has pointed.

Large personal stockholdings are monopolized by a propertied class which need no longer be tied to the particular enterprises in which it has a shareholding. While directors may not even hold a significant minority stake in the companies which they direct, they are, nevertheless, major shareholders in a large number of companies. Mills (1956, 147) has argued that this constitutes a 'managerial reorganization of the propertied class', a restructuring of the mediation of strategic control which does not alter the basic features of the system. He also maintains that

The growth and interconnections of corporations . . . have meant the rise of a more sophisticated executive elite which now possesses a certain autonomy from any specific property interest. Its power is the power of property, but that property is not always or even usually of one coherent and narrow type. It is, in operating fact, class-wide property [ibid., 122].

Domhoff has shown very clearly what this involves: 'Family A does not own Company X while Family B owns Company Y, as it may have been in the past; instead, Family A and Family B both have large stockholdings in Companies X and Y, as does Family C, which used to be the sole owner of Company Z' (Domhoff 1967, 40). Property has been 'depersonalized' (Birnbaum 1969, 12), just as possession has become impersonal. The managerial stratum is now merely 'the most active and influential part of the propertied class' (Baran and Sweezy 1966, 46; Sweezy 1951). The basis of this process was discussed by Hilferding, who argued that the central feature of 'finance capitalism' was the growth of a reliable stock exchange. Hilferding holds that 'only through the securities market does the capitalist attain independence of the fate of the particular enterprise in which he has invested his money' (Hilferding 1910, cited in Sweezy 1942, 258). The consequence is that the propertied class has a common interest in the business system as a whole (Domhoff 1967, 40).

The most forceful statement of the thesis of the managerial reorganization of the propertied class is that of Zeitlin, who argues that 'corporations are units in a class-controlled apparatus of appropriation; and the whole gamut of functionaries and owners of capital participate in varying degrees, and as members of the same social class, in its direction' (Zeitlin 1974, 1079). That is,

Although the largest banks and corporations might conceivably develop a relative autonomy from *particular* proprietary interests, they would be limited by the *general* proprietary interests of the principal owners of capital. To the extent that the largest banks and corporations constitute a new form of class property ... the 'inner group' ... of interlocking officers and directors, and particularly the finance capitalists, become the leading organizers of this class-wide property [Zeitlin 1976, 901].

The trend towards management control and control through a constellation of interests is directly associated with this managerial reorganization of the propertied class. This is not to say that millionaires and wealthy families no longer exist – far from it. Rather, direct access to particular controlling positions by virtue of personal shareholdings is of declining importance in modern industrial capitalism.

Evidence from France and Scandinavia suggests that managerial reorganization is not yet such a marked feature of these societies. Bleton remarks that the great families of the Parisian high bourgeoisie are no longer so prominent in the running of French industry. As enterprises age, so the interests involved in them become dispersed (Bleton 1966, 134, 144). Bertaux has summarized the trend towards the 'socialization' of property as follows: 'the structure of capital ... is no longer a structure of isolated molecules (family enterprise) but a structure of large groups, which are not dominated by one or two families but in which many families possess a small part' (Bertaux 1977, 78). France is characterized by a continuing mixture of direct family capital and 'managerially reorganized' capital (Meynaud 1964, 157). Direct family ownership is even more important in Sweden, as shown in Table 37. In 1963, seventeen groups of owners had majority, dominant, or strong minority interests in companies which accounted for 36 per cent of manufacturing industry. The Wallenberg family alone controlled 15 per cent (Commission on Concentration 1968, 37; Therborn 1976).

Table 37 *Millionaires with business interests in the 282 largest Swedish companies (1963)*

Wealth (million SKr)	% in 20 largest shareholders of a company	% with board memberships
1–2	14	8
2–3	24	12
3–5	41	22
5–10	51	25
10–15	59	44
15–20	82	64
More than 20	100	60
Number	553	303

SOURCE: Commission on Concentration (1968), 48.

In a study of the 122 largest companies in Norway, Higley *et al.* examined the differences between personally owned companies and corporations with respect to interlocking directorships (see Table 38). They concluded that there was evidence of a

. . . transformation from an earlier structure which contained numerous independent and sometimes competing leaders, most of whom owned in whole or in part the companies they led, to a structure of interlocking professional leaders who command large corporations which dominate their industries and branches but which, because of the large amounts of capital, long lead times, and large markets necessary to their operations, are dependent on each other for capital supplies and cooperative arrangements in production and marketing [Higley *et al.* 1976, 145].

The American evidence has been explained in terms of the gradual structuration of an 'upper class', the most sophisticated formulation being that of Berkowitz (1975), who argues that the structure of the privileged class in the USA has developed from a segmental structure of family compacts to a systemic upper class.[5] Family compacts are sets of loosely interconnected families engaged in similar business activities. Typically, partnerships between families are established in order to extend the capital base of an undertaking and this results in intermarriage. Thus, kinship relations and capital

Table 38   *Interlocking directorships in Norwegian business organizations (1967)*

No. of interlocks per organization	Corporations	Personally owned companies	Foreign corporations	Associations	Totals
0	9	25	3	1	38
1	7	9	2	0	18
2–5	18	15	6	2	41
6–10	11	3	3	3	20
More than 11	10	1	0	0	11
Totals	55	53	14	6	128

SOURCE: Higley *et al.* (1976), 143, table 3–1.

NOTE: The data involve 122 top companies and the six main business associations.

mobilization reinforce one another. When capital requirements go beyond the means of the partners, incorporation of the firm allows capital to be mobilized from non-family sources. Solidified family dynasties (which Berkowitz terms 'elites') in which the 'family' and the 'firm' are structurally separated are the outcome of this process, and the upper class exists as an extensive kinship network within which various 'cliques' can be identified around particular firms. Zeitlin has characterized these dynastic families as 'kinecon groups':

> The corporation is the legal unit of ownership of large-scale productive property. The set of interrelated kin who control the corporation through their combined ownership interests and strategic representation in management constitute the kinecon group [Zeitlin *et al.* 1975, 110].

During the early years of this century, the major dynasties became more closely linked, as bank credit rather than kinship became the most important source of capital. The merging of a number of local and regional dynasties led to the emergence of the 'Money Trust' and the financial empires. Family fortunes became relatively dissociated from particular firms, and the kinecon groups acquired an interest in the economy as a whole. Berkowitz argues that

> In family compacts, the structure of the 'family' and the system of capital mobilization are identical. . . . In what I refer to as 'elites', whole institutions begin to perform many of the functions which were previously carried on by family compacts through kinship ties, the *way* in which

someone is connected into this system is still important. Thus while the system of kinship among these elites approximates a single extended family, membership within a particular clique within this network, in part, determines one's access to resources. In upper class kinship systems this is no longer true: while the fact of being connected into the network or not is important, *how* one is connected is far less so [Berkowitz 1975, 208].

The nature of this 'upper class' is brought out clearly by Goldsmith and Parmelee, who argue that controlling shareholdings by family interest groups in the 1930s were restricted to specific holding companies, although families had smaller holdings in a large number of companies (1940, 115 ff.). Though they had diversified financial interests in the economy as a whole, their controlling interests remained particularized. Mills's analysis suggests that this structure has been transformed into a unified national upper class in which regional divisions are of secondary importance. The depersonalized structure of managerially reorganized property involves an upper class centred on the major cities but having truly national interests (Mills 1956, 47, 62; Sweezy 1951; Domhoff 1967, 12). As Domhoff argues, 'wealthy families from all over the country, and particularly from major cities . . . are parts of interlocking social circles which perceive each other as equals, belong to the same clubs, interact frequently, and freely intermarry' (Domhoff 1974, 86).

In view of the trends discussed in earlier chapters, it can be suggested that the internal structure of the propertied class is transformed from a system of family compacts to a unified national class. That is, the propertied class undergoes a managerial reorganization. The evidence available on countries such as France, Sweden and Norway suggests that these countries are still characterized by dynastic families, though in France they are coming under increasing pressure from foreign capital and from sectors of the propertied class which have already become 'technocratic' (Morin 1974). The internal structure of the propertied class is directly related to the changing pattern of interdependencies in an advanced economy (Mann 1977*b*; Elias 1970*a*, 138 ff.).

The structuration of the propertied class

Structuration is the process through which structures are made to persist or become transformed. To study the structuration of a propertied class is to analyse the mechanisms through which its privileged position is reproduced over time. My concern here is with the mechanisms of 'mediate structuration', that is, the long-term processes through which closure and monopolization are achieved. The analysis will focus on the social institutions through which class structuration is mediated (Giddens 1976b, 120–3). Giddens has argued that class structuration proceeds along two dimensions: integration and recruitment. That is, the solidarity and cohesion of a privileged class depends upon the quality and quantity of inter-actions between its members and upon the ability of the class to restrict entry to the privileged positions which it enjoys (Giddens 1973, 120).

Integration is necessary because the propertied class has no monolithic unity; it comprises various 'segments'. The propertied class is internally differentiated into segments 'having a relatively distinct location in the social process of production and, consequently, its own specific political economic requirements and concrete interests which may be contradictory to those of other class segments with which, nonetheless, it shares essentially the same relationship to ownership of productive property' (Zeitlin *et al.* 1976, 1009). In his original formulation of the thesis of the managerial revolution, Burnham had discussed the changing balance of power between 'managers', 'finance executives' and 'finance capitalists', and more recent studies have followed this lead. The most extensive study of this kind is that of Villarejo, who found three major categories of company directors: the 'propertied rich', 'executives' and 'outside' directors. The latter group includes bankers, lawyers and other businessmen. More than half of the directors of top American com-panies were active or retired executives. About a fifth were major stockholders – the propertied rich – and about a third of these also held executive posts. Outside directors sit on the board as representa-tives of large holdings or because of their legal and financial skills (Villarejo 1961b, 52; Domhoff 1967, 58 ff.; Smigel 1964; Smith 1970, 48). A study by Soref found that outside directors came from a more 'exclusive' social background than executive directors and that they tended to hold a large number of directorships, giving them a broad interest in intercorporate affairs (Soref 1976, 360). Useem calls these directors, following Zeitlin, the 'inner group' of the propertied class. The inner group is concerned mainly with integrating the activities of the business world and was found to sustain a class awareness – a sense of common identity and community (Useem 1978, 238). This class awareness served as a diffuse mechanism of integration but did not involve specific political concerns or a consciousness of opposition. (See also: Seider 1974; 1977; Christ 1970.)

Integration of the various segments of the propertied class, therefore, is brought about by a division of labour between the segments themselves. Full-time executives concern themselves with the management of particular companies, while non-executive directors 'manage' the system as a whole. These non-executive directors are the core of the propertied class, which has its interests dispersed throughout the system which they manage. The major mechanism of integration pointed to in these studies is the informality and communication deriving from a common social background. Indeed, this has been central to the whole discussion of social class so far. In Britain, this has been analysed in relation to the changing balance of power between landed, industrial and financial segments of the propertied class. From within the theory of capitalist society Aaronovitch has stated the argument:

The capitalist class itself, at first politically managed by the aristocracy and landed gentry, underwent a complex process by which the most powerful groups of industrial and trading capitalists married into and merged with the aristocracy and big landed gentry. . . . But the outcome of capitalist competition and the fusion of banking and cognate capital with industrial capital has been, inevitably, the emergence of a small, oligarchic set of groupings who are the upper caste of the class which dominates capitalist society as a whole [Aaronovitch 1961, 70].

A number of studies have confirmed some aspects of this view. It is generally accepted that the fusion of industrial and financial interests with the older landed interests resulted in the creation of an 'establishment'. Rubinstein claims that in the early years of this century 'there took place the collapse of the three old elites and their merger into one elite, dominated by the South of England and finance' (Rubinstein 1976, 124). Drawing on evidence from the Parker Tribunal (1957), Lupton and Wilson documented the high degree of integration characteristic of the City establishment (Lupton and Wilson 1959; Sampson 1962; Stanworth and Giddens 1974*a*, 99 ff.). In this fusion, the values of the old landed class, the ideals of civilized gentlemanly behaviour, were fostered and maintained in the public schools and Oxbridge (Elias 1939*a*; Dunning 1977; Coleman 1973), and these values were passed on to the leaders of various institutions, whatever their social origins (Rex 1974*b*). A common background and pattern of socialization, reinforced through intermarriage, club memberships, etc., generated a community feeling among the members of the propertied class. This feeling could be articulated into a class awareness by the most active members of the class.

In the USA as well there is evidence that the propertied class is tightly integrated through similar mechanisms. Baltzell has argued that the American upper class is

. . . a group of *families*, whose members are descendants of successful individuals (elite members) of one, two, three or more generations ago. These families are at the top of a *social class* hierarchy; they are brought up together, are friends, and are intermarried one with another; and, finally, they maintain a distinctive style of life and a kind of primary group solidarity which sets them apart from the rest of the population [Baltzell 1958, 7].

It is facts such as these which led Mills to assert that ' "Interlocking Directorate" is no mere phrase: it points to a solid feature of the facts of business life, and to a sociological anchor of the community of interest, the unification of outlook and policy, that prevails among the propertied class' (Mills 1956, 123). Interlocking directorships between the members of the core of the propertied class reinforce the values and ideas of that class and so consolidate the integration of the class. The informality engendered in networks of kinship and friendship and by shared ideas enables the network of interlocking directorships to function as an efficient system of communication. 'A consequence of multiple participation is the maintenance of well-oiled communication channels through which business deals of a wide variety can be furthered when need be' (Sonquist *et al.* 1975, 199).

The problem of recruitment has received a considerable amount of attention from within the theory of industrial society. It is held that the increased need for skilled, professional managers cannot be met from within the ranks of the propertied families. Kerr *et al.* discuss this problem as the disappearance of 'patrimonial management':

When the family enterprise expands, its patrimonial form is undermined. To find technicians, engineers, and administrators with the requisite knowledge, training, and skill, it must go beyond blood relatives. As the number of professionals in the patrimonial enterprise expands, the members of the family find it increasingly difficult to maintain their control ·
There comes a point where the interests of the family are better promoted by turning over the operation of the enterprise to competent professiona

managerial careerists. This is what happened in the case of hundreds of family enterprises in the United States, and the same trend is apparent in the larger enterprises in England, Germany, and even France and Italy today [Kerr *et al.* 1969, 151–2; Banks 1964, 48].

Taken in conjunction with the supposed 'separation of ownership from control', this trend is held to bring about a gradual but definite shift in the composition of the dominant class, a shift from propertied to managerial personnel (Dahrendorf 1959, 47; Crosland 1962, 73). Evidence from a study by Bendix, however, shows that the proportion of 'heirs' in the American business elite has actually increased over the course of the present century. Both heirs and 'bureaucrats' have grown in number at the expense of self-made entrepreneurs. Bendix (1956, 229–30) notes that all three types of businessmen tend to come 'from families which already occupied a privileged economic position'. Without producing direct evidence, however, Bendix suggests that family management is characteristic of small enterprises, and Aron (1967, 116) claims that it is 'possible only in those instances where the heirs show the necessary ability'.

A study by Taussig and Joslyn found that, in the 1930s, 58 per cent of American business leaders came from a business background, only 13 per cent being professional managers. This study showed the importance of education for business leadership, even among those who were heirs (Taussig and Joslyn 1932). More recent research has emphasized both the restrictions on mobility and the importance of education (Warner and Abegglen 1955, 14, 22, 25, 208; Dye 1976, 152; Mace 1971).

In Britain, a study of directors in large firms in the 1950s found that 58 per cent had been educated at public schools and that 57 per cent had some kind of high-level qualification. More than half of all the directors came from a business background, 44 per cent having fathers who had been directors. Just under one-fifth of the directors inherited their positions. The heirs were found to have the highest level of qualification of all directors. Nearly three-quarters had spent their whole career in business, a third having spent their career solely in large firms. In all, about three-quarters of the directors had some kind of 'commercial' training, while a quarter had a 'technical' training. Those directors trained in engineering or science tended to be single directors in engineering or chemical firms; those directors trained in law and accountancy tended to be multiple, outside directors (Copeman 1955, 89, 92–5, 105, 120; Clements 1958, 173 ff.). Nichols found that in the 1960s the situation was very similar: a large number of directors were unqualified, only a small number had science qualifications, and the most frequent single qualification was a training in accountancy. He did find, however, some evidence that professional management training was becoming more widespread (Nichols 1969, 81–3, 93; Marceau and Whitley 1978). A study of company chairmen by Stanworth and Giddens suggested that, while recruitment in manufacturing industry had opened up a little, banking remained an exclusive occupation (Stanworth and Giddens 1974*a*, 89). In view of the centrality of banks in corporate networks, it is important to investigate this more fully. Table 39 presents the results of a major investigation into the education of directors in British commercial banks.

Table 39   *Educational background of British commercial bank directors* (*1939–70*)

			%	
Type of education	*1939*	*1950*	*1960*	*1970*
Major public schools	60·9	66·9	61·1	62·7
Other public schools	7·3	9·5	12·2	17·2
All public schools	68·2	76·4	73·3	79·9
Oxford and Cambridge	45·3	51·5	52·8	60·4
Other universities	4·5	1·8	4·5	8·2
All universities	49·8	53·3	57·3	68·6

SOURCE: Boyd (1973), 84, table 11, and 92, table 19.

Table 39 shows a clear and significant upward trend in both public school and university attendance. The clearing-bank directors were becoming more highly educated, but they were obtaining this education at the traditional privileged institutions. Examining the fathers of these directors, Boyd found that about half had appeared in *Who's Who* and that the directors who had not come directly from this privileged background had achieved their mobility through the public schools and Oxbridge (Boyd 1973, 96, 102, 110). Thus recruitment to the leadership of British business remained restrictive, though formal educational qualifications are becoming of greater importance.

A study which related the careers of French business leaders to the ownership characteristics of firms found that chairmen of the board (*Président directeur général*) came predominantly from business backgrounds and were educated in scientific schools such as the *polytechniques* (Monjardet 1972, 133; Marceau 1977, 133; Lautman 1966). Monjardet found that those who did not come from a business background had to compensate for this through the possession of educational diplomas. Chairmen of companies subject to bank control were always from an exclusive social background, always had technical diplomas, and had frequently *'pantouflé'* from administrative careers in the state. By contrast, chairmen in family firms were either lowly educated heirs or dependent employees. Those who chaired firms which were controlled through a constellation of interests, having the majority of their shares held by a small but diverse group, were managed by neutral arbitrators or by directors of one of the shareholding companies. These managers were both exclusive in social background and highly qualified (Monjardet 1972, 139 ff.).[6]

Business leaders in the capitalist industrial societies are still drawn overwhelmingly from the propertied class, yet this class supplements direct inheritance with possession of educational diplomas. While technical expertise and education generally are increasingly prominent factors in executive recruitment, this does not preclude the continued dominance of propertied families. Stanworth and Giddens argue that

. . . the persistence of familial ties with the economic leadership of the very large companies is a notable phenomenon. This tends to be masked by the declining importance of 'inherited control' of the sort in which an entrepreneur passes on 'his' firm to his son. This obviously drops away among the giant corporations; but it does not signal the disappearance of less immediate forms of 'inheritance', whereby members of the same family continue to be prominently represented on the board [Stanworth and Giddens 1975, 24].

If the established families are able to monopolize access to the education system, they can ensure that those most qualified for controlling positions in the corporate system are none other than their own scions. The greater the monopolization of education, the greater the closure of the upper class and, therefore, the more secure will be the established families in the overall process of class reproduction.

The evidence I have presented suggests that, while class domination still persists, the mechanisms of this domination have changed. Although private ownership is of considerable importance, it is not always sufficient to ensure a leading position in the corporate world.

E

Baran and Sweezy (1966, 29) have argued that 'stock ownership, wealth, connexions, etc., do not as a rule enable a man to control or to exercise great influence on a giant corporation from the outside. They are rather tickets of admission to the inside, where real corporate power is wielded.' Braverman has amplified this point and claims that severance of the direct personal link between capital and its individual owner has involved a transition from a 'personal' link between ownership and strategic control to a 'class' link. Recruitment is based on technical expertise rather than on personal connections, and technical expertise is monopolized by the propertied class (Braverman 1974, 257–8). The link between legal ownership and control over capital has changed from a personal to an impersonal link and from a reliance on wealth to a reliance on 'cultural assets'.

Bourdieu, from whom the term 'cultural assets' is taken, expresses this transformation in terms of a move from the personal mode of class domination appropriate to the mechanical solidarity of the traditional market society, to the 'structural mode of class domination' characteristic of the organic solidarity of an administered oligopoly involving highly interdependent firms, complex networks of power, and bureaucratized enterprises. There has been a change in the mode of executive recruitment and, therefore, in the mode of reproduction of the system. Selection and promotion are now dependent on educational certificates rather than being directly dependent on personal property:

The family enterprise run at least partially by its proprietors can overlook formal criteria in the recruitment of its leaders because the possession of property titles to the enterprise and/or its appurtenances by the proprietary family guarantees possession of the attributes and qualities considered socially necessary (for example, 'standing' or 'sense of authority') and the symbolic capital (notably personal relations) necessary for management of the enterprise: in assuring its own reproduction, the family assures at the same time the production of personnel endowed with the social competence (and often also the technical competence) necessary for running the enterprise. The tendential transformation of 'individual possessory holdings' within 'power systems' renders inoperative the means by which the enterprise can assure the managerial personnel endowed with the characteristics, and notably the class habitus, required. It is as if possession of an educational title, and particularly a diploma from a *Grande École*, which tends to become a necessary (though not sufficient) condition of access to positions of economic power, constitutes, like the possession of a property title in another stage of the system, a sort of syncretic index guaranteeing possession of most of the properties and qualities with which the leaders of the large integrated firms must be endowed in order to occupy positions of power in the apparatus of the enterprise [Bourdieu *et al.* 1973, 66].

The modern structural mode of domination requires agents with a high level of technical competence. The dominant class has transformed the institutions through which it reproduces itself and so is able to continue to control the economy; the reproduction of class domination operates through the mediation of the school (ibid., 77, 80–2). Whereas the personal mode of domination involved the 'direct transmission of social positions between the holder and the inheritor designated by the holder himself', the structural mode of domination operates in an indirect way at the level of the class as a whole: transmission of social positions within the dominant class 'rests on the *statistical* aggregation of the isolated actions of individuals or collective agents who are subject to the same laws, those of the educational market (ibid., 83).

This transition involves what Parkin sees as a move from collectivist rules of exclusion to individualist rules of exclusion. Increasingly, recruitment is based on rules which refer to the specific attributes of individuals which fit them for positions. In particular, this involves what Miller has called 'credentialism', 'reliance upon examination certificates as a means of controlling entry to valued positions in the division of labour' (Parkin 1974*a*, 7). But this is not a straightforward transition from 'ascription' to 'achievement', although it may have the appearance of a meritocracy. Achievement of an educational title depends upon a person's cultural patrimony (*patrimoine culturel*). The new mode of domination

... limits the powers of the family which, in the old mode of reproduction, controlled the totality of the mechanisms of reproduction from fertility and marriage to inheritance – by which the transmission of patrimony ensures the transmission of the social positions to which the patrimony gives access – and also, to a considerable extent, education. But this is only to restore them in another form, at the level of the class, through the intermediary of the better hidden mechanisms of social statistics which are capable, such is the logic of probability, of conferring on the class in its totality the properties which it refuses to its various elements taken separately [Bourdieu *et al.* 1973, 83–4].

The inherited cultural assets of an upper-class background are amplified through the educational system, access to which is still dependent upon wealth. Thus wealth can be converted into cultural assets. Inheritance of cultural assets is possible only for those 'endowed with the means of appropriating it for themselves', and since these means are differentially distributed between social classes

. . . it is sufficient to give free play to the laws of cultural transmission for cultural capital to be added to cultural capital and for the structure of the distribution of cultural capital between social classes to be thereby reproduced [Bourdieu 1971, 73; Bourdieu and Passeron 1970].

Even if this form of closure is incomplete and a certain degree of social mobility occurs, this need not threaten the reproduction of the class structure, since 'the controlled mobility of a limited category of individuals, carefully selected and modified by and for individual ascent, is not incompatible with the permanence of structures' (Bourdieu 1971, 71). Stability of class relations will occur so long as the occupants of dominant positions are endowed with the system of predispositions, the 'habitus', which generates actions that contribute to the reproduction of the structure.

Thus, to the extent that ownership and strategic control are no longer directly connected, the mechanisms of cultural patrimony and the educational market together ensure that the corporate economy remains under the control of the capitalist class as a whole. To the extent that ownership and strategic control are *not* actually separated, the mechanisms of personal domination will continue to operate. As Meynaud puts it:

Without any doubt at all, modern capitalism has considerably modified its practices; but if the method of recruitment of the managerial circle has undergone any noticeable changes, it does not seem to me that either the unity or even the homogeneity of this group is seriously compromised [Meynaud 1964, 175].

There is a privileged class of propertied families which are increasingly autonomous from particular proprietary interests. This class is able to secure a degree of closure sufficient to reproduce the positions of its members within the broader structure which it reproduces. Industrial capitalism shows a long-term tendency for the direct connection between private family property and strategic control to be broken. Nevertheless, it is also evident that propertied interests are still of central importance: a large number of companies are controlled by private owners, many executives are drawn from those who hold large blocks of shares in the corporation, and directors and executives are drawn from a pool of wealthy families.

The managerial reorganization of the propertied class has resulted in a structure of interdependent families and corporations. The families involved in this structure are the nucleus of a social class which reproduces itself over time. The propertied class is 'the social class formed around the core of interrelated principal owners of capital' (Zeitlin 1976, 901). The most important mechanisms of class structuration are commonalty of social background, the direct transmission of property, and the indirect transmission of cultural patrimony. Social class relations are reproduced on the basis of the 'resources' provided by the relations of possession with which they are associated. In class structuration, individuals are recruited in such a way that their actions reproduce the structure of class relations. As Bourdieu (1971; 1974) argues, structures comprise sets of constraints upon action, such that agents with particular 'habitus' are selected out. The practices generated by these habitus are precisely those which serve to reproduce the structure. Structures are human products and emerge as consequences, frequently unintended, of definite social practices. Thus the attempt to 'open' education to a broader social intake may in fact have strengthened the position of a propertied class which could no longer rely exclusively on the direct inheritance of positions.

6 The economy and the state

A major trend in the development of industrial capitalism has been the expanding scale of economic activity. The theory of industrial society has focused on the *concentration of production* in bigger technical units. The imperatives of large-scale industry are held to generate powerful managerial technostructures as well as counter-vailing worker and consumer groups (Galbraith 1952; Kerr *et al.* 1960). The arena of competition for these interest groups is the state, with the government acting as referee. Power generates counter-vailing power, and so the economic policy of the state reflects the competition of the more or less equal groups. Political leaders form a professional body performing the essentially technical function of policy formulation (Aron 1960, 269). The theory of capitalist society sees the central process as the *centralization of control* over larger units of capital and the consequent 'monopolization' of the economy. The formation of cartels, trusts and other types of monopoly are the means through which the dominant class, against its will, brings about the incipient socialization of production. This class also dominates the state machinery and so constitutes a ruling class. As a consequence, an increasingly centralized state can be used to buttress the economic power of the monopolies (Lenin 1917*a*; Ryndina and Chernikov 1974, 198). Many aspects of these arguments have, of course, been countered in previous chapters. The aim of the present chapter is to consider the consequences of economic concentration and centralization. Specifically, I shall examine the implications which these processes have for the state mediation of economic relations.

Market behaviour and capital accumulation

There has undoubtedly been a trend towards both technical concentration and financial centralization, the sectors of the economy dominated by large companies having increased steadily since at least the 1880s. The emerging 'mesoeconomic' firms have developed a diversified product range and a wide geographical spread of activity and so have adopted characteristic forms of internal administration (Chandler 1962; 1976; Holland 1975). Evidence from many countries suggests that large firms have developed and continued to grow, not through investment in new plant, but through the acquisition of other companies. The main mechanism of concentration and centralization is the merger. In Britain, observers agree that concentration has increased, but they disagree about the rate and extent of this trend.[1] It is widely recognized that since the 'Great Depression' of the 1870s and 1880s there have been three main bursts of merger activity. From 1880 to the First World War many small family firms amalgamated into cartels and trusts and so laid the foundations of many of the giant firms which later developed. These mergers were, however, mainly concerned with sales and output and did not result in integrated large-scale production. The post-war boom of 1919–20 initiated a period of mergers and reorganizations in which the emerging large firms were consolidated, though many were still being formed as holding companies exercising only a loose financial control over autonomous subsidiaries. The merger boom of the 1950s and 1960s produced a considerable restructuring of the large companies as more and more of them adopted an integrated divisional structure (Hannah 1975; Pollard 1962; Prais 1976; Aaronovitch and Sawyer 1975; Channon 1973). These movements of centralization and restructuring have affected industrial and financial companies alike, although diversification and multidivisional organization have only recently become characteristic of financial companies (Channon 1977). There is considerable debate over how concentration should be measured and over its precise extent (Utton 1970; Hart *et al.* 1973; Walshe 1973; Evely and Little 1960). But it has been suggested by Meeks and Whittington (1975; 1976) that the share of the top 100 companies in net assets has risen from 46 per cent in 1948, through 57 per cent in 1957, to 65 per cent in 1969. Prais has estimated that the share of these same firms in total output increased from 27 per cent in 1953 to 41 per cent in 1970 (Prais 1976, 4; Jewkes 1977).

The trend of concentration in the USA and Canada has followed a similar pattern to that in the UK. By 1929, the top 100 US manufacturing corporations accounted for 40 per cent of manufacturing assets, and this figure had risen to 49 per cent by 1962 (Means 1964, 15). Even the conservative estimates made by Jewkes show that the top 100 firms accounted for 33 per cent of manufacturing output in 1972 (Jewkes 1977, 15). Miller's data suggest that the top 500 accounted for 65 per cent of sales and 79 per cent of profits of all industrial firms and employed one-fifth of the non-agricultural labour force. Similarly, the top fifty banks had more than half of all bank assets and deposits, and the top ten insurance companies had 57 per cent of insurance company assets (Miller 1975, 3–5). There is, furthermore, considerable concentration within the top 100 itself: a quarter of manufacturing assets in 1962 were held by the top twenty companies, and the top five held half of the assets of the twenty largest companies (Mueller 1964, 23). Similarly, Jewkes estimates that, while the top 100 companies in 1977 accounted for 33 per cent of industrial output, the top fifty accounted for 25 per cent (Jewkes 1977, 15).

In Thompson's study of Canadian companies, which drew on US information as well, it was shown that company mergers led to few economies of scale: acquired plants tended to be run as parallel operations rather than being integrated into a restructured production process (Thompson 1978, 12). Prais found that while mergers in Britain had brought about financial centralization, the proportion of the labour force employed in large plants had remained constant: the centralization of financial resources had resulted in little or no restructuring at the technical level (Prais 1976). A study by Morvan shows that the proportion of the labour force employed in establishments of more than 1000 people varied from high levels of 28 to 30 per cent in the USA, West Germany and Holland, to low levels of 13 to 17 per cent in Italy, Japan and France (Morvan 1972, 221). A recent study suggests that in Europe financial centralization has been more significant than technical reorganization, though Germany is perhaps an exception (George and Ward 1975; Daems and Van Der Wee 1974).

The growth in the scale of business has led to much discussion on how the behaviour of large firms is to be explained. In particular, the dominance of the giant companies has raised the question of whether these companies are able to override the constraints of market competition. Means has argued that the relative importance of market and non-market controls must always be assessed empirically: 'Where policies with respect to the use of resources are only limited and not dominated by market controls, the nonmarket controls become a significant factor making for more or less effective use of resources' (Means *et al.* 1939, 154). Banks and the state, for example, may be able to influence corporate strategy within the range of alternatives possible. 'In many producing units there is a wide latitude of choice in price policy, and economic controls not operating through the market are in effect' (ibid.). Where a number of companies have overlapping ranges of action, a bank may be able to influence them into adopting particular strategies within the area of overlap in order to further its own interests. Fitch and Oppenheimer (1970c, 77, 81) argue that giant corporations are engaged in relations of 'reciprocity' in which intercorporate sales and purchases are not based on market factors but on considerations such as the wishes of their bankers. From a different point of view, Bell has claimed that the loosening of market constraints permits the large corporation to 'judge society's needs in a more conscious fashion and . . . to do so on the basis of some explicit conception of the "public interest" ' (Bell 1974, 283). Clearly, a consideration of these possibilities requires a closer analysis of the nature of market constraints themselves.

The position of a corporation in a system of market relations involves what Karpik (1972) calls a 'logic of action' for that corporation. Companies are located in structural conditions which limit their actions by imposing certain 'principles' upon them. The behaviour of the company in relation to these structural limits determines the limits it will face in the future. The dynamics of intercorporate relations are to be found, in part, in the logic of action which the market structure imposes on each company. Owing to the imperfect information about market conditions which each company possesses, the structural limits are altered in an unconscious unintended way. For this reason, firms cannot be sure that they, or their competitors, will not bring about the conditions for their own disappearance. The larger are the individual firms within a particular market – that is, the greater is the degree of concentration – the more dependent are the firms on one another and the less able are they to reduce the level of market uncertainty. As Elias argues in his discussion of 'game models': 'as power differentials lessen between interdependent individuals and groups there is a diminishing possibility that any participants . . . will be able to influence the overall course of the game' (1970a, 96). In the market, each corporation is faced with a broad range of action (Marris 1964, 47) which it can influence but not totally determine. The actual pattern of limits within a market is determined as the unintended consequence of the behaviour of the various companies involved in that market.

The implications of market concentration have been discussed by many writers, stretching back at least to Robinson (1933) and Chamberlin (1933). These writers formulated theories of 'imperfect' or 'monopolistic' competition as alternatives to the classical economic theories of atomistic, perfect competition. More recently, theories of 'oligopoly' have been put forward. In oligopoly, prices are tacitly administered by a few large firms; 'prices are no longer an impersonal force selecting the efficient man, forcing him to adopt the most efficient mode and scale of operations and driving out the inefficient and incompetent' (Galbraith 1952, 43; Kefauver 1966). According to Galbraith the normal pattern of development in an industry is that of a steady decline in the number of firms until a point of stability is reached, involving a handful of large firms and a fringe of smaller hangers-on. Following the initial accumulation of capital and the disappearance of weak firms, there are almost insuperable barriers to entry into the industry. The occurrence of this process in all industries means that eventually 'a small number of large corporations are responsible for a very substantial proportion of all industrial activity' (Galbraith 1952, 38). With the large corporation as a 'price maker' rather than a 'price taker', each market is organized around 'administered prices'. This is not to say that oligopolistic market prices cease to be 'the unintended outcome of the self-regarding actions of the numerous units that compose it' (Baran and Sweezy 1966, 63). The price-setting activities of the large corporation are still influenced by those of its competitors, and lack of knowledge about the intentions of competitors generates the typical uncertainty, or 'anarchy', of the market mechanism. This uncertainty can be reduced by a tacit prohibition on price competition, which permits firms to pursue a more or less rational pricing policy. So long as the dominant corporations can reach such agreement, the group as a whole can pursue a monopoly pricing policy and so secure monopoly profits. Competition in non-price areas – advertising, brand differentiation, etc. – then involves a struggle over the distribution of these monopoly profits among the various firms (Baran and Sweezy 1966, 66–8; Lipsey 1966, 343 ff.; Paish 1967, 212 ff.; Baran 1957, 196 ff.; Holland 1975, 56). Competition involves cutting the costs of production, since lower costs lead to advantages in the struggle for market shares; the firm with the lowest costs can best afford advertising, research and development, and so on. Success and failure in cost reduction are the mechanisms of oligopolistic competition; and cost-cutting competition is systematically generated in an oligopolistic market (Baran and Sweezy 1966, 76–9). As Giddens argues,

Even in the most 'organized' of the capitalist economies, the private appropriation of profit through the investment of capital remains the ultimate regulator of productive activity – situations of oligopoly or monopoly, involving in some sense the direct 'administration' of prices by producers, may entail a 'reallocation' of revenue on capital from the more to the less competitive industries, but do not directly cut through the conditions of capitalist production [Giddens 1973, 143, 161].

The structural limits on corporate behaviour are manifested in the pressures of competition. The 'logic of action' for a corporation located in an oligopolistic market is to engage in competitive cost-reduction in order to improve its share of the market. But can this be described as a strategy of profit maximization? And what compels a firm to observe these limits? According to Baran and Sweezy (1966, 37), large corporations are involved in a 'systematic temporal search for highest practicable profits'. In a given market situation, this level of profit is generally the greatest increase in profits which will not ruin later opportunities. Short-term profit maximization would involve 'a reckless and wholly irrational pursuit of immediately realizable profit, regardless of any longer term consideration' (Miliband 1968, 54). But this is neither the only nor the most rational form of profit seeking. Mandel has claimed that the modern corporation eschews such 'reckless' hedonism:

In conditions of monopolistic competition short-term profit maximization is a completely senseless goal. Company strategy aims at *long-term profit maximization*, in which factors such as domination of the market, share of the market, brand familiarity, future ability to meet demand, safeguarding of opportunities for innovation, i.e., for growth, become more important than the selling price which can be obtained immediately or the profit margin which this represents [Mandel 1972, 232; Aaronovitch and Sawyer 1975, 42 ff.; Westergaard and Resler 1975, 165].

Marketing policies aimed at size, strength and growth are aspects of a strategy of long-term profit seeking (Baran and Sweezy 1966, 51; Marris 1964, 59, 107 ff.; Blackburn 1965, 172; Child 1969, 49), but it may be somewhat misleading to call this profit 'maximization'. Alchian has argued that companies are not maximizers, since market uncertainty is the obverse of the conditions for rational maximization. Rather, the market selects companies for survival according to their success in realizing profits. In order to survive, a company must merely do better than its actual competitors; it does not need to adopt some hypothetical 'maximum'. Companies may adopt any of a number of procedures and criteria in the calculations they make in pursuing their strategies, but the inherent uncertainty of market relations is such that their actions can be successful only if market conditions permit. Because companies have imperfect knowledge of current market conditions, and must predict future conditions on the basis of this knowledge, strategies for survival cannot follow an absolute and unambiguous norm of maximization. No matter whether companies attempt to 'maximize', to 'optimize' or to achieve 'social responsibility', they will survive only if their actual behaviour is compatible with market conditions (Alchian 1950; Becker 1962). The policies described above as typical of the large corporation can be seen as the most rational attempts possible to cope with market conditions:

The compelling constraint . . . is that the firm's health, indeed its survival, depend on the relation within it of revenues and costs. . . . Pursuit of profit does not mean that management spends much of its time contemplating profit as such but that its time is spent on decisions regarding the planning, providing, pricing, and selling of products, which govern revenue, and the organizing, equipping, and carrying on of production, together with the purchase of labour, supplies, and other requirements, which govern costs. . . . This is the essence of profit-seeking and of capitalist behaviour in employing resources [Peterson 1965, 9; Baumol 1962].

The corporation, is therefore, a long-term profit seeker. It attempts to secure a relation of revenue to costs which will give it the best chance of survival in the market.

It is important to note that not all corporations are profit seekers in the sense defined above. Companies which are subsidiaries of other companies will have their behaviour subordinated to the strategy of their parent company. The parent company, as the effective unit of capital, is the unit of profitability. This same point may be extended to other company groupings. Writing of family interest groups, Anderson *et al.* claim that 'While all of these concerns are independent enterprises, with complete freedom to determine their own policies, it seems hardly likely, in view of the extent to which they are owned by the same people, that anyone of them would pursue a course which was prejudicial to the interests of the others' (Anderson *et al.* 1941, 24). It is in this light that the notion of 'reciprocity' put forward by Fitch and Oppenheimer can be considered. Fitch has argued that all corporations which engage in reciprocal non-market trading with other corporations must be considered as subordinate elements of broader units of capital. In particular, bank-centred groupings comprise sets of individual companies subordinated to the profitability of the bank (Fitch 1972, 126). In Chapter 4 certain problems of this theory have already been suggested and O'Connor has rightly pointed out that if banks operated in this way then industrial companies would soon go out of business and the banks could no longer make profits at their expense (O'Connor 1971). However, the fact remains that, within the limits of their market situation, companies may follow strategies which do not bring them as high a profit as might have been earned, but which are profitable enough to allow them to survive. It is necessary to consider both market and non-market determinants of corporate behaviour. The balance of power between companies may well determine the distribution of profit, and hence the pattern of capital accumulation (Thompson 1977), but profit will be available for distribution only if market limits are observed.

This discussion shows that the behaviour of companies depends not merely upon their market situation, but also upon the non-market influences to which they are subjected. Companies owned by the same family may be operated as a group, and companies located in bank-centred networks of communication may be influenced by the companies to which they are connected. But this argument has often been taken much further, and it has been claimed that the fundamental determinant of corporate behaviour is the mode of control. Bell's claim that management-controlled companies pursue a strategy related to the 'public interest' is only a particularly extreme statement of this point of view. Dahrendorf (1959, 46), for example, has argued that 'Never has the imputation of a profit motive been further from the real motives of men than it is for the modern bureaucratic manager. Economically, managers are interested in such things as rentability, efficiency, and productivity.' Similarly, Shonfield (1965, 377) states that 'the manager, who is not the owner, is neither driven into automatic responses by the forces of the market place nor guided by the exclusive desire to make the maximum profit on behalf of his shareholders.' Changes in patterns of industrial control are held to create the conditions under which management may exercise a certain amount of discretion and so may move away from an exclusive concern with profit. Monsen and Downes (1965), for example, argue that, while the shareholders of a company look for a steady divided income and capital gains, managers seek to maximize their lifetime incomes. (See also Crosland 1962, 87–8.) In the previous chapter I suggested that no hard-and-fast distinction could be made between 'capitalists' and 'managers' – those who run the major corporations are the kernel of a privileged, propertied class. However, it may be true that companies which are majority- or minority-owned by particular owners are run differently from companies with no dominant ownership interest. Pahl has claimed that firms with family or other majority owners will pursue long-term growth and capital appreciation as a way of maintaining the value of the capital invested. On the other hand, companies owned by financial institutions will have to make high dividend payouts in order to meet the pension and insurance commitments of the financial interests (Pahl 1977a, 15; Wilson Report 1977, 22). In this view the transformation of ownership patterns leads to more money coming out of the company in the form of income and so limits the amount available for investment by the firm. In a study of the top 200 US companies it was found that there was some very slight tendency for 'owner-controlled' companies to be more profit-able than those with no dominant ownership interest. The main factors associated with profitability, however, were the size of the firm and market factors such as barriers to entry (Kamerschen 1968). A similar study found that owner-controlled firms showed a better return on their capital (Monsen *et al.* 1968; Larner 1970, 29). In Britain, Radice studied eighty-nine large firms over the period 1957–67 and found that owner-controlled companies had both a higher profit rate and a higher growth rate than management-controlled companies. However, Radice found that profitability was inversely related to size and that owner-controlled companies were mainly smaller companies: low profitability was not a character-istic of management control as such, but of large size (Radice 1971, 558–61).

Clearly, no firm conclusions can be drawn about the relationship between mode of control and profitability.[2] It may be that companies with different modes of control are subject to different non-market controls and that, for this reason, their behaviour will be affected. A dominant ownership interest, for example, may be able to make a company act at a particular point in the range of possibilities open to it in its market situation. Similarly, the directors and top execu-tives may be able to benefit themselves excessively through salaries, fees, pensions, and so on, at the expense of dividend payouts. There is little firm evidence on which to test these possibilities. Indeed, the reason why the evidence is inconclusive is probably that any such effects on profitability will be extremely small. Profit seeking involves a surplus of revenue over costs, and, since the surplus is always small in relation to revenue and costs, behaviour aimed at marginally altering the size of the surplus is unlikely to have a significant influence on the overall corporate strategy (Peterson 1965; Lieberson and O'Connor 1972).

The possibilities discussed above raise the important question of the relationship between, on the one hand, corporate strategy and the objective market constraints to which it relates and, on the other hand, the personal motives and orientations of those who manage the large corporations. I have argued that market and non-market constraints together determine corporate strategy. But this strategy is formulated and implemented by a particular personnel with particular interests. It follows from the argument above that, while socially responsible managers may pursue 'soulful' policies in an attempt to usher in 'People's Capitalism', their companies are unlikely to survive if this policy involves a departure from long-term profit seeking. The imperatives of the market are such that firms which do not make profits will not survive. The management of a large corporation is limited by the effective demand generated in the market and is constrained to meet this demand through techniques and policies which allow them to earn a rate of profit which does not fall too far below the average (Blackburn 1965, 168–9). Such market constraints are likely to generate the type of managerial personality which is subjectively oriented to these same constraints. This occurs through the 'selective and moulding effects of institutions on the personnel that operates them' (Baran and Sweczy 1966, 49; Bourdieu 1974; Gerth and Mills 1954, 165 ff.). Corporate careers depend upon contribution to the success of the company, and managers tend to acquire the personality which meets the needs of the system. The corporate goals of size, strength and growth – i.e. profitability – 'become the subjective aims of the business world because they are the objective requirements of the system' (Baran and Sweezy 1966, 53; Parsons 1940).

Top managers are drawn from the wealthiest section of society, they often have a considerable financial stake in their own company, they are the major individual owners of company shares, they are selected and moulded so as to follow the principle of long-term profitability, and if their companies depart from this principle then bankruptcy or decline will follow. Furthermore, to the extent that professional managers have a high level of technical competence and have systems of technical knowledge and information processing available to them, they are able to pursue profits with a greater efficiency than was possible in the past. The professional manager is, perhaps, better able to interpret market constraints than was the traditional entrepreneur. As Blackburn argues, 'Improved methods of interpreting the market only make the manager's subordination to it more complete' (Blackburn 1965, 170; Baran and Sweezy 1966, 40, 58: Pahl and Winkler 1974, 118). Mandel has claimed that the whole panoply of scientific management and business administration is an attempt to plan the various factors which are under the control of the firm so as to reduce the complexity of an inherently uncertain market. Companies plan for the stability which derives from reducing the imperfections of their knowledge and thus they improve their chances of survival in the search for profit (Mandel 1972, 233).

No company can dissociate itself from the objective constraints of the market, and these constraints will often be backed up by the board representation of ownership and banking interests. Board representation is also a possible basis for 'non-market' control, and it would be unlikely if the exercise of influence did not result in certain reciprocal trade-offs in which each interest pushes its own advantage in seeking to come to a mutually beneficial decision. But director links generate interlocking directorships, and it was argued in Chapter 4 that the main function of a network of interlocking directorships is to reduce the complexity of the environment in areas which are beyond the control of any single company. Companies will attempt to plan those factors subject to their control, and they will interlock with one another up to the particular level of interlocking which is necessary for optimizing their relations with one another. Interlocking directorships are a stabilizing force in essentially uncertain market conditions, since multiple directors bring a breadth of knowledge about corporate affairs to the deliberations of each company board on which they sit. The network of interlocks is a network of communication and, as such, too much interlocking produces too much 'damping down', and too little interlocking produces riskiness that is due to lack of information. The flow of capital between corporations is reinforced by the flow of information, and it is in this way that market and non-market controls interact to determine the overall pattern of capital accumulation.

The emergence of a political economy

What are the consequences of the mesoeconomic trends discussed above for the long-term development of industrial capitalism? The theory of capitalist society holds that, under conditions of atomistic competition, capital flows freely from the less to the more profitable sectors, and that there is a consequent tendency for the rate of profit earned by each unit of capital to be equalized. Under 'monopoly' conditions, companies earn 'super-profit' on top of average profit, and so the economy as a whole shows no equalization of actual profit rates, since the market entry barriers inhibit the free movement of capital. Unprofitable sectors stagnate and require state support if they are to survive, and, at the same time, existing monopolies are able to attract the capital required to finance their own highly profitable activities. Whereas an average rate of profit is still earned in the 'competitive' sectors of the economy, higher profits are earned in the 'monopoly' sectors. The dynamics of the rate of profit are to be found in the organic composition of capital (the ratio of constant capital to variable capital), and competitive conditions generate a rising organic composition of capital owing to the continual displacement of labour (variable capital) in favour of machinery (constant capital). Thus competition generates a tendency for the rate of profit to fall. This 'law' is a law of tendency, since various factors may counteract its operation: increasing the 'rate of exploitation' by ensuring that wages fall below the value of labour power; export of capital to secure wage goods at a lower price and to exploit low wage economies; and so on (Kozlov 1977, 447 ff., 214 ff.). Monopoly conditions, where there is no one average rate of profit, will also affect the operation of this law, and the nature of this effect has been hotly disputed in orthodox and less orthodox Marxist circles.

Without getting too involved in these disputes, it is necessary to follow through some of the implications which have been drawn about trends in company profitability, since these are important for an understanding of the empirical data. Some writers have suggested that Marx's 'law' operates only under conditions of atomistic competition – in economies dominated by oligopolistic conditions, laws distinct from those discussed by Marx will operate (Szymanski 1973). Indeed, Marx himself claimed that the mere existence of joint-stock companies counteracted the tendency of the rate of profit to fall. His economic theory holds that this tendency depends upon an equalization of the rate of profit throughout the economy, and Marx remarks that joint-stock companies 'do not necessarily enter into the equalization of the general rate of profit' (1894, 428) because companies need only yield *interest* payments such as dividends. Capital invested in stock companies does not enter into the dynamics of the rate of *profit*. If it were included in the calculation, it would indicate a lower rate than the 'seemingly existing rate, which is decisive for the capitalists' (ibid., 235). Owing to the distinction between interest and profit, an economy dominated by corporations – independently of whether the economy is 'monopolized' – will not necessarily exhibit a falling rate of profit. This area of uncertainty in Marxist economics has produced not only discussions of the status of the 'law of value' (Becker 1971; Kosonen 1977; Kemp 1978) but also criticism of the very notion of tendential laws (Hussain 1977; Cutler *et al.* 1977). Nevertheless, many arguments have been put forward to show that state intervention is a direct consequence of the effect of oligopoly on profits. Since the law of value is the 'mechanism by which the nature of the commodity as value determines the social division of labour' (Kosonen 1977, 371), the failure of this 'law' to operate properly under 'monopoly' conditions means that balanced accumulation over the various sectors of the economy is not possible without the intervention of a body which is not itself limited by the criterion of profitability.[3] The state, as such a body, can discriminate against one sector and in favour of another through taxes, subsidies and general expenditure, and so can bring about the restructuring of capital which private capital itself is incapable of producing (Urry 1977, 12–13).

A considerable literature has arisen over the trends in profitability which underlie these arguments.[4] For Britain, Glyn and Sutcliffe have shown that the share of profit in company net output fell from 25 per cent in 1950 to 12 per cent in 1970. They argue that 'the basic reason for the decline in the profit share was the squeezing of profit margins between money wage increases on the one hand and progressively more severe international competition on the other' (Glyn and Sutcliffe 1972, 65). Over the same period, the pre-tax rate of profit fell from 17 per cent to 10 per cent, the post-tax rate falling from 7 per cent to 4 per cent. The implicit argument is that the falling *share* of profit results in an actualization of the tendency for a falling *rate* of profit. Glyn and Sutcliffe relate the decline in profitability to liquidity problems and to a lack of internal investment funding. Falling profitability leads industrial corporations to a greater dependence on bank loans and state subventions. This trend, they argue, is common to all the advanced capitalist economies, though its severity is greater in some – such as Britain – than in others. This is supported by Castells, who documents falling profitability in the USA, Britain, Germany and France (Castells 1976, 33–4; Winkler 1976). In the USA, the ratio of profits to wages has shown a cyclical tendency since the war, though the share of profit has fallen since 1950 (Castells 1976, 61; Boddy and Crotty 1974). Rowthorn has produced similar evidence and adds that rising state expenditure has itself resulted in a further squeeze on profit margins (Rowthorn 1976, 66–7). It would appear that a lack of profitability leads the state to spend more money, and that growing state expenditure exacerbates the profitability problem which it was intended to solve.

In Britain, state expenditure grew from between 25 and 30 per cent of GNP in the 1920s through 40 per cent in the late 1940s, to 50 per cent in the late 1960s – a smooth trend interrupted only by the Second World War, which raised state expenditure to 75 per cent of GNP in 1943 (Gough 1975, 61). As Table 40 shows, state expenditure in all advanced capitalist societies has risen to a similar level.

Table 40   *State expenditure as a percentage of GDP (1972)*

	UK	France	W. Germany	Italy	USA	Japan
Total expenditure	39·8	36·7	38·0	40·0	34·3	20·0
Total revenue	37·9	38·0	39·0	34·7	31·4	22·6

SOURCE: Gough (1975), 59.

NOTE: These figures exclude state-owned productive concerns. The figure for Japan is an estimate.

Three broad categories of state expenditure can be identified: collective provision, demand management and central planning. The state has attempted to ensure collective provision of welfare, education, housing, transport, etc., as well as providing military and police activities. These and other activities are increasingly taken over by the state when they are essential supports of economic activity which cannot be met by private capital, whether this is because of the sheer scale of expense involved or because such provision is not sufficiently profitable for private initiative (Gough

1975, 66–7; Pahl 1977*b*; Kidron 1968). Welfare expenditure encompasses spending on pensions, social security and unemployment benefit, as well as social work and the health services, and has been a rapidly growing item of expenditure. Similarly, the education and training of the labour force, at all levels, takes a large portion of national expenditure, as does 'infrastructural' expenditure on transport, posts, communications, housing and other urban facilities (Pickvance 1976). Thus many activities are provided directly by central or municipal authorities, nationalized corporations, and so on, in order to provide on a collective basis those services which cannot be provided privately. Collective provision is not, of course, merely a 'subsidy' to private capital, but its general function has been to underwrite continued private accumulation (Yaffe 1973, 226; Frankel 1970, 136).

The second major item in state expenditure is demand management. The state has attempted to maintain aggregate expenditure at a level of demand which is sufficient to prevent stagnation and depression. Such policies aim to iron out economic fluctuations so as to maintain acceptable levels of unemployment, inflation and growth, and so as to secure some balance in foreign payments. While the state may not be able to eradicate economic fluctuations, it has been able to influence their timing and intensity (Fine and Harris 1976*b*, 102). Demand management need not involve extra items of expenditure, since, in general, spending on collective provision can be timed and phased in order to serve as an instrument of demand management. But 'Keynesian' demand management can lead imperceptibly to state involvement in the planning and restructuring of capital. To the extent that certain sectors of the economy are in need of aid or inducement, the state can engage in specific activities involving additional expenditure (Fine and Harris 1976*b*, 107; Yaffe 1973, 216–17; Guttman 1976). Giddens has argued that

the operation of 'unfettered' capitalism, first of all, tends to create definite 'weaknesses' in certain sectors of the economy: for these are frequently the sectors into which the state moves. Moreover, the very occurrence, and widening scale, of crises makes evident the generic instability of capitalism if no direct control is maintained by the state over certain of the key aspects of economic organization [Giddens 1973, 151; Warren 1971].

Economic relations are mediated through the state, but the form of mediation varies from one period to another. Atomistic competition existed in national economies – the territorial boundaries of the nation state defined the boundaries of interdependent economic processes. At this stage, the state facilitated private production by securing its general preconditions: law and order, guaranteeing the currency, raising taxation, and so on. This 'facilitative' mediation was of the kind legitimized in the ideology of *laissez-faire*, which was itself grounded in a belief in the self-regulating nature of atomistic competition. As atomistic market structures were undermined by the evolving giant corporations, so state mediation became more 'supportive' of private capital. The state took on responsibilities for collective provision and demand management. As oligopolistic markets matured and profitability problems became more pressing, so state mediation became 'interventionist'. The state had positively to intervene, to impose itself between economic interests, in an attempt to solve these problems. Capitalist production has always involved the periodic fluctuations of the business cycle, but the unprecedented depression of the 1920s and 1930s initiated a series of state-sponsored economic reforms and saw the beginnings of the so-called 'welfare' or 'social' state (Dalton 1974, 63–4; Winkler 1976; 1977; Hill 1977; Westergaard 1977). The national economy became a political economy, two hundred years after the emergence of the discipline of political economy.

From the early 1960s, state intervention has involved attempts at direct planning. Moves towards central planning occurred first in France and Japan and then began in other capitalist economies, the last countries to begin planning being Germany and the USA (Warren 1972; Vernon 1974*a*; Halliday 1975, 53–60: Lockwood 1965*a*, 501 ff.; Holland 1972; Causer 1978). Long-term planning of a 'global' or 'comprehensive' kind involves the coordination of private and public expenditure as well as incomes policy and policies of restructuring or regenerating business (Habermas 1973, 34; Miliband 1968). By promoting mergers and joint ventures and by playing an active role in the economy, governments have attempted both to plan and to ensure the implementation of their plans. As Shonfield (1965, 66) argues:

The effort to secure an enlarged area of predictability for business management . . . has encouraged long-range collaboration between firms. Governments in their anxiety to increase the area of the predictable for the purposes of economic planning have encouraged firms within an industry to evolve agreed policies on the basis of their common long-range interests.

Attempts at central planning involve an attempt to move away from the 'anarchic', 'nature-like' pattern of development inherent in unregulated market relations. The move towards greater concentration and oligopolistic competition creates a greater potential for coordination, and state planning has attempted to consolidate and further this move. Thus Berle has claimed that early capitalism and the modern economy differ in so far as under the former system

. . . no one individual could seriously affect or direct the actions of other individuals: he could only decide for himself. Results in an economic system of that kind were thus attained without conscious intent or decision by anyone; they were the product of an unplanned aggregate. Mid-twentieth century capitalism has been given the power and the means of a more or less planned economy, in which decisions are or at least can be taken in the light of their probable effect on the whole community [Berle 1955, 23; Habermas 1973, 33–4)].

Berle's argument is that planning reduces market uncertainty and so enables conscious political direction of the economy. The next section will discuss whether, in Giddens's words, 'the main characteristic of the mediation of control . . . is increasing ascendancy of political control over decision-making in the economic sphere' (1973, 173). Does the emerging political economy signal the undermining of capitalist relations of production?

The mechanisms of state intervention

In the above discussion 'the state' has been introduced as an unproblematic term. In fact, the state and its mechanisms of intervention are matters of considerable dispute. The state is a set of institutions defined in public and constitutional law as having two monopolies in a given territory: a fiscal monopoly over taxation and the money supply, and a monopoly over the use of violence. The state is a public legal form which is institutionally separate from private economic activities (Hintze 1900; 1906; Pašukanis 1924; Elias 1939b; 1970b; Hirsch 1974). Discussion on the state in recent sociology has concerned not so much the legal form as its 'social function'. The various social apparatuses which undertake the functions of a legally defined state may not, for example, possess the unity of action required to make the legal monopolies of the state into effective monopolies. In the debate over state intervention in the economy, two divergent views on the social function of the state have emerged: the 'instrumentalist' and the 'structuralist' views.[5]

According to the instrumentalist view common to the theory of industrial society and many Marxist writings, the state is a neutral means which social groups can use either to maintain or to transform social relations. State intervention in the economy is, therefore, determined by the background and recruitment of political leaders and by the direct pressure which can be applied to them. While the theory of industrial society depicts the state as the referee for a plurality of interest groups, writers influenced by the Marxist tradition have tended to see the state as the locus of a power elite (Bottomore 1964; Nicholls 1974; Mintz *et al.* 1976; Perry and Gillespie 1976; Domhoff 1976). In the theory of capitalist society, the statement that 'The executive of the modern state is but a committee for managing the common affairs of the whole bourgeoisie' (Marx and Engels 1848, 82) is taken as implying that the state is an instrument of class domination because its apparatuses are dominated by the capitalist class.

The structuralist view holds that the effect of the state on social relations follows from its structure: certain determinants of social development are not topics of political debate because the 'selectivity' built into the state apparatus excludes them from consideration. These processes of 'non-decision-making' are reinforced by fiscal limitations on the state which derive from its dependence upon taxation and borrowing (Bachrach and Baratz 1970; Lukes 1974; Poulantzas 1968; Offe 1972e). It is possible to build on the debate generated by the confrontation of these two views in order to arrive at a more satisfactory understanding of the mechanisms of state intervention.[6]

State expenditure must be financed through borrowing or through taxation, and this certainly creates a fiscal dependence of the state on profitable private business. The state is constrained to carry out those general policies which the competing units are unwilling or unable to support, but which are essential for private business and for continued capital accumulation. State expenditure on 'collective commodities' such as education and infrastructure can become forms of 'social investment', which increase the productivity of labour, or 'social consumption', which lower the reproduction costs of labour power (Habermas 1973, 55; O'Connor 1973; Offe 1975a; Castells 1972). Offe has claimed that policies of vocational training, regional development, scientific research and industrial reconstruction can be seen as aspects of a process of 'administrative recommodification': the state carries out in an administrative mode what unregulated market relations cannot do (Offe and Ronge 1975; Schroyer 1975; Strinati 1978). While this expenditure involves a subtraction from the total funds available for private investment, it is 'indirectly productive' in the long run, since it involves an alteration in the social conditions of reproduction of capital: 'it systematically alters the conditions under which surplus value can be appropriated from productive labour' (Habermas 1973, 56). Without getting involved in the tortuous debate over productive and unproductive labour in Marxist economics, it is easy to see that expenditure which improves the position of private capital in the long run has short-run effects which are the exact opposite. In order to finance its expenditure, the state must borrow or raise taxation; it must take funds away from the private sector. Private capital may be unwilling or unable to provide the facilities upon which its long-term survival depends, but it must, willingly or unwillingly, pay for the collective provision of these facilities. A rise in state expenditure involves a deduction from current private investment funds. For this reason, the productivity of capital must be sufficient to meet both the immediate needs of capital and the needs of the state (Mattick 1969; Fine and Harris 1976*b*, 102–5; Yaffe 1973, 225). When state expenditure is growing, productivity must also increase, or there will be a contraction in the rate of capital accumulation. While past state expenditure may be increasing the productivity of capital, a portion of this increased productivity is required to finance present and future expenditure. It is in this way that an increase in state expenditure creates the need for further state expenditure. O'Connor (1973, 9, 40) concludes that 'The socialization of costs and the private appropriation of profits creates a fiscal crisis, or "structural gap", between state expenditures and state revenues'.

The state is located within certain definite constraints which limit its possible actions. If it is to survive, the state must observe these limits, though there is, logically, nothing to stop any particular state from adopting a course of action which would lead to its own destruction, just as there is nothing to stop a company from going bankrupt through failing to observe market constraints. The selectivity of the state derives from certain institutionalized 'exclusion rules' which enable it to distil a policy from the particular interests that are pressed upon it, and which enable it to suppress interests that threaten the system. When the state is structured in this way, it constitutes a part of the overall system of class domination (Offe 1972*b*; Sardei-Biermann *et al.* 1973). Institutionalization of such principles restricts the range of activities which political leaders are willing to consider. In this way, state policy can function as 'a specific form of expressing the general interests of capital' (Altvater 1972, 99; Israel 1974; Hirsch 1977). However, state intervention involves autonomous decision-rules which do not merely reflect the economic logic of capitalism but which do enable it to recognize the imperatives of capitalist production. The state must arrive at a logic of action in terms of which its attempts to maintain production *as such* require it, thereby, to maintain *capitalist* production (Offe 1975*b*; 1972*f*; Habermas 1973, 60). When the state realizes the need to intervene, it will act on the basis of what are perceived to be the main problems, and so its policies may not correspond to the objective needs of capital accumulation. As Goldthorpe has argued in another context, it is necessary to 'explain why the social actors through whose agency the change occurs *should* act in such ways, and with such outcomes, that the functional exigencies are in fact met' (1974, 277). State intervention does not follow from some inexorable teleology; it follows from the activities of the state apparatuses operating under constraints of which the state personnel may be only partly aware. There is no necessity that the state should carry out the functions which are required for continued capital accumulation.

How, then, are these principles of action institutionalized? Institutionalization is an unintended consequence of the attempts made by particular interests to influence the state. Over time, a structure is built up which has the 'bias' of past pressures built into it. This bias creates a predisposition for the state to respond in the future in the same way as it has in the past. Unsuccessful responses lead to failure and so are not institutionalized. State apparatuses are, therefore, formed through a complex adaptive process (Luhmann 1968). It is in responding to the myriad *particular* interests that certain principles of action are structured into state practices. The restructuring of the state over time is a result of the changing practices of units of capital, and other social groups, in the face of altered environmental circumstances. Of crucial importance in this process are the state personnel. Occupants of positions within the state are selected and moulded in such a way that their personal interests in maintaining their positions and their public duties in protecting the state both coincide with the objective requirements of continued capital accumulation which have been structured into the state apparatuses they run (Hirsch 1977, 122; Offe 1972*a*).

While I am not here attempting to give a general picture of the modern state and its processes of policy formation, it is necessary to give some evidence that the most important influences on the state are business interests. This has, of course, been a major theme of the instrumentalist view, according to which business interests can lobby the state, monopolize recruitment to top positions, and influence the implementation of policies which they have not themselves sponsored. The most persuasive statement of this has been that of Mills, who postulated the existence of a 'power elite' in the USA. Mills claimed that business influence was most significant at Cabinet level because

Within American political institutions, the centre of initiative and decision has shifted from Congress to the executive. . . . Accordingly, it is in the executive chambers, and in the agencies and authorities and commissions and departments that stretch out beneath them, that many conflicts of interest and contests of power have come to a head – rather than in the open arena of politics of an older style [Mills 1956, 229].

Top-level political decision-makers are no longer elected representatives but appointed political outsiders who have spent more years out of politics than in politics. Because businessmen 'occupy the command posts' of the state (ibid., 267), the political executive is very sympathetic to the business lobby. In an important criticism of this argument, Rose restated the pluralist case. Although business has a great potential influence over government because of its ability to move liquid capital resources from one location to another, Rose argued that its actual influence was far less than Mills suggested (Rose 1967, 102–3; Presthus 1973). Business leaders form a loose coalition of sub-groupings with divergent interests, and their influence is greatest in relation to economic policy issues: business leaders 'exercise their influence mainly on issues affecting production, occasionally on issues affecting consumption and distribution of wealth, and ordinarily very little on issues that do not affect wealth directly or primarily' (Rose 1967, 89). Even this circumscribed statement recognizes an important political role for business, and many recent studies of American politics have shown the channels through which business influence is exercised (Domhoff 1967; 1974; 1975; Kolko 1969). Rose questions studies of background and recruitment on the basis of a comparison of the Eisenhower and Kennedy administrations. He suggests that in the Eisenhower administration 36 out of 120 members were from a business background, while the Kennedy administration showed only 6 out of 100 from this background. Business dominance of politics 'was a quirk of the Eisenhower Administration' (Rose 1967, 122), and not the continuing phenomenon which Mills had thought. More recent work has thrown some doubt on Rose's conclusion. Over the period 1897–1973, 76 per cent of Cabinet members had come from a business background, and in every administration the figure was at least 60 per cent. The average figure has been higher since the Second World War, and particularly since the Eisenhower period (Freitag 1975; Mintz 1975).

A similar picture of the relation between business and the state has been produced for Britain, where the political leadership was once drawn from the landed aristocracy but is now firmly rooted in the business sector (Guttsman 1963; 1974; Johnson 1973; Miliband 1969). It is clear that the state in industrial capitalism is closely associated with the propertied class and that the direct pressure of business interests is sufficient to institutionalize the principles of action discussed above. It is now possible to examine the consequences which follow from this.

Habermas argues that, when the state intervenes to resolve economic crises, the 'crises tendencies' do not disappear but are 'displaced' into the internal structure of the state itself. The state attempts to compensate for economic blockages to capital accumulation, and in doing so it creates distinct political problems. The fiscal crises of the state and its consequences for capital accumulation have already been discussed, and Habermas recognizes additional problems of administrative inefficiency (Habermas 1973, 39–40, 47).[7] As Habermas (1973, 53) argues, state economic policy

. . . depends today on concrete power constellations that are no longer *predetermined* by an autonomously effective mechanism of the labour market. Today the state has to fulfil functions that can be neither explained with reference to prerequisites of the continued existence of the mode of production, nor derived from the immanent movement of capital. This movement is no longer realized through a market mechanism that can be comprehended in the theory of value, but is a result of the still effective economic driving forces and a political counter control in which a *displacement of the relations of production* finds expression.

When the state does attempt to act in the general interests of capital, it can do so only at the cost of generating new problems of finance and administration. While it may be possible, in principle, for the state to move at least some of the way towards directive planning of the economy without undermining capitalist production, there are definite obstacles to the achievement of full planning. Mandel has shown that market uncertainties lead to internal corporate planning, since the individual company is able to ensure the precise coordination of all the factors under its control. However, just as corporations cannot cooperate to the point of eliminating the remaining uncertainties, so no state agency is capable of securing coordination of the competing corporations (Mandel 1972, 233; Braverman 1974, 269). No planning authority has sufficient control over production to ensure that the economy as a whole is planned. State planning, argues Mandel, is strictly a form of 'programming', since there are two crucial elements of uncertainty in the decision-making of the planners. First, planning is based on investment plans which are projections of past tendencies and which, therefore, cannot fully take account of changing market conditions. Second, the various units of capital have conflicting interests and will, therefore, co-operate only to a limited degree (Mandel 1972, 235–6). Habermas extends this argument by pointing out further limits to administrative rationality. This rationality is limited not merely by the 'reactive' character of planning to autonomously determined capitalist decisions but also by factors internal to the state. First, the various agencies of the state are themselves imperfectly coordinated. Second, each agency is dependent upon its clients for information:

It is possible to show that the authorities, with little informational and planning capacity and insufficient coordination among themselves, are dependent on the flow of information from their clients. They are thus unable to preserve the distance from them necessary for independent decisions. Individual sectors of the economy can, as it were, privatize parts of the public administration, thus displacing the competition between individual social interests into the state apparatus [Habermas 1973, 62; Miliband 1977, 96].

Offe has argued, for example, that planning requires 'technocratic' rather than 'bureaucratic' procedures of decision-making and that the administrative problems of the state preclude effective technocratic procedures. Bureaucratic procedures require that there be a political determination of goals in order that the state agencies can react in an *ad hoc* way to such problems as emerge. Decision-making involves a 'case-by-case muddling through' (Offe 1972*b*, 39–40; Hirsch 1977, 120–1). These procedures do not depend upon an independent formulation of the needs of capital accumulation, and so it is more than likely that policy will run counter to these needs. Longstreth has shown that government policy in Britain has tended to follow such bureaucratic procedures: parliament and ministers determined the general goals of economic policy, and the constraints upon policy were set by the Treasury and the Bank of England on the basis of their close links with the financial interests of the City of London. The main concern was to use fiscal means to influence Britain's short-term financial position, particularly the maintenance of the international value of the pound and the role of sterling as a reserve currency (Longstreth 1977*a*; 1977*b*; Westergaard and Resler 1975, 200 ff.). As state expenditure grew and the need to intervene became more compelling, there were attempts to adopt technocratic procedures. Instead of relying on politically defined goals, the state had to determine what results its policies should achieve. It was necessary to set up agencies in which the needs of the economy could be identified and appropriate policy measures formulated. Bodies such as the National Economic Development Council were set up as a means of bringing together the various economic interests. As Nettl has argued, these bodies involve a restriction of the circle of decision-makers to business and union leaders who then attempt to construct a policy which is in the 'national interest' (Nettl 1965; Parry 1969, 91; Hirsch 1970; Jessop 1978*a*). The basic problem of the attempt to establish technocratic procedures is whether NEDC and other 'QUANGOS'[8] can attain the necessary independence from particular interests to form a conception of the general interest. In particular, the incorporation of trades-union representatives on these bodies makes the problem of consensus far greater. The state may not even be able to formulate the policy which it is incapable of implementing! As Habermas (1973, 63) argues, 'Rationality deficits are the unavoidable result of a snare of relations into which the advanced-capitalist state fumbles and in which its contradictory activities must become more and more muddled.'

The theory of capitalist society is certainly correct to point to the connection between the centralization of control over capital and the growth of state intervention, though this connection is far weaker than the notion of 'state monopoly capitalism' implies. Indeed, state intervention in the economy has generated a whole new set of problems for both private business and the state. The theory of industrial society is perhaps right to emphasize that the state is not solely the preserve of business interests, but it overlooks the extent to which the selectivity built into the structure of the state ensures that the struggle between competing groups is far from equal. I have attempted to show that the actual trends in market behaviour and its state mediation are misconceived in each of the theories. The political economy which has developed is still based on capitalist principles, though many Marxist writers overemphasize its continuity with early capitalism, and proponents of the theory of industrial society overstate the extent of the transformation which has occurred.

7 The internationalization of capital and the multinational company

The international dimension of industrial capitalism has been one of the most hotly disputed themes within the two theories which have structured my investigations. The theory of industrial society sees the 'underdeveloped' societies undergoing a transition from tradition to modernity, a transition which has exact parallels with the modernization of the now industrialized world. The difference between the 'developed' and the 'underdeveloped' societies is merely a 'technological gap', and multinational companies spread the benefits of advanced technology and its associated 'modern' social and cultural features. The theory of capitalist society relates under-development to the internal problems of the monopolized capitalist economies. Faced with inadequate domestic investment opportunities, because of the tendency of the rate of profit to fall, capitalists export capital to those areas where there is a plentiful supply of cheap labour and politically protected markets. This theory holds that the main consequence of the monopolization of national industry is the displacement of competition from the national to the international level. The struggle between rival imperialist powers replaces the struggle between competing firms. A full discussion of these rival views would require a discussion of the voluminous literature on the sociology of development, and such a discussion cannot be given here.[1] In this chapter I shall concentrate upon the general features of the world economic system and upon the role of the so-called multinational company. In line with the rest of this book I shall focus upon the implications for the advanced capitalist industrial economies.

The movement of international capital

The development of the modern world system began with the rise of mercantile capitalism in Europe. By the late fifteenth and early sixteenth centuries, an international commercial economy had developed from within the confines of rival absolutist states (Waller-stein 1974a and 1974b; Anderson 1974). From the sixteenth century to the eighteenth century there was a Europe-centred world market for agricultural produce. The profit earned from the privileged position of the strong states of Western Europe was the basis for the industrial 'take-off' of the eighteenth and nineteenth centuries (Hoogvelt 1976, 68–77; Palloix 1969, 179; Sutcliffe 1972; Amin 1975; Kay 1976). From the late nineteenth century to the Second World War, the key feature of the world economic system was not international exchange of commodities but the internationalization of money capital: the export of capital from the European core to the 'underdeveloped' periphery did indeed occur on a massive scale and permitted the development of export-oriented sectors in the peripheral economies (Palloix 1973).

By 1855 the volume of British overseas investment was £230m.; and by 1914 this figure had risen to £4000m. In the first half of the nineteenth century the financial centre of the City of London, which had grown through the financing of overseas trade and the financing of government expenditure, was lending money to Europe, Latin America and the USA. The real take-off for foreign investment occurred with the conjunction of the railway boom, which began in the 1830s and 1840s, and the decline of domestic investment opportunities after 1870 (Cottrell 1975; Cairncross 1953; Hobson 1914; Kennedy 1976). In the period from 1855 up to the First World War, the major destinations for British investment were the railway companies of the USA, Canada, Australia and Argentina, though ranching, timber and mining in these countries also attracted much British capital. In 1914, British investment in Canada accounted for three-quarters of all foreign capital, but by 1955 this same proportion was accounted for by American capital, The growth of US trade was associated with growing US investment abroad: by the mid-1950s the USA bought 60 per cent of Canadian exports and provided 75 per cent of Canadian imports (see Table 41). Similarly, while over half of all foreign investment in Australia in 1964 was British, the American share had risen to a third (Aitken 1959a, 7–8; Blyth and Carty 1956; Encel 1970, 337; Brash 1970).

The growth of US investment since 1918, and particularly since 1945, has been associated with a transition from 'portfolio invest-ment' to 'direct investment'. In the early years of the present century, 90 per cent of all international capital movements was portfolio investment – ownership of foreign stocks and shares by domestic

Table 41 *Foreign investment in Canada (1900–64)*

% of total by:	1900	1918	1926	1933	1946	1957	1964
USA	14	36	53	61	72	76	78
UK	85	60	44	36	23	17	13
Other	1	4	3	3	5	7	9
Totals	100	100	100	100	100	100	100

SOURCE: Adapted from Dunning (1970), 192, table 1.

interests – but this proportion had fallen to one-fifth by the 1960s. Direct investment for productive purposes increased markedly during the 1930s and became the predominant form of overseas investment over the next thirty years. Unlike portfolio investment, direct investments are generally made by corporations and involve some control over decision-making in the 'host' economy. As Dunning (1972, 13) argues:

... while portfolio capital is mainly supplied by individuals and institutions to different foreign individuals and institutions, through the mechanism of the capital market, direct investment ... is usually accomplished without any change in ownership at all. Essentially it represents the vertical or horizontal geographical extension of a firm's activities and must thus be viewed in the light of its overall objectives.

Direct investment is a consequence of the growth of the large corporation and is the form of overseas investment characteristic of modern industrial capitalism.

Table 42 *US direct foreign investment (1929–68)*

Area	% of total investment stake in:			
	1929	1949	1959	1968
Europe	19	14	16	30
Canada	25	31	33	33
Latin America	33	39	35	17
Other	23	15	16	20
Totals	100	100	100	100

SOURCE: Adapted from Barratt Brown (1974), 208–9, table 20.

F

It can be seen from Table 42 that a marked change occurred in the direction of American foreign investment during the 1960s. A fairly constant one-third of all US investment has gone to Canada, but there has been a substantial shift from Latin America to Europe. The most favoured sites for US investment are other industrialized economies (Magdoff 1970). By the early 1970s, US investment in Canada took $21075m. from a total of $67702m. Within Europe, Britain received $7158m. and West Germany $4252m. Furthermore, the rate of increase of US investment in Europe is twice that in Canada (Vernon 1971*a*, 19; Hughes 1973, 161). Figures for British foreign investment in the 1960s show that the total was equivalent to just under 10 per cent of net domestic investment and that the total foreign assets of British companies (£6000m.) was divided equally between the developed and the 'underdeveloped' nations, although investment in Europe was growing more rapidly. Increasingly, the advanced economies are investing in one another rather than in the Third World. Barratt Brown has estimated that about half of all their capital exports are to one another (Barratt Brown 1974; Dunning 1970, 49–50).

Although the absolute amount of international capital movement has increased since 1914, its relative significance for each domestic economy has diminished. Emmanuel estimates that British foreign assets in 1914 amounted to twice the British national income, while US foreign assets in 1974 amounted to a mere fifth of US national income (Emmanuel 1976, 759). However, both the relative and the absolute significance of foreign investment for each 'host' economy has increased. In Australia and Canada, foreign direct investment is no longer limited to the railways and to pastoral concerns, but is predominantly in the important sectors of manufacturing industry. Wheelwright and Miskelly have estimated that 36 per cent of the share capital of the top 200 Australian companies in the 1960s was owned abroad. The British portion of this, which is still channelled through the City of London, is concentrated in petroleum, chemicals, non-ferrous metals, iron and steel, food processing, textiles and electrical engineering. American capital is also concentrated in petrol, chemicals, metals and food but is equally strong in motor vehicles and agricultural equipment (Wheelwright and Miskelly 1967, cited in Encel 1970, 338). In Canada, total foreign ownership of industry and commerce declined from 38 per cent before the Second World War to 32 per cent in 1954, but US ownership increased from 19 to 25 per cent in the same period (Drache 1970,

25). As Table 43 shows, foreign investment has increasingly moved into manufacturing industry. In Canada, more than 50 per cent of manufacturing assets (particularly the automobile, chemical and electrical industries) were owned by U S interests.

Table 43   *Foreign investment in Canada by sector (1926–62)*

Sector	% in each sector which was foreign-owned in:				
	1926	1948	1957	1959	1962
Manufacturing	38	42	50	51	54
Petroleum and gas	—	—	64	62	63
Mining and smelting	37	—	56	59	—
Railways	55	—	30	—	—
Other utilities	32	—	15	—	—
Merchandizing and construction	—	—	—	9	9

SOURCE: Constructed from Porter (1965), 267; Safarian (1966), 14; Drache (1970), 24.

NOTE: A dash in a column indicates data not available.

American investment in Europe began first in Britain after the Second World War and spread to the rest of Europe between 1950 and 1957, although the 1960s were the period of rapid expansion. This investment is highly concentrated by industry and by company: 85 per cent of total U S investment in Europe is in four industries (vehicles, chemicals, mechanical engineering, and electrical and electronic engineering), and 40 per cent of U S investment in Britain, Germany and France is made by General Motors, Ford and Exxon (Hughes 1973, 162–4; Turner 1970; Hodges 1974, 53). American companies in Europe account for only 6 per cent of manufacturing sales, although the figure is highest in Britain, at 10 per cent, and lowest in Italy, at 3 per cent (Vernon 1971a, 21). The real significance of U S dominance lies in the importance of American ownership in specific industries which are oligopolistic and have an advanced technology:

. . . the more narrowly one chooses to define an 'industry', the more commonly one encounters extreme rates of U S participation. In Italy, during the 1960s, U S enterprises were reported as controlling 100 per cent of the ballbearing industry and most of the heavy electric industry; in Great Britain, more than 75 per cent of the carbon black industry, more than 40 per cent of the computer industry; in France, more than 90 per cent of the carbon black output, more than 40 per cent of the telegraph and telephone equipment and more than 35 per cent of the tractor and agricultural machinery output [Vernon 1971a, 24; Steuer *et al.* 1973, 91].

The internationalization of production itself, associated with the growing importance of international banking (Junne 1976), has transformed the world economic system. The basic mechanism of this system is no longer trade between separate national economies but the operations of multinational companies. The overseas sales and production of the world's largest corporations now account for a substantial proportion of their total output (Rowthorn 1971). The centre of the world economic system comprises the advanced industrial economies of the USA, Western Europe and Japan, and the growth of the multinational company has tied these economies very closely together. Within the 'multinational' companies, there occurs 'an internal circulation of products among its subsidiaries in place of a circulation of commodities' between separate companies (Palloix 1973, 68), and this fact means that important areas of 'national' economic decision-making may lie beyond the powers of particular national states. The next section of this chapter will examine this thorny problem.

The multinational company and the national economy

Behind the considerable terminological dispute over the words 'international', 'plurinational', 'multinational' and 'transnational' company, lies an important matter of fact. This concerns whether a company operating in many countries from its own national base is able to adopt a corporate strategy which makes the frontiers of nation states irrelevant to its operation. Some of the earliest forms of European capitalist enterprise – such as the British East Africa Company, the Hudson's Bay Company, etc. – traded internationally, but multinational production is a fairly recent phenomenon. The central point of contention is whether a 'global strategy' of production involves a fundamental change in business activity (Michalet 1976; Franko 1976).

Vernon has defined the multinational company as 'a cluster of corporations of different nationalities that are joined together through bonds of common ownership, that respond to a common strategy, and that draw on a common pool of human and financial resources' (Vernon 1971b, 694; 1971a, 11–15). Like product diversification, geographical diversification results from the characteristic features of big business. Once a product line has become standardized, market entry barriers are weakened and profitability falls. In consequence the large company must move into newer markets where it can increase its advantages in relation to its smaller competitors. These markets may be either new product markets or foreign markets for the original product, where indigenous interests are unable to match the scale and complexity of the technology required. Diversification is a consequence of the market constraints within which large companies operate. At the same time, diversification can lead to further growth, since the super-profits earned in one advantaged market situation can be used as funds for investment in a new market (Vernon 1971*a*, 26–7; 1977, chapter 5; Kurth 1975; Michalet 1976, 106 ff.). The logic of this 'product cycle' impels the multinational company to adopt a 'global strategy' in terms of which the profitability of the parent concern is the yardstick for assessing the contribution of particular subsidiaries or branches. The multinational company operates worldwide in the same way as large national companies operate within their own national markets. As Heilbronner has claimed,

. . . we must view the world of very large, expansive national enterprises, extending their operations abroad, as a change in degree, not kind, from the world of very large expansive enterprises still contained within national borders [Heilbronner 1976, 73; Papandreou 1973, 109].

The conglomerate as a whole is the unit of capital for which profitability is assessed, and the subordination of subsidiaries to this strategy means that they will not behave in the same way as local firms. What this means is that the price-making power of the large company can be transferred to the markets in which its subsidiaries operate:

. . . when setting a price . . . the multinational enterprise is released from certain constraints that would ordinarily inhibit an unintegrated business. Although the multinational system as a whole must make a profit in order to survive, each of the affiliates in the system does not independently have to meet that test. Moreover, the price in any given transaction between a pair of affiliates need not be tested against competing offers in the open market [Vernon 1977, 128; Martinelli and Somaini 1973, 71; Brooke and Remmers 1970, 68–76].

Vernon argues that it was during the 1960s that multinational companies underwent the structural transformation from a system of separate national units to a system with centralized financial control. A consequence of this strategy is a preference for wholly owned subsidiaries rather than mere minority or majority ownership. Table 44 shows that US and European companies have indeed moved towards total ownership of subsidiaries, though the less established Japanese companies show no such tendency yet.

Table 44   *Ownership status of foreign subsidiaries in industrial economies (1970)*

Ownership	180 US companies		135 European companies		61 Japanese companies	
	No.	*%*	*No.*	*%*	*No.*	*%*
Wholly owned	2612	72·5	1788	55·8	6	13·0
Majority-owned	657	18·2	802	25·0	8	17·4
Minority-owned	302	8·4	404	12·6	30	65·2
Unknown	32	0·9	213	6·6	2	4·4
Totals	3603	100·0	3207	100·0	46	100·0

SOURCE: Calculated from Vernon (1977), 34, table 4.

NOTE: Subsidiaries in the Third World are not included. This distorts the picture for Japan, most of its subsidiaries being in Asia (see Weinstein 1976). Percentage figures for Japan are included for illustrative purposes only.

The development of this structure of strategic control has important consequences for the flow of funds between parent and subsidiary. While subsidiaries of multinational companies are able to obtain funds externally or from their own resources, established subsidiaries are net providers of funds to their parent. About two-thirds of the funds employed by subsidiaries derive from their own cash flow, the next most important source being local financial interests. The main flow of funds from parent to subsidiary occurs when the subsidiary is first set up. Thereafter, the subsidiary is a long-term provider of capital to the parent, so enabling the multinational company to set up further subsidiaries which will, in their turn, provide the parent with more capital (Brooke and Remmers 1972, 30 ff.; House 1977, 5).[2] Two of the major mechanisms for transferring funds from one part of the company to another, and thereby of 'hiding' profits, are transfer pricing and charges against income. Transfer pricing involves the discretionary pricing in intra-company transfers of goods and services with little regard for market criteria, and charges against income involve direct payment to head office of interest, royalties, fees, etc. These mechanisms are supplemented by various after-tax payments, such as dividends, and capital transfers, such as trade credit and repayment of internal loans (Brooke and Remmers 1970, 172 ff.; Hoogvelt 1976, 85–8; Hughes 1973, 172–3). While these internal transfers accord with the 'global strategy' of the multinational company, they can also defer or reduce taxation by moving funds from high tax areas to a low tax area. This frequently involves the establishment of a 'base company' which holds the shares of the overseas subsidiaries, acts as an intermediary for sales within the group, and provides management services, etc. Such 'tax havens' as Switzerland, Liechtenstein, Panama, the Bahamas and the Netherlands Antilles are popular locations for base companies (Brooke and Remmers 1970, 206 ff.; Raw *et al.* 1971). It would be wrong to see these transfers in conspiratorial terms. Rather, they must be seen as reflections of the logic of the situation within which multinational companies are located. Holland (1976, 153) argues that 'transfer pricing is not a conspiracy against the public interest, but a necessary means of maintaining a world competitive position once competing multinationals are transfer pricing'.

The flow of funds from subsidiary to parent raises the crucial problems of the 'nationality' of the multinational company and of the relationship between the company, its 'host' states and its 'home' state. These questions cannot be resolved merely by postulating that the nationality of those exercising strategic control determines corporate behaviour, but neither is it the case that the nationality of the controllers is irrelevant (Vernon 1971a, 150; Magdoff and Sweezy 1969). This problem has been raised in Europe in the face of 'the American challenge' (Servan-Schreiber 1968), but has probably been discussed most fully in Canada (Gonick 1970). Porter, for example, has argued that the 'satellite' position of the Canadian economy is manifest in the fact that much of the strategic decision-making process lies outside the country. The significance of this does not lie in a supposed 'foreign threat', since 'to argue that national sentiments and the "national interest" would supplant the historical and inexorable norms of capitalist enterprise is to reveal an ignorance of the capitalist economy' (Porter 1965, 269). Its significance lies in the fact that the development of the Canadian economy reflects 'the imperatives of more advanced areas' (Aitken 1959a, 3): patterns of capital accumulation in Canada are subordinate to patterns of accumulation in Britain and the USA. It is true that managers of foreign subsidiaries 'do not formulate policy, they administer it. The decisions they make are routine in the sense that they are constrained by budgetary allocation made at head office' (Levitt 1970, 77). But the 'Americanization' of strategic control does not merely reduce the amount of strategic decision-making which occurs within a particular area, but determines the whole pattern of accumulation of that area. Foreign investment in Canada has produced, reproduced and consolidated Canada's position in the world economic system. It has created a set of objective constraints within which greater Canadian participation in decision-making could have only a limited impact on Canada's world role. Extending Canadian participation within a system that is already constrained by the international pattern of accumulation will not, in itself, remedy the structural distortions of the Canadian economy.[3] Put more generally, the strategies of multinational companies produce and reproduce the structure of the world economic system within which those companies arose. Multinational companies are produced by the world economic system and contribute to its reproduction and transformation (Michalet 1976, 113 ff.).

The main point at issue in relation to the 'nationality' of the multinational company is not national sentiment but the fact that centralized decision-making is associated with the repatriation of profits to the base country, and the fact that this repatriation inhibits or distorts capital accumulation in the 'host' economy (Amin 1973, 211, 236; Hymer 1972). Table 45 shows the financial centres of 7034 overseas companies analysed in 1969. 'Nationality' determines the flow of funds and so determines the world pattern of capital accumulation. The growth of the 'centre' of the world economy occurs at the expense of the 'periphery'. Yet important differences arise within the centre itself. The challenge presented to European business by the growth of US multinationals after the Second World War was manifest in the pattern of accumulation between Europe and the USA. And the recent expansion of European and Japanese multinationals has again altered this pattern. In areas such as Europe, where there is a complex interweaving of international capital movements, the development of each national economy is significantly influenced by the operation of foreign multinationals. The European pattern of accumulation emerges as the unintended consequence of the intersecting strategies of the multinational companies.

The size of the multinational companies gives them an enhanced

Table 45 *Financial centres of multinational subsidiaries (1969)*

Nationality	No. of units	% of units
USA	2816	40·0
Britain	1651	23·5
W. Germany	801	11·4
France	471	6·6
Switzerland	349	4·9
Netherlands	222	3·2
Sweden	219	3·1
Belgium	197	2·7
Italy	101	1·5
Denmark	82	1·2
Norway	78	1·1
Austria	38	0·6
Spain	9	0·2
Totals	7034	100·0

SOURCE: Adapted from Evan (1976), 214, table 14.2.

NOTE: The units in this table are subsidiaries of companies located in foreign financial centres. No information is given for Canada or Japan.

ability to determine in which national economies they will operate. In consequence they unwittingly produce and reproduce the structure of the world economic system. Their effects on particular national economies may further undermine the limited capacity of the state to control the economy:

The capacity of any government to command a particular firm to undertake a specified task in support of public policy, such as settling in a backward region or holding down a key price, has been reduced; large firms now have a capacity that they never had before for choice between competing nations [Vernon 1977, 63].

The 'fundamental dilemma' of the modern state, according to Vernon, is to reconcile national control over economic events, with the recognition that accumulation is determined by external forces beyond its control (Vernon 1976, 256; Hughes 1973, 166, 169; Holland 1976, 56, 152–3).

The consequences of foreign direct investment for the 'host' economy have generally been seen in terms of the process of 'disarticulation' or structural distortion of the national economy, and this process has been analysed most extensively in the context of the

Third World. 'Disarticulation' means that the economy 'is made up of sectors, of firms, which are juxtaposed and not highly integrated among themselves, but which are, each on its own, strongly integrated in entities whose centres of gravity lie in the centres of the capitalist world' (Amin 1971, 289). There are 'empty boxes' in the inter-industrial tables, such that 'the density of the flow of external exchanges of these atoms [is] much greater, and that of the flow of internal exchanges very much less' than in the countries of the capitalist core (Amin 1973, 237). It is possible to extend this point to argue that the activities of multinational companies, within the centre itself, produce various symptoms of disarticulation: the external linkages of certain industries which are dominated by foreign capital become more important than their linkages with other national industries. Thus, Murray (1971, 96) has argued that such tendencies bring about a 'growing territorial non-coincidence between extending capital and its domestic state'. He claims that

There is . . . a tendency for the process of internationalization to increase the potential economic instability in the world economy at the same time as decreasing the power of national governments to control economic activity even within their own borders [Murray 1971, 102–3; Picciotto and Radice 1973, 63; Mandel 1972, 316; Mandel 1970].

But there is no simple undermining of state power. The state's limited ability to control the economy is certainly curtailed by the internationalization of capital. Some of the tendencies towards 'corporatism' (discussed in the previous chapter) which *strengthen* the social power of the state derive in part from the opposition of small businesses and workers to the multinational companies. Furthermore, because greater economic interdependence leads to greater economic instability in both the national and the international spheres, large corporations seek a closer relationship with their home state and so strengthen its power. Corporatist or 'mercantilist' policies may be in the interests of internationalized capital as well as in the interests of those who oppose it (Holloway 1976, 4). As Warren (1971, 139) argues,

. . . there is always necessarily a link between the 'extended capital' and its home government by virtue of the inter-connections between national taxation systems, international (company) law and private appropriation of profits – with their ramifications into the balance of payments and growth rate of the domestic economy.

It would seem that the activities of multinational companies within the advanced industrial economies certainly exacerbate many of the problems discussed in earlier chapters. But there is no fundamental qualitative change consequent upon the internationalization of production. Problems which were formerly internal to each national economy are translated to the level of the world economic system, and the latter acquires a structure of its own, which international flows of capital reproduce.

Contrary to the theory of industrial society, I have shown for the 'modern' societies that the 'technological gap' follows from the characteristic development of the large corporation. Differences in technology are associated with the power to protect markets and generate definite patterns of capital accumulation for the world economic system. The multinational companies are not benign agents of 'modernization', but produce and reproduce the structure of an international system. There is considerable evidence that, while the theory of capitalist society may have overstated the case for 'state monopoly capitalism', international competition does complement competition within national economies, and that the 'anarchy' of the world economic system undermines any national economic coordination which might be achieved.

8 The corporation in capitalist society: some conclusions

In this book I have attempted to depict the significance of the business corporation in capitalist society and I have related this to the main contending theories of industrial capitalism. The facts do not, of course, speak for themselves. The empirical data presented in this book have, by and large, been collected and analysed by researchers working within the theoretical and conceptual tradition defined by the interplay of these two contending theories. The attempt to defend one theory at the expense of the other has generated a distinct research problematic: the problems investigated in empirical research are defined in terms of the concepts and themes of these two theories. Very few writers can be unambiguously regarded as proponents of one or other theory in its pure form. My presentation of the theory of industrial society and the theory of capitalist society in Chapter 1 was concerned with the underlying theoretical structures common to a large number of writers.

The confrontation of theory and data in empirical research on the business corporation has led many of the most sophisticated researchers to go beyond the limits of their initial theoretical formulations. As a result, a considerable amount of empirical information has been produced, and much of this has been brought together in earlier chapters. But no comparable theoretical advances have been made. The dominance of the two contending theories has had both positive and negative effects on empirical research. Theoretical choice has frequently been defined in terms of ideological choice: it is assumed that in order to counter the arguments of supporters of a particular theoretical position it is necessary to force one's data into the categories of its mirror-image theory. Research on interlocking directorships is a case in point. Radical writers have generally assumed this phenomenon to be important and have, often by default, presented their research in terms of the categories of the theory of capitalist society. Other writers opposed to Marxism have tended to argue that interlocking directorships are unimportant features of modern business. In turn, those who believe interlocking directorships to be important have reacted by overstating their significance, and so have confirmed the prejudices of their opponents. Similarly, research on the 'separation of ownership from control' has suffered from theoretical prejudices – radical writers believing it necessary to argue against any suggestion that the institution of property has undergone any transformation at all, and liberal writers seeing the 'separation' as the cornerstone of their anti-Marxist arguments. Many of these arguments have been reviewed in the first four chapters of this book, and I tried to go beyond such sterile disputes so as to uncover the real trends of development in industrial capitalism.

This is, of course, to put the case too simply. The theory of industrial society and the theory of capitalist society have certainly proved inadequate as interpretations of industrial capitalism. But I have not simply demonstrated their inadequacies in relation to 'raw' data: the implication of my argument is that my own attempt to order the findings of empirical research must itself have involved definite theoretical assumptions. I cannot pretend to have a generalized explanatory theory of the dynamics of industrial capitalism, but a particular theoretical interpretation is explicitly contained in the chapters of this book. In this conclusion I propose to review the inadequacies of the two contending theories and to present a schematic outline of my own interpretation. This outline is presented in Table 46.

In Chapter 2 I showed the relationship between legal forms and social relations. Those with a legal entitlement to the ownership of joint-stock companies no longer have exclusive detention of a particular set of assets. They have the right to a beneficial participation in the fruits of company operations. Shareholders may increasingly be regarded on a par with other creditors. The theory of industrial society is correct to follow Berle and Means in recognizing this as a fact. It is incorrect, however, to assume that actual social practice corresponds to these legal prescriptions. Shares still carry votes in company affairs, and those who can mobilize votes in sufficient numbers will be able to determine corporate behaviour. Effective possession lies with those who can benefit from the *de facto* disenfranchisement of the small shareholder. Chapter 3 demonstrated that effective possession is increasingly becoming 'impersonalized': power over corporate affairs is passing from the hands of individual persons to impersonal organizations. The massive growth of

Table 46   *Trends in the development of industrial capitalism*

	Early capitalism	Late capitalism
Legal form of ownership	Exclusive detention	Beneficial participation
Social relation of possession	Personal possession	Impersonal possession
Mode of strategic control	Private ownership	Control through a constellation of interests
Mode of funding	Entrepreneurial capital	Finance capital
Mode of class structuration	Personal domination	Structural domination
Structure of market	Atomistic competition	Oligopolistic competition
Mode of state mediation	Facilitative	Interventionist
Movement of international capital	Portfolio investment	Direct investment

NOTE: The terms 'early' capitalism and 'late' capitalism are used purely as a matter of convenience in an attempt to avoid some of the more misleading labels.

'institutional' shareholdings is thrusting the insurance companies, pension funds, banks, etc., into a position of effective possession of industrial companies. These financial companies are themselves, as shown in Chapter 4, increasingly subject to impersonal possession. A complex system of intercorporate shareholdings and credit relations is emerging, within which particular corporations are controlled by the specific constellations of interest which have effective possession. At present, the major capitalist economies are undergoing a transition from personal to impersonal possession, and so many family-controlled companies are still in evidence. But the overall trend of development seems clear.

I have argued, however, that this emerging situation must not be seen as control by 'finance capitalists', or as 'bank control'. The theory of capitalist society misreads the growth of 'institutional' shareholdings as an extension and consolidation of the close relationship which existed between the banks and industry at the end of the nineteenth century in Germany. I have shown that most of the capitalist industrial economies have moved past the period of bank dominance. The power of the investment banker in the USA, for example, reflected the huge capital requirements of US corporations in their formative years. Banks no longer have this kind of immense power, even when they lend to large corporations. Funds for investment no longer come from the entrepreneur or his immediate family and associates. These funds are provided as 'finance' from outside, whether this be through bank loans or through the stock exchange. When corporations today fund their investment from 'internal' sources, their dependence on stockmarket valuations and their creditworthiness with their bankers mean that internal funding is also an indicator of the importance of finance capital. The providers of capital certainly have considerable power to determine corporate strategy, but this power is more restricted and more circumscribed than is assumed in the theory of capitalist society. Large industrial corporations and major banks confront one another as equals, each being constrained by its controlling constellation of interests. Banks are, however, located at the centres of spheres of influence. Through the mechanism of the interlocking directorship a network of relations between companies is built up, and this network is the means through which business information can be transmitted. Because of their centrality in the communication network, banks are able to exercise considerable influence over the policies of industrial corporations and so can affect what happens in companies where they have no direct power. The communication of information through interlocking directorships is an important way of reducing the uncertainties facing large corporations. The business system as a whole is able to achieve a certain degree of coordination, and the banks play an important role in this.

These developmental trends in industrial capitalism have not been associated with the demise of the capitalist class. In Chapter 5, I showed that a propertied class still exists and that it derives its advantages from ownership of company shares and participation in strategic control. The 'impersonal' structure of possession has not resulted in a loss of power by wealthy persons. The distributional consequences of capitalist relations of production continue to privilege some people at the expense of others. Yet the propertied class has undergone a transformation and is no longer merely a collection of individually powerful families. There has been a managerial reorganization of the propertied class. Wealthy families hold shares in a large number of companies and they form a pool from which corporate managers are recruited, though these managers may not come from families having a substantial ownership stake in the companies which they run. The propertied class has interests throughout the corporate system and is able to ensure its continuity over time through the monopolization of social and cultural assets as well as the monopolization of wealth. Those who head the major corporations and the constellations of interests which control them are increasingly characterized by the possession of some kind of educational diploma, and so the educational system becomes a crucial mechanism in ensuring class domination of the economy. Class domination takes a 'structural' form, because the transmission of social positions is less and less a matter of personal inheritance and more and more a matter relating to the structure of the class as a whole.

The economic system which is dominated by this propertied class involves a small number of large companies in which the bulk of all corporate assets are concentrated. These companies are surrounded by a fringe of small and medium-sized firms in which some of the features of atomistic competition are still to be found, but the large companies themselves have considerable market power and engage in oligopolistic competition. Corporate strategy is constrained by the market conditions in which corporations act, and thus corporate behaviour is limited by market factors as well as by the non-market factors of power and influence. The conditions of oligopolistic competition, discussed in Chapter 6, have led the state to take a more and more interventionist role. The state can no longer merely facilitate private production; it must aim to direct and restructure economic activity in numerous ways. It is necessary not only for many items of expenditure to be taken on by the state itself, but also for the state to attempt to plan and coordinate production. While the development of industrial capitalism has brought about these pressures on the state, the consequences of state intervention may exacerbate the very conditions which it was intended to alleviate. State intervention generates profitability and productivity problems for private capital, and it generates fiscal, administrative and legitimation problems for the state itself. The imperfections of state intervention derive from and contribute to the imperfections and uncertainties of the corporate system itself. Contrary to the theory of capitalist society, private capital and the state have not fused into a system of state monopoly capitalism; but neither is the state a neutral arbiter of competing social conflicts. I have tried to show that state intervention has definite social effects, and that these effects follow from the structure of the state and from its connections with the propertied class which dominates the economy.

Internationally, as shown in Chapter 7, oligopolistic competition is translated into the worldwide activities of the multinational company. The foreign investments of the advanced capitalist economies are no longer portfolio investments in foreign shares and bonds, but involve direct ownership by corporations of overseas subsidiaries. Increasingly, the pattern of accumulation within each national economy is influenced by the particular conjunction of national and foreign companies which operate within its boundaries. As the multinational companies of each of the advanced economies turns its international activities to other advanced economies, so the development of the national economies of the USA, Western Europe, Japan, Canada and Australia become more dependent upon one another. This interdependence further exacerbates the domestic economic problems faced by each national state. An interdependent world economic system has developed and has altered some of the conditions under which each of its constituent national economies can develop. Neither 'imperialism' nor 'modernization' is an adequate concept for the analysis of this world economic system.

I have given here the briefest outline of my argument, and the reader should refer back to the main chapters for detailed documentation of the argument. It is clear, I hope, that the theories of industrial society and of capitalist society have outlived their usefulness. They have together enabled research to produce a considerable amount of data. But the implications which I have drawn from these data suggest that the two theories should be finally buried. The theoretical interpretation of the corporation in capitalist society that I have given in this book is the basis upon which it is necessary to advance if we are to arrive at an alternative explanatory theory which has the empirical scope of the two rejected theories as well as being capable of generating further empirical advances.

Notes

1 Contending theories of industrial capitalism

1 In Britain the legal form is that of the 'joint-stock company', or simply 'company', while American law speaks of 'corporations'. French and German equivalents are *société anonyme* and *Aktiengesellschaft*. In this book I use the terms company and corporation interchangeably to refer to these legal forms and their equivalents.

2 The figures in this paragraph are based on calculations from *The Times 1000* for 1974–5.

3 Europe is here defined as Western Europe together with Norway and Sweden but excluding Britain.

4 The term 'mesoeconomic' refers to that sector which is intermediate between the macro- and microeconomic levels of the economy.

5 Various attempts to measure economic concentration can be found in Hannah (1975), Aaronovitch and Sawyer (1975), Prais (1976) and Jewkes (1977).

6 In a discussion of approaches to social stratification, John Goldthorpe (1972) has identified a 'liberal' perspective and a 'Marxist' critique which come close to the contrasting approaches discussed here.

7 I am not concerned here with Giddens's claim that the theory of industrial society is associated with a 'positivist' philosophy of science (Giddens 1976a, 727). See also Fay (1975, 57 ff.).

8 Earlier statements of some of the themes can be found in more popular works such as Drucker (1951) and Mayo (1949).

9 This viewpoint underlies much of the so-called 'functionalist' theory of stratification. See Davis and Moore (1945) and Parsons (1954a).

10 'Institutional' share ownership refers to shares held by investment organizations such as insurance companies, investment trusts, unit trusts, savings banks, etc.

11 General discussions of pluralism can be found in Parry (1969), Nicholls (1974) and Keller (1963).

12 In this chapter I discuss the work of orthodox Marxist writers. Marx's own discussion of these issues is reviewed in the following chapter.

13 The concept of 'finance capital' originated in the works of Kautsky

(1902), Hilferding (1910) and Luxemburg (1913). For a general review, see Kiernan (1974).

14 See also: Haxey (1939), Gollan (1956), Harvey and Hood (1958), Frankel (1970), Rochester (1936, ch. 8) and Perlo (1957, ch. 15). Similar arguments can be found in Lenin (1917*b*), although this also contains some non-instrumentalist arguments on the state. For criticisms of the notion of state monopoly capitalism, see Jessop (1978*b*), Wirth (1973).

2 Property relations and the mediation of control

1 Berle and Means somewhat confusingly term these two aspects 'passive' and 'active'. I prefer not to follow the usage in this context.
2 Similar distinctions to those made by Bettelheim can be found in Morin (1974, 21), De Vroey (1975*a*, 3), Carchedi (1975, 48–9) and Wright (1976, 11).
3 This discussion clearly relates to the old problem of 'methodological individualism' (O'Neill 1973). On the autonomy of collective actors, see Coleman (1974, 41–3) and Jessop (1976, 17–18).
4 This problem is alluded to in Cutler *et al.* (1977, 307) but its full importance is not realized.
5 Also relevant on this point are Marx (1885) and Carchedi (1975).
6 See also Villarejo (1961*a*, 49), Domhoff (1967, 50), Barratt Brown (1968*a*, 53–4) and Francis (1977). Perhaps the earliest formulation of the position that control over the 'managerial function' was to be defined in terms of control over recruitment to top management was in Weber (1921). For a discussion of Weber, see Zeitlin (1974, 1091–2), which attempts to sketch the types of decisions involved.
7 Compare the distinction between power and metapower in Baumgartner *et al.* (1975).
8 The distinction between strategic control and operational management which has been drawn here can be found, often implicitly, in numerous sources, although Pahl and Winkler (1974, 115) are the first writers to make the distinction an explicit point of reference in their work. For the background, see: Parsons (1956, 30–1), Peterson (1965, 2), Juran and Louden (1966), Lundberg (1969, 169), Jancovici (1972, 80), Burch (1972, 18), Westergaard and Resler (1975, 163), Poulantzas (1974, 119) and Soref (1976, 362).
9 In this book I ignore the technical distinction between 'stocks' and 'shares' and use the terms interchangeably.
10 This 'proxy' is the form on which the shareholder who does not wish to attend a company meeting is invited to delegate a board member to vote on his behalf, normally in favour of management's own proposals.
11 One of the best-studied proxy fights between a management group and

a minority shareholder is Rockefeller's battle over the control of Standard Oil in Indiana in 1929. See Baum and Stiles (1965, 13), Baran and Sweezy (1966, 32 ff.), Fitch and Oppenheimer (1970*a*, 88), Blumberg (1975, 93).

12 Morin (1974) somewhat misleadingly terms this a situation of 'technocratic control'. See also Barratt Brown (1968*a*, 43–4) on 'coordinating controllers'.

13 In the following discussion I shall concentrate on mechanisms for *maintaining* control. I shall not explicitly discuss those involved in *attaining* control. See Chevalier (1970, 42) and Blumberg (1975, 92, 145).

14 See also Zeitlin's paradigm for studying corporate control (Zeitlin *et al.* 1975, 110 ff.), and also Marris (1964, 15) and Mace (1971).

3 Capital ownership and strategic control

1 I am not here concerned with Dahrendorf's argument that classes can be generated outside the economy wherever 'authority' relations occur.

2 In this chapter I follow Berle and Means in confining my attention to ownership of non-financial corporations.

3 The term 'fiduciary' refers to those organizations which hold their assets 'in trust' for their beneficiaries. Examples would be savings banks, mutual insurance companies, unit trusts, etc. In practice, the distinction between fiduciary institutions and other business enterprises is of little significance. This is discussed further in Chapter 4.

4 Burch notes here and elsewhere that inclusion of private, non-quoted companies would increase the number of family-controlled corporations.

5 Florence allocated companies to the 'marginal' category if the beneficiaries of large nominee holdings could not be identified.

6 As should be clear from the discussion, it is important to know whether 'British' data refer to Britain as a whole or merely to England and Wales. In this chapter I have used 'England' whenever Scottish companies were not included. The number of Welsh companies in such studies is unknown but is undoubtedly negligible.

7 Norwegian law distinguishes between 'personally owned' companies and 'corporations'.

4 Finance capital and strategic control

1 It is important to distinguish between the general usage of 'financial company' to refer to those companies operating in the monetary sphere, and the specific usage of 'finance capital' defined above. A good description of the 'financial sector' in Britain is contained in Revell (1973).

2 For a brief discussion of the struggle through which the Prudential and other financial institutions forced the management of Distillers to increase their offer of compensation to thalidomide victims, see Blumberg (1975), 134–5.

3 An interlocking directorship occurs when one person sits on the boards of two or more companies and so creates an 'interlock' between them. Such people are generally referred to as 'multiple directors'. In France and Germany, researchers have used the more general terms *liaisons personnelles* and *personell Verflechtungen*. These general terms are usually qualified to the effect that they relate to the equivalents of the board of directors, the *conseil d'administration* and the *Aufsichtsrat*. For general reviews of investigations into interlocking directorships, see Fennema and Schijf (1978) and Titscher (1977).

4 Hughes *et al.* (1977) contains trend data for Scotland analagous to those given for the U S A by Bunting and Barbour (1971).

5 Further information can be found in Helmers *et al.* (1975). The limited evidence available for France suggests that the corporate network is denser than in the USA (Morin 1974, 31–3, tables 2 and 3). On Belgium see Daems (1975), chapters 2 and 3; Daems and Van Der Wee (1974).

6 For further evidence on interlocking directorships, see: Higley *et al.* (1976) for Norway; Gustavsen (1976) for Norway and Sweden; Lim and Anderson (1976) for Malaysia.

7 In view of the specific sense in which 'finance' has been used in this chapter, I prefer to speak of 'internal funding' than 'internal finance'.

8 This study measures internal funding on a slightly different basis from that of Thompson (1977).

9 This has been argued by one of Scotland's major investment managers: De Vink (1970).

10 See also Farace and Wigand (1975) and Renn (1975).

11 See also Luhmann (1971; 1970; 1975c).

5 The corporation and the class structure

1 Weber identifies only three social classes: the working class, the petit-bourgeoisie and the propertyless intelligentsia. This list is followed by a section heading, 'The Classes Privileged Through Property or Education', and it is likely that Weber here intended to discuss dominant social classes. However, none of this section was ever written. Both Parsons's translation (Weber 1921) and Giddens's commentaries (1971; 1973) incorrectly treat this section heading as the name of a fourth social class. In fact, the social classes are ordered in Greek and section headings are numbered in Roman. It is clear from the German text that Weber's whole discussion of 'social class' was incomplete.

2 Here and elsewhere I use the term 'cultural assets' instead of Bourdieu's

term 'cultural capital', since 'capital' is a rather misleading word in this context. I am grateful to Ilya Neustadt for clarifying this point.

3 'Status' is preferable to both 'estate' and 'status group' as a translation of *Stand*.

4 Considerable dispute has arisen in recent years over the precise figures on income and wealth distribution in Britain during the 1970s. The disputants have analysed variations in year-to-year proportions and have tried to extrapolate from these. It is still too early to see whether these are minor fluctuations around a long-term constant proportion, whether they indicate a change of trend, or whether they reflect the peculiar economic features of the 1970s. See: Atkinson (1972), Polanyi and Wood (1974), Diamond Report (1975*a*).

5 The distinction between 'segmental' and 'systemic' class structures is taken from Mann (1977*a*; 1977*b*).

6 For evidence on Canada and Australia, see: Porter (1965), 122, 246–7, 275–8; Clement (1975), 192, 173–8; Encel (1970), 391–5.

6 The economy and the state

1 In much of the work in this area, 'concentration' is used as a generic term for both technical concentration and financial centralization. In the discussion which follows, the context should make clear what is implied.

2 On the dependence of 'profit' on accounting practices, and therefore on the relative nature of any such measure, see Cutler *et al.* (1978).

3 Marx's analysis of reproduction and accumulation can be found in Marx (1885).

4 See Fine and Harris (1976*a*), Gamble and Walton (1976) and Yaffe (1973).

The main discussion in these and other sources concerns the relation between calculations of profit in money terms and calculations in 'value' terms. However, even those who propose the method of value analysis recognize that the immediate determinant of company behaviour is money profit.

5 The distinction drawn here has been made by a number of other writers. See in particular: Offe (1972*b*), Wolfe (1974), Gold *et al.* (1975), Mollenkopf (1975), Esping-Anderson *et al.* (1976), Abromeit (1976) and Miliband (1977).

6 The main contributions to the debate on the state can be followed through Poulantzas (1968), Miliband (1969), Poulantzas (1969), Miliband (1970), Miliband (1973), Laclau (1975), Poulantzas (1976). The outcome of this debate is adequately summarized in Jessop (1978*b*), and in the contributions to Poulantzas (1977) and Holloway and Picciotto (1978). A particularly persuasive statement of the structuralist view is to be found in the work of Luhmann (1968; 1975*a*; 1975*b*).

7 Habermas terms this the 'rationality crisis' and relates it to broader sociocultural problems of legitimation which cannot be discussed here. On the displacement of economic crisis tendencies, see Wirth (1973); Gerstenberger (1976); Meier (1976). On legitimation problems, see Habermas (1976), Part 4. Habermas's general approach to sociology is discussed in Scott (1978).

8 'Quasi-autonomous non-governmental organizations' in Whitehall jargon.

7 The internationalization of capital and the multinational company

1 A useful source on the sociology of development is Hoogvelt (1976).

2 More detailed accounts of multinational operations can be found in Sampson (1973; 1975), and Cronjé *et al.* (1976).

3 Some of these issues are raised in relation to Scotland in Scott and Hughes (1976) and Scott *et al.* (1976)

Bibliography

In all cases the date of first publication follows the author's name. Occasionally an additional date appears after the publisher's name, and refers to the English language edition.

AARONOVITCH, S. (1955) *Monopoly: A Study of British Monopoly Capitalism*. London: Lawrence and Wishart

AARONOVITCH, S. (1961) *The Ruling Class*. London: Lawrence and Wishart

AARONOVITCH, S., and SAWYER, M. C. (1975) *Big Business*. London: Macmillan

ABELL, P. (1974) 'Mathematical sociology and sociological theory'. In Rex (1974*a*)

ABROMEIT, H. (1976) 'Zum Verhältnis von Staat and Wirtschaft in gegenwärtige Kapitalismus' ('The relation of state and economy in contemporary capitalism'), *Politische Vierteljahresschrift*, 17/1

AITKEN, H. G. J. (1959*a*) 'The changing structure of the Canadian economy'. In Aitken (1959*b*)

AITKEN, H. G. J. (1959*b*) *The American Impact on Canada*. Cambridge University Press

ALCHIAN, A. A. (1950) 'Uncertainty, evolution and economic theory', *Journal of Political Economy*, 58/2

ALDRICH. H. (1978) 'Organisation sets, actions sets, and networks'. In Starbuck (1978)

ALLEN, G. C. (1940) 'The concentration of economic control'. Extracts in Livingston *et al.* (1973)

ALLEN, M. P. (1974) 'The structure of interorganizational elite cooptation', *American Sociological Review*, 39

ALLEN, M. P. (1976) 'Management control in the large corporation', *American Journal of Sociology*, 81/4

ALTVATER, E. (1972) 'Notes on some problems of state intervention', *Kapitalistate*, 1 and 2

AMIN, S. (1971) *Accumulation on a World Scale*. New York: Monthly Review Press, 1974

AMIN, S. (1973) *Unequal Development*. Sussex: Harvester Press, 1976

AMIN, S. (1975) 'Toward a structural crisis of world capitalism', *Socialist Revolution*, 23

ANDERSON, D., *et al.* (1941) *Final Report to the Temporary National Economic Committee on the Concentration of Economic Power in the United States*. Washington: Government Printing Office for the US Senate

ANDERSON, P. (1964) 'Origins of the present crisis', *New Left Review*, 23

ANDERSON, P. (1974) *Lineages of the Absolutist State*. London: New Left Books

ANSOFF, H. I. (1965) *Corporate Strategy*. New York: McGraw-Hill

ANTITRUST COMMITTEE (1965) *Interlocks in Corporate Management*. Antitrust Subcommittee of the Committee on the Judiciary, House of Representatives, 89th Congress, 1st session. Washington: Government Printing Office

ARON, R. (1960) 'Classe sociale, classe politique, classe dirigeante' ('Social class, political class, ruling class'), *European Journal of Sociology*, 1/2

ARON, R. (1964) *La Lutte des classes* ('Class Struggles') Paris: Gallimard

ARON, R. (1967) *The Industrial Society*. London: Weidenfeld and Nicolson

ARON, R. (1968) *Progress and Disillusion*. Harmondsworth: Penguin, 1972

ATKINSON, A. B. (1972), *Unequal Shares*, Harmondsworth: Penguin, 1974

ATKINSON, A. B. (1973*a*) 'The distribution of income in Britain and the US'. In Atkinson (1973*b*)

ATKINSON, A. B. (ed.) (1973*b*) *Wealth, Income and Inequality*. Harmondsworth: Penguin

ATKINSON, A. B. (1975) *The Economics of Inequality*. Oxford University Press

AVERITT, R. (1968) *The Dual Economy*. New York: W. W. Norton

BABEAU, A., and STRAUSS-KAHN, D. (1977) *La Richesse des français* ('The Wealth of the French'). Paris: Presses Universitaires de France

BACHRACH, P., and BARATZ, M. (1970) *Power and Poverty*. New York: Oxford University Press

BALTZELL, E. D. (1958) *Philadelphia Gentlemen*. Glencoe, Ill.: Free Press

BANKS, J. A. (1964) 'The structure of industrial enterprise in industrial society'. In Halmos (1964)

BANKS, J. A. (1970) *Marxist Sociology in Action*. London: Faber and Faber

BARAN, P. A. (1957) *The Political Economy of Growth*. Harmondsworth: Penguin

BARAN, P. A., and SWEEZY, P. M. (1966) *Monopoly Capital*. Harmondsworth: Penguin, 1968

BARRATT BROWN, M. (1968*a*) 'The controllers of British industry'. In Coates (1968)

BARRATT BROWN, M. (1968*b*) 'The limits of the welfare state'. In Coates (1968)

BARRATT BROWN, M. (1974) *The Economics of Imperialism*. Harmondsworth: Penguin

BARRY, B. (1976) *Power and Political Theory*. London: Wiley

BAUM, D. J., and STILES, N. B. (1965) *The Silent Partners: Institutional Investors and Corporate Control*. Syracuse University Press

BAUMGARTNER, T., *et al.* (1975) 'Metapower and relational control in social life', *Social Science Information*, 14/6

BAUMGARTNER, T., *et al.* (1978) *Power, Conflict and Exchange in Social Life*. University of Oslo, Institute of Sociology

BAUMOL, W. J. (1962) 'On the theory of expansion of the firm', *American Economic Review*, 52

BEARDEN, J., *et al.* (1975) 'The nature and extent of bank centrality in corporate networks'. Paper to the American Sociological Association

BECKER, G. S. (1962) 'Irrational behaviour and economic theory', *Journal of Political Economy*, 70/1

BECKER, J. F. (1971) 'On the monopoly theory of monopoly capitalism', *Science and Society*, 35/4

BECKER, J. F. (1973) 'Class structure and conflict in the managerial phase', *Science and Society*, 37/3 and 4

BECKER, L. C. (1977) *Property Rights*. London: Routledge and Kegan Paul

BEED, C. S. (1966) 'The separation of ownership from control', *Journal of Economic Studies*, 1/2

BELL, D. (1953) 'The prospects of American capitalism'. In Bell (1961)

BELL, D. (1957) 'The breakup of family capitalism'. In Bell (1961)

BELL, D. (1958) 'Is there a ruling class in America?' In Bell (1961)

BELL, D. (1961) *The End of Ideology*. New York: Collier-Macmillan

BELL, D. (1974) *The Coming of Post-Industrial Society*. London: Heinemann

BENDIX, R. (1956) *Work and Authority in Industry*. New York: Wiley

BENSON, J. K. (1977) 'Organisations: a dialectical view', *Administrative Science Quarterly*, 22

BERKOWITZ, S. D. (1975) *The Dynamics of Elite Structure*. Thesis for the degree of PhD, Brandeis University

BERLE, A. A. (1955) *The Twentieth Century Capitalist Revolution*. London: Macmillan

BERLE, A. A. (1960) *Power Without Property*. New York: Harcourt Brace

BERLE, A. A. (1963) *The American Economic Republic*. London: Sidgwick and Jackson

BERLE, A. A., and MEANS, G. C. (1932) *The Modern Corporation and Private Property*. New York: Macmillan, 1947

BERTAUX, D. (1977) *Destins personnels et structure de classe* ('Personal Destinies and Class Structure'). Paris: Presses Universitaires de France

BETEILLE, A. (ed.) (1969) *Social Inequality*. Harmondsworth: Penguin

BETTELHEIM, C. (1970) *Economic Calculation and Forms of Property*. London: Routledge and Kegan Paul, 1976

BIRNBAUM, N. (1969) *The Crisis of Industrial Society.* Oxford University Press

BIRNBAUM, P. (1971) *La Structure du pouvoir aux États-Unis* ('The Structure of Power in the United States'). Paris: Presses Universitaires de France

BLACKBURN, R. (1965) 'The New Capitalism'. In Blackburn (1972)

BLACKBURN, R. (1967) 'The Unequal Society'. In Blackburn and Cockburn (1967)

BLACKBURN, R. (ed.) (1972) *Ideology in Social Science.* London: Fontana

BLACKBURN, R., and COCKBURN, A. (eds.) (1967) *The Incompatibles.* Harmondsworth: Penguin

BLETON, P. (1966) *Le Capitalisme français* ('French Capitalism'). Paris: Éditions Ouvrières

BLOOMFIELD, J. (ed.) (1977) *Class, Hegemony and Party.* London: Lawrence and Wishart

BLUMBERG, P. I. (1975) *The Megacorporation in American Society.* Englewood Cliffs, NJ: Prentice-Hall

BLYTH, C. D., and CARTY, E. B. (1956) 'Non-resident ownership of Canadian industry', *Canadian Journal of Economics and Political Science,* 22/4

BODDY, R., and CROTTY, J. (1974) 'Class conflict, Keynesian policies and the business cycle', *Monthly Review,* 26

BOLTANSKI, L. (1973) 'L'Espace positionnel' ('Positional Space'), *Revue française de sociologie,* 14/1

BOTTOMORE, T. B. (1964) *Elites and Society.* Harmondsworth: Penguin

BOTTOMORE, T. B. (1965) *Classes in Modern Society.* London: Allen and Unwin

BOURDIEU, P. (1971) 'Cultural reproduction and social reproduction'. In Brown (1973)

BOURDIEU, P. (1974) 'Avenir de classe et causalité du probable' ('Class future and the causality of the probable'), *Revue française de sociologie,* 15/1

BOURDIEU, P., and PASSERON, J. C. (1970) *Reproduction in Education, Society and Culture.* London: Sage, 1977

BOURDIEU, P., et al. (1973) 'Les Stratégies de reconversion: Les classes sociales et le système d'enseignement' ('Reconversion strategies: social classes and the system of education'), *Social Science Information,* 12/5

BOYD, D. (1973) *Elites and their Education.* Windsor: NFER

BRANDEIS, L. D. (1914) *Other People's Money and How the Bankers Use It.* New York: Harper and Row, 1967

BRASH, D. T. (1970) 'Australia as host to the international corporation'. In Kindleberger (1970)

BRAVERMAN, H. (1974) *Labour and Monopoly Capital.* New York: Monthly Review Press

BROOKE, M. Z., and REMMERS, A. L. (1970) *The Strategy of Multinational Enterprise*. London: Longman

BROOKE, M. Z., and REMMERS, A. L. (1972) *The Multinational Corporation in Europe*. London: Longman

BROWN, R. (ed.) (1973) *Knowledge, Education and Cultural Change*. London: Tavistock

BUCKLEY, W. (1967) *Sociology and Modern Systems Theory*. Englewood Cliffs, NJ: Prentice-Hall

BUKHARIN, N. (1915) *Imperialism and World Economy*. London: Merlin Press, 1972

BUKHARIN, N., and PREOBRAZHENSKY, E. (1920) *The ABC of Communism*. Harmondsworth: Penguin, 1962

BUNTING, D., and BARBOUR, J. (1971) 'Interlocking directorates in large American corporations, 1896–1964', *Business History Review*, 45/3

BURCH, P. H. (1972) *The Managerial Revolution Reassessed*. Massachusetts: Lexington Books

BURNHAM, J. (1941) *The Managerial Revolution*. Harmondsworth: Penguin, 1945

BURNS, T. R., and BUCKLEY, W. (eds.) (1976) *Power and Control*. London: Sage

CAIRNCROSS, A. K. (1953) *Home and Foreign Investment*. Cambridge University Press

CARCHEDI, G. (1975) 'On the economic identification of the new middle class', *Economy and Society*, 4/1

CASTELLS, M. (1972) *The Urban Question*. London: Edward Arnold, 1977

CASTELLS, M. (1976) *La Crise économique et la société américaine* ('The Economic Crisis and American Society'). Paris: Presses Universitaires de France

CAUSER, G. (1978) 'Private capital and the state in western Europe'. In Giner and Archer (1978)

CHAMBERLIN, E. (1933) *The Theory of Monopolistic Competition*. Harvard University Press

CHANDLER, A. D. (1962) *Strategy and Structure*. MIT Press

CHANDLER, A. D. (1976) 'The development of modern management structure in the US and UK'. In Hannah (1976)

CHANNON, D. F. (1973) *The Strategy and Structure of British Enterprise*. London: Macmillan

CHANNON, D. F. (1977) *British Banking Strategy and the International Challenge*. London: Macmillan

CHEVALIER, J.-M. (1969) 'The problem of control in large American corporations', *The Antitrust Bulletin*, 14

CHEVALIER, J.-M. (1970) *La Structure financière de l'industrie américaine* ('The Financial Structure of American Industry'). Paris: Cujas

CHILD, J. (1969) *The Business Enterprise in Modern Industrial Society*. London: Collier–Macmillan

CHRIST, T. (1970) 'A thematic analysis of the American business creed', *Social Forces*, 49

CITOLEUX, Y., *et al.* (1977) 'Les Groupes de sociétés en 1974' ('Company groups in 1974'), *Économie et statistique*, 87

CLARKE, S. (1977) 'Marxism, sociology, and Poulantzas's theory of the state', *Capital and Class*, 2

CLARKE, W. M. (1967) *The City in the World Economy*. Harmondsworth: Penguin

CLEMENT, W. (1975) *The Canadian Corporate Elite*. Toronto: McClelland Stewart

CLEMENTS, R. V. (1958) *Managers: A Study of their Careers in Industry*. London: Allen and Unwin

COATES, K. (ed.) (1968) *Can the Workers Run Industry?* London: Sphere

COLE, G. D. H. (1934) *What Marx Really Meant*. Connecticut: Greenwood Press, 1970

COLE, G. D. H. (1948) *The Meaning of Marxism*. University of Michigan Press, 1964

COLE, G. D. H. (1955) *Studies in Class Structure*. London: Routledge and Kegan Paul

COLEMAN, G. H. (1973) 'Gentlemen and players', *Economic History Review*, 26

COLEMAN, J. (1974) *Power and the Structure of Society*. New York: W. W. Norton

COMMISSION ON CONCENTRATION (1968) 'Ownership and influence in the economy'. Extract from *Commission on Industrial and Economic Concentration*. Stockholm: Government Publications Office. In Scase (1976)

CONNELL, R. (1976) *Ruling Class, Ruling Culture*. Cambridge University Press

COOK, K. S. (1977) 'Exchange and power in networks of interorganisational relations', *Sociological Quarterly*, 18

COPEMAN, G. H. (1955) *Leaders of British Industry*. London: Gee

CORRIGAN, P., *et al.* (1977) 'The state as a relation of production'. Paper to British Sociological Association, Sheffield

COTTRELL, P. L. (1975) *British Overseas Investment in the Nineteenth Century*. London: Macmillan

COX, E. B. (1963) *Trends in the Distribution of Stock Ownership*. University of Pennsylvania Press

CREWE, I. (ed.) (1974) *British Political Sociology Yearbook*. Volume 1. London: Croom Helm

CRISP (1962) *Morphologie des groupes financiers belges* ('Morphology of Belgian Financial Groups'). Brussels: CRISP

CROMPTON, R., and GUBBAY, J. (1977) *Economy and Class Structure*. London: Macmillan

CRONJÉ, S., *et al.* (1976) *Lonrho*. Harmondsworth: Penguin

CROSLAND, C. A. R. (1962) *The Conservative Enemy*. London: Cape

CROUCH, C. (ed.) (1978) *British Political Sociology Yearbook*. Volume 5. London: Croom Helm.

CUTLER, A. *et al.* (1977) *Marx's 'Capital' and Capitalism Today*. Volume 1. London: Routledge and Kegan Paul

CUTLER, A., *et al.* (1978) *Marx's 'Capital' and Capitalism Today*. Volume 2. London: Routledge and Kegan Paul

CUYVERS, L., and MEEUSEN, W. (1976) 'The structure of personal influence of the Belgian holding companies', *European Economic Review*, 8/1

CUYVERS, L. and MEEUSEN, W. (1978) 'A time-series analysis of concentration in Belgian banking and holding companies'. Paper to European Consortium for Political Research, Grenoble

DAEMS, H. (1975) *The Holding Company*. PhD thesis, Katholieke Universiteit Te Leuven

DAEMS, H., and VAN DER WEE, H. (eds.) (1974) *The Rise of Managerial Capitalism*. The Hague: Martinus Nijhoff

DAHRENDORF, R. (1959) *Class and Class Conflict in an Industrial Society*. London: Routledge and Kegan Paul

DAHRENDORF, R. (1967) *Conflict After Class*. London: Longman

DAHRENDORF, R. (1968) *Society and Democracy in Germany*. London: Routledge and Kegan Paul

DALTON, G. (1974) *Economic Systems and Society*. Harmondsworth: Penguin

'DARRAS' (1966) *Le Partage des bénéfices* ('The Distribution of Advantages'). Paris: Éditions de Minuit

DAVIS, K., and MOORE, W. E. (1945) 'Some principles of stratification', *American Sociological Review*, 10/2

DAY, A. C. L. (1974) 'The nation's wealth – who owns it', *Observer*, 20 January

DE ALESSI, L. (1973) 'Private property and dispersion of ownership in large corporations', *Journal of Finance*, 28/4

DE VINK, P. H. J. (1970) 'Should institutional management get involved in company management situations?', *The Investment Analyst*, 26 May

DE VROEY, M. (1973) *Propriété et pouvoir dans les grandes entreprises* ('Property and Power in Large Enterprises'). Brussels: CRISP

DE VROEY, M. (1975a) 'The separation of ownership and control in large corporations', *Review of Radical Political Economics*, 7/2

DE VROEY, M. (1975b) 'The owners' interventions in decision-making in large corporations', *European Economic Review*, 6

DE VROEY, M. (1976) 'The measurement of ownership and control in large corporations: a critical review'. Document de travail, No. 718, CRIDE

DIAMOND REPORT (1975*a*) *Royal Commission on the Distribution of Income and Wealth.* Report No. 1, Cmnd. 6172. London: HMSO

DIAMOND REPORT (1975*b*) *Royal Commission on the Distribution of Income and Wealth.* Report No. 2, Cmnd. 6173. London: HMSO

DOMHOFF, G. W. (1967) *Who Rules America?* Englewood Cliffs, NJ: Prentice-Hall

DOMHOFF, G. W. (1971) *The Higher Circles: The Governing Class in America.* New York: Vintage Books

DOMHOFF, G. W. (1974) *The Bohemian Grove.* New York: Harper and Row

DOMHOFF, G. W. (1975) 'Social clubs, policy-planning groups and corporations', *Insurgent Sociologist,* 5/3

DOMHOFF, G. W. (1976) 'I am not an "instrumentalist" ', *Kapitalistate,* 4/5

DOOLEY, P. C. (1969) 'The interlocking directorate', *American Economic Review,* 59

DRACHE, D. (1970) 'The Canadian bourgeoisie and its national consciousness'. In Lumsden (1970)

DRUCKER, P. F. (1951) *The New Society: The Anatomy of the Industrial Order.* London: Heinemann

DUNNING, E. G. (1977) 'Power and authority in the public schools'. In Gleichmann *et al.* (1977)

DUNNING, J. H. (1970) *Studies in International Investment.* London: Allen and Unwin

DUNNING, J. H. (ed.) (1972) *International Investment.* Harmondsworth: Penguin

DYE, T. R. (1976) *Who's Running America?* Englewood Cliffs, NJ: Prentice-Hall

EATON, J. (1963) *Political Economy.* New York: International Publishers

EDWARDS, G. W. (1938) *The Evolution of Finance Capitalism.* London: Longmans Green

EISENBERG, M. A. (1969) 'The legal roles of shareholder and management in modern corporate decision-making', *California Law Review,* 57/1

ELIAS, N. (1939*a*) *Über den Prozess der Zivilisation* ('On the Process of Civilization'). Volume 1. Frankfurt: Suhrkamp, 1977

ELIAS, N. (1939*b*) *Über den Prozess der Zivilisation* ('On the Process of Civilization'). Volume 2. Frankfurt: Suhrkamp, 1977

ELIAS, N. (1970*a*) *What is Sociology?* London: Hutchinson, 1978

ELIAS, N. (1970*b*) 'Processes of state formation and nation building', *Transactions of the 7th World Congress of Sociology,* Volume 3

EMMANUEL, A. (1976) 'The multinational corporations and inequality of development', *International Social Science Journal,* 28/4

ENCEL, S. (1970) *Equality and Authority.* London: Tavistock

ERICKSON, C. (1959) *British Industrialists: Hosiery and Steel.* Cambridge University Press

ERRITT, M. J., and ALEXANDER, J. C. D. (1977) 'Ownership of company shares', *Economic Trends*, September. London: HMSO

ESPING-ANDERSON, G. *et al.* (1976) 'Modes of class struggle and the capitalist state', *Kapitalistate*, 4/5

EVAN, W. (1976) *Organization Theory*. New York: Wiley

EVELY, R., and LITTLE, I. M. D. (1960) *Concentration in British Industry*. Cambridge University Press

FARACE, R. V., and WIGAND, R. T. (1975) 'The communication industry in economic integration: the case of West Germany'. Paper to International Communication Association, Chicago

FAY, B. (1975) *Social Theory and Political Practice*. London: Allen and Unwin

FENNEMA, M., and SCHIJF, H. (1978) 'Analysing interlocking directorates'. Paper to European Consortium for Political Research, Grenoble

FINE, B., and HARRIS, L. (1976a) 'Current issues in Marxian economic theory', *Socialist Register*

FINE, B., and HARRIS, L. (1976b) 'State expenditure in advanced capitalism: a critique', *New Left Review*, 98

FITCH, R. (1971) 'Reply to James O'Connor', *Socialist Revolution*, 7

FITCH, R. (1972) 'Sweezy and corporate fetishism', *Socialist Revolution*, 12

FITCH, R., and OPPENHEIMER, M. (1970a) 'Who rules the corporations?', Part I, *Socialist Revolution*, 4

FITCH, R. and OPPENHEIMER, M. (1970b) 'Who rules the corporations?' Part II, *Socialist Revolution*, 5

FITCH, R., and OPPENHEIMER, M. (1970c) 'Who rules the corporations?', Part III, *Socialist Revolution*, 6

FLEMMING, J. S., and LITTLE, I. M. D. (1974) *Why We Need A Wealth Tax*. London: Methuen

FLORENCE, P. S. (1947) 'The statistical analysis of joint stock company control', *Statistical Journal*, Part I

FLORENCE, P. S. (1953) *The Logic of British and American Industry*. London: Routledge and Kegan Paul. Rev. ed. 1961

FLORENCE, P. S. (1961) *Ownership, Control, and Success of Large Companies*. London: Sweet and Maxwell

FRANCIS, A. (1977) 'Families, firms, and finance capital'. Unpublished paper, Imperial College, London

FRANKEL, H. (1970) *Capitalist Society and Modern Sociology*. London: Lawrence and Wishart

FRANKO, L. G. (1976) *The European Multinationals*. London: Harper and Row

FREITAG, P. J. (1975) 'The Cabinet and big business: a study of interlocks', *Social Problems*, 23/2

G

GALBRAITH, J. K. (1952) *American Capitalism*. Massachusetts: Riverside Press

GALBRAITH, J. K. (1967) *The New Industrial State*. London: Hamish Hamilton

GAMBLE, A., and WALTON, P. (1976) *Capitalism in Crisis*. London: Macmillan

GEORGE, K. D., and WARD, T. S. (1975) *The Structure of Industry in the EEC*. Cambridge University Press

GERSTENBERGER, H. (1976) 'Theory of the state', *German Political Studies*, 2

GERTH, H., and MILLS, C. W. (1954) *Character and Social Structure*. London: Routledge and Kegan Paul

GESSELL, G. A., and HOWE, E. J. (1941) *A Study of Legal Reserve Life Insurance Companies*. Monographs of the Temporary National Economic Committee, Number 28. Washington: Government Printing Office for the US Senate

GIDDENS, A. C. (1971) *Capitalism and Modern Social Theory*. Cambridge University Press

GIDDENS, A. C. (1973) *The Class Structure of the Advanced Societies*. London: Hutchinson

GIDDENS, A. C. (1976a) 'Classical social theory and the origins of modern sociology', *American Journal of Sociology*, 81/4

GIDDENS, A. C. (1976b) *New Rules of Sociological Method*. London: Hutchinson

GILBERT, F. (ed.) (1975) *The Historical Essays of Otto Hintze*. Oxford University Press.

GINER, S., and ARCHER, M. S. (1978) *Contemporary Europe: Social Structures and Cultural Patterns*. London: Routledge and Kegan Paul

GINSBERG, M. (1953) *Sociology*. Oxford University Press

GLEICHMANN, R. R., et al. (eds.) (1977) *Human Figurations*. Amsterdams Sociologisch Tijdschrift

GLYN, A., and SUTCLIFFE, B. (1972) *British Capitalism, Workers and the Profit Squeeze*. Harmondsworth: Penguin

GOLD, D., et al. (1975) 'Some recent developments in Marxist theories of the capitalist state', *Monthly Review*, 25

GOLDSMITH, R. W. (1958) *Financial Intermediaries in the American Economy since 1900*. Princeton University Press

GOLDSMITH, R. W., and PARMELEE, R. C. (1940) *The Distribution of Ownership in the 200 Largest Nonfinancial Corporations*. Monographs of the Temporary National Economic Committee, Number 29. Washington: Government Printing Office for the US Senate

GOLDTHORPE, J. H. (1972) 'Class, status and party in modern Britain', *European Journal of Sociology*, 13

GOLDTHORPE, J. H. (1974) 'Theories of industrial society', *European Journal of Sociology*, 12/2

GOLLAN, J. (1956) *The British Political System*. London: Lawrence and Wishart

GONICK, C. W. (1970) 'Foreign ownership and political decay'. In Lumsden (1970)

GORDON, R. A. (1936) 'Stockholdings of officers and directors in American industrial corporations', *Quarterly Journal of Economics*, 50

GORDON, R. A. (1938) 'Ownership by management and control groups in the large corporations', *Quarterly Journal of Economics*, 52

GORDON, R. A. (1945) *Business Leadership in Large Corporations*. Washington: Brookings Institution

GOUGH, I. (1975) 'State expenditure in advanced capitalism', *New Left Review*, 92

GUSTAVSEN, B. (1976) 'The social context of investment decisions', *Acta Sociologica*, 19

GUTTMAN, R. (1976) 'State intervention and the economic crisis', *Kapitalistate*, 4/5

GUTTSMAN, W. L. (1963) *The British Political Elite*. London: McGibbon and Kee

GUTTSMAN, W. L. (1974) 'The British political elite and the class structure'. In Stanworth and Giddens (1974*b*)

HABERMAS, J. (1973) *Legitimation Crisis*. London: Heinemann, 1976

HABERMAS, J. (1976) *Zur Rekonstruktion des historischen Materialismus* ('The Reconstruction of Historical Materialism'). Frankfurt: Suhrkamp

HABERMAS, J., and LUHMANN, N. (1971) *Theorie der Gesellschaft oder Sozialtechnologie* ('Theory of Society or Social Technology'). Frankfurt: Suhrkamp

HADLEY, E. M. (1970) *Antitrust in Japan*. Princeton University Press

HALL, S. (1977) 'Rethinking the "base and superstructure" metaphor'. In Bloomfield (1977)

HALL, S., *et al.* (1957) 'The insiders', *Universities and Left Review*, 1/3

HALLIDAY, J. (1975) *A Political History of Japanese Capitalism*. New York: Pantheon Books

HALMOS, P. (ed.) (1964) *The Development of Industrial Societies*. Sociological Review Monograph, No. 8

HANNAH, L. (1975) *The Rise of the Corporate Economy*. London: Methuen

HANNAH, L. (ed.) (1976) *Management Strategy and Business Development*. London: Macmillan

HARBURY, C. D. (1962) 'Inheritance and the distribution of personal wealth in Britain'. In Atkinson (1973*b*)

HARBURY, C. D., and MCMAHON, P. C. (1974) 'Intergenerational wealth transmission and the characteristics of top wealth leavers in Britain'. In Stanworth and Giddens (1974*b*)

HART, P. E., *et al.* (1973) *Mergers and Concentration in British Industry.* Cambridge University Press

HARVEY, J., and HOOD, K. (1958) *The British State.* London: Lawrence and Wishart

HAXEY, S. (1939) *Tory M P.* London: Gollancz

HEILBRONNER, R. L. (1976) *Business Civilization in Decline.* Harmondsworth: Penguin, 1977

HELMERS, H. M., *et al.* (1975) *Graven naar Macht* ('Channels of Power'). Amsterdam: Van Gennep

HERMAN, E. S. (1973) 'Do bankers control corporations', *Monthly Review* 25/2

HIGLEY, J. *et al.* (1976) *Elite Structure and Ideology.* Oslo: Universitetsforlaget

HILFERDING, R. (1910) *Das Finanzkapital* ('Finance Capital'). Vienna: Ignaz Brand

HILL, R. C. (1977) 'Two divergent theories of the state', *International Journal of Urban and Regional Research*, 1/1

HINDESS, B. (1977) 'The concept of class in Marxist theory and Marxist politics'. In Bloomfield (1977)

HINTZE, O. (1900) 'The formation of states and constitutional development'. In Gilbert (1975)

HINTZE, O. (1906) 'Military organisation and the organisation of the state'. In Gilbert (1975)

HIRSCH, J. (1970) 'Scientific-Technical progress and the political system', *German Political Studies*, 1

HIRSCH, J. (1974) *Staatsapparat und Reproduktion des Kapitals* ('State Apparatus and the Reproduction of Capital'). Frankfurt: Suhrkamp. Chapters 1 and 5 translated in Holloway and Picciotto (1978)

HIRSCH, J. (1977) 'Remarques théoriques sur l'état bourgeois et sa crise' ('Theoretical remarks on the bourgeois state and its crisis'). In Poulantzas (1977)

HIRST, P. (1977) 'Economic classes and politics'. In Hunt (1977)

HOBSBAWM, E. J. (1968) *Industry and Empire.* Harmondsworth: Penguin, 1969

HOBSON, C. K. (1914) *The Export of Capital.* London: Constable

HODGES, M. (1974) *Multinational Corporations and National Government.* Farnborough: Saxon House

HOERNING, K. H. (1971) 'Power and social stratification', *Sociological Quarterly*, 12

HOLLAND, S. (ed.) (1972) *The State as Entrepreneur.* London: Weidenfeld and Nicolson

HOLLAND, S. (1975) *The Socialist Challenge.* London: Quartet

HOLLAND, S. (1976) *Capital Versus the Regions.* London: Macmillan

HOLLOWAY, J. (1976) 'Some issues raised by Marxist analyses of European integration', *Conference of Socialist Economists Bulletin*, 13

HOLLOWAY, J., and PICCIOTTO, S. (1977) 'Capital, crisis and the state', *Capital and Class*, 2

HOLLOWAY, J., and PICCIOTTO, S. (1978) *State and Capital*. London: Edward Arnold

HOOGVELT, A. (1976) *The Sociology of the Developing Societies*. London: Macmillan

HOSELITZ, B. F. (1960) *Sociological Aspects of Economic Growth*. Glencoe, Ill.: Free Press

HOSELITZ, B. F., and MOORE, W. E. (1966) *Industrialisation and Society*. Paris: Mouton

HOUSE, J. D. (1977) 'The social organisation of multinational corporations: Canadian subsidiaries in the oil industry', *Canadian Review of Sociology and Anthropology*, 14/1

HUGHES, M. D. (1973) 'American investment in Britain'. In Urry and Wakeford (1973)

HUGHES, M. D., *et al.* (1977) 'Trends in interlocking directorships: an international comparison', *Acta Sociologica*, 20/3

HUNT, A. (ed.) (1977) *Class and Class Structure*. London: Lawrence and Wishart

HUSSAIN, A. (1976) 'Hilferding's finance capital', *Bulletin of the Conference of Socialist Economists*, 13

HUSSAIN, A. (1977) 'Crises and tendencies of capitalism', *Economy and Society*, 6/4

HYMER, S. (1972) 'The multinational corporation and the law of uneven development'. In Radice (1975)

ISRAEL, J. (1974) 'The welfare state: a manifestation of advanced capitalism', *Acta Sociologica*, 17/4

JANCOVICI, E. (1972) 'Informatique et entreprise' ('Information and enterprise'), *Sociologie du travail*, 14/1

JEIDELS, O. (1905) *Das Verhältnis der deutschen Grossbanken zur Industrie mit besonderer Berücksichtigung der Eisenindustrie* ('The Relation of the Large German Banks to Industry with Particular Reference to the Steel Industry'). Leipzig: Duncker und Humblot

JENKINS, R. (1970) *Exploitation*. London: MacGibbon and Kee

JESSOP, B. (1976) 'On the commensurability of power and structural constraint'. Paper to EGCS Symposium

JESSOP, B. (1978a) 'Capitalism and democracy'. In Littlejohn *et al.* (1978)

JESSOP, B. (1978b) 'Remarks on some recent theories of the capitalist state', *Cambridge Journal of Economics*, 1/4

JEWKES, J. (1977) *Delusions of Dominance*. London: Institute of Economic Affairs

JOHNSON, R. W. (1973) 'The British political elite, 1955–1972', *European Journal of Sociology*, 14/2

JOHNSON, T. J. (1977*a*) 'What is to be known?', *Economy and Society*, 6/2
JOHNSON, T. J. (1977*b*) 'The professions in the class structure'. In Scase (1977)
JUNNE, G. (1976) 'Multinational banks, the state and international integration', *German Political Studies*, 2
JURAN, J., and LOUDEN, J. K. (1966) *The Corporate Director*. New York: American Management Association

KAMERSCHEN, D. R. (1968) 'The influence of ownership and control on profit rates', *American Economic Review*, 58
KARPIK, L. (1972) 'Les Politiques et les logiques d'action de la grande entreprise industrielle' ('The policies and logics of action of the large industrial enterprise'), *Sociologie du travail*, 14/1
KAUTSKY, K. (1902) *The Social Revolution*. New York: Dial Press, 1925
KAY, G. (1976) *Development and Underdevelopment*. London: Macmillan
KEFAUVER, E. (1966) *In a Few Hands*. Harmondsworth: Penguin
KELLER, S. (1963) *Beyond the Ruling Class*. New York: Random House
KEMP, T. (1978) 'Marx on the formation of an average rate of profit', *Labour Review*, 2/2
KENNEDY, W. P. (1976) 'Institutional responses to economic growth: capital markets in Britain to 1914'. In Hannah (1976)
KERR, C. *et al.* (1960) *Industrialism and Industrial Man*. Harmondsworth: Penguin, 1973
KIDRON, M. (1968) *Western Capitalism Since the War*. Harmondsworth: Penguin, 1970
KIERNAN, V. G. (1974) *Marxism and Imperialism*. London: Edward Arnold
KINDLEBERGER, C. P. (ed.) (1970) *The International Corporation*. Massachusetts: MIT Press.
KLEIN, L. R., *et al.* (1956) 'Savings and finances of the upper income classes', *Oxford Institute of Statistics Bulletin*, 18
KNOWLES, J. C. (1973) 'The Rockefeller financial group'. MSS Modular Publications, Module 343
KOLKO, G. (1962) *Wealth and Power in America*. London: Thames and Hudson
KOLKO, G. (1969) *The Roots of American Foreign Policy*. Boston: Beacon Press
KOSONEN, P. (1977) 'Contemporary capitalism and the critique of political economy', *Acta Sociologica*, 20/4
KOZLOV, G. A. (1977) *Political Economy: Capitalism*. Moscow: Progress
KREJCI, J. (1976) *Social Structure in Divided Germany*. London: Croom Helm
KURTH, J. R. (1975) 'The international politics of post-industrial societies'. In Lindberg (1975)

KUUSINEN, O. V., *et al.* (1959) *Fundamentals of Marxism–Leninism*. New York: Crowell-Collier and Macmillan, n.d.

KUZNETS, S. (1953) *Shares of Upper Income Groups in Incomes and Savings*. New York: National Bureau of Economic Research

KUZNETS, S. (1961) *Capital in the American Economy*. Princeton University Press

LACLAU, E. (1975) 'The specificity of the political: the Poulantzas–Miliband debate', *Economy and Society*, 4/1

LAMPMAN, R. (1959) 'The share of top wealth holders in the United States'. In Atkinson (1973*b*)

LAMPMAN, R. (1962) *The Share of Top Wealth Holders in National Wealth*. Princeton University Press

LARNER, R. J. (1966) 'Ownership and control in the 200 largest non-financial corporations: 1929 and 1963', *American Economic Review*, 56

LARNER, R. J. (1970) *Management Control and the Large Corporation*. New York: Dunellen

LAUTMAN, J. (1966) 'Les Milieux de décision' ('Places of decision'). In 'Darras' (1966)

LAWRENCE, P., and LORSCH, J. (1967) *Organization and Environment*. Harvard University Press

LEINHARDT, S. (ed.) (1977) *Symposium on Social Networks*. New York: Academic Press

LENIN, V. I. (1917*a*) *Imperialism: The Highest Stage of Capitalism*. Moscow: Progress Publishers, 1966

LENIN, V. I. (1917*b*) *The State and Revolution*. Moscow: Progress, 1969

LENSKI, G. (1966) *Power and Privilege*. New York: McGraw-Hill

LEVINE, J. H. (1972) 'Spheres of influence', *American Sociological Review*, 37

LEVINE, J. H., and ROY, W. S. (1977) 'A study of interlocking directorates'. In Leinhardt (1977)

LEVITT, K. (1970) *Silent Surrender: The Multinational Corporation in Canada*. Toronto: Macmillan

LEVY, A. B. (1950) *Private Corporations and their Control*. 2 vols. London: Routledge and Kegan Paul

LIEBERSON, S., and O'CONNOR, J. R. (1972) 'Leadership and organizational performance: a study of large corporations', *American Sociological Review*, 37/2

LIM, M. H., and ANDERSON, M. (1976) 'Concentration of wealth and power in the top corporations in Malaysia'. Paper to Malayan Economic Association

LINDBERG, L., *et al.* (eds.) (1975) *Stress and Contradiction in Modern Capitalism*. London: D. C. Heath

LIPSET, S. M. (1960) *Political Man*. London: Heinemann

LIPSEY, R. G. (1966) *An Introduction to Positive Economics*. London: Weidenfeld and Nicolson

LITTLEJOHN, G. J., *et al.* (eds.) (1978) *Power and the State.* London: Croom Helm

LIVINGSTON, J., *et al.* (eds.) (1973) *The Japan Reader.* Volume 1. Harmondsworth: Penguin, 1976

LOCKWOOD, D. (1964) 'Social integration and system integration'. In Zollschan and Hirsh (1964)

LOCKWOOD, W. W. (1964) *The Economic Development of Japan.* Princeton University Press

LOCKWOOD, W. W. (1965*a*) 'Japan's "new capitalism" '. In Lockwood (1965*b*)

LOCKWOOD, W. W. (1965*b*) *The State and Economic Enterprise in Japan.* Princeton University Press

LONGSTRETH, F. (1977*a*) 'The state and national economic planning in a capitalist society'. Paper to British Sociological Association, Sheffield

LONGSTRETH, F. (1977*b*) 'The City, industry and the state'. Paper to Conference of Socialist Economists

LUHMANN, N. (1968) 'Sociology of political systems', *German Political Studies*, 1 (1974)

LUHMANN, N. (1970) *Soziologische Aufklärung* ('Sociological Explanation'). Volume 1. Opladen: Westdeutscher

LUHMANN, N. (1971) 'Sinn als Grundbegriff der Soziologie' ('Meaning as a basic concept of sociology'). In Habermas and Luhmann (1971)

LUHMANN, N. (1975*a*) *Macht* ('Power'). Stuttgart: Enke

LUHMANN, N. (1975*b*) *Legitimation durch Verfahren* ('Legitimation through Procedure'). Neuwied: Luchterhand

LUHMANN, N. (1975*c*) *Soziologische Aufklärung* ('Sociological Explanation'). Volume 2. Opladen: Westdeutscher

LUKES, S. (1974) *Power.* London: Macmillan

LUMSDEN, I. (ed.) (1970) *Close the 49th Parallel: The Americanization of Canada.* University of Toronto Press

LUNDBERG, F. (1937) *America's Sixty Families.* New York: Vanguard Press

LUNDBERG, F. (1969) *The Rich and the Super Rich.* London. Nelson

LUPTON, C., and WILSON, C. (1959) 'The social background and connections of top decision-makers'. In Urry and Wakeford (1973)

LUXEMBURG, R. (1913) *The Accumulation of Capital.* London: Routledge and Kegan Paul, 1951

LYDALL, H. F. (1959) 'The long-term trend in the size distribution of income', *Journal of the Royal Statistical Society*, Series A, 122/1

LYDALL, H. F., and LANSING, J. B. (1959) 'A comparison of the distribution of personal income and wealth in the United States and Great Britain'. In Atkinson (1973*b*)

LYDALL, H. F., and TIPPING, D. G. (1961) 'The distribution of personal wealth in Britain'. In Atkinson (1973*b*)

MACE, M. L. (1971) *Directors: Myth and Reality*. Harvard University Press
MCCLELLAND, D. C. (1961) *The Achieving Society*. New York: Van Nostrand
MACPHERSON, C. B. (1973) *Democratic Theory*. Oxford: Clarendon Press
MAGDOFF, H. (1970) 'The American empire and the US economy'. In Rhodes (1970)
MAGDOFF, H., and SWEEZY, P. M. (1969) 'Notes on the multinational corporation', *Monthly Review*, 21
MANDEL, E. (1969) *Marxist Economic Theory*. London: Merlin
MANDEL, E. (1970) *Europe Versus America*. London: New Left Books
MANDEL, E. (1972) *Late Capitalism*. London: New Left Books, 1975
MANKOFF, M. (ed.) (1972) *The Poverty of Progress*. New York: Holt, Rinehart and Winston
MANN, M. (1977a) 'States ancient and modern'. To appear as chapter 5 of Mann (forthcoming)
MANN, M. (1977b) 'Class and the nation state'. To appear as chapter 6 of Mann (forthcoming)
MANN, M. (forthcoming) *The Sources of Social Power*
MARCEAU, J. (1977) *Class and Status in France*. Oxford University Press
MARCEAU, J., and WHITLEY, R. (1978) 'Management education in Britain and France'. In Littlejohn *et al.* (1978)
MARCUS, H. (1970) *Die Macht der Mächtigen* ('The Power of the Powerful'). Dusseldorf: Droste
MARIOLIS, P. (1975) 'Interlocking directorates and control of corporations'. *Social Science Quarterly*, 56/3
MARRIS, R. (1964) *The Economic Theory of 'Managerial' Capitalism*. London: Macmillan
MARTINELLI, A., and SOMAINI, E. (1973) 'Nation states and multinational corporations', *Kapitalistate*, 1
MARX, K. (1857) 'Introduction' to *Grundrisse*. Harmondsworth: Penguin, 1973
MARX, K. (1885) *Capital*. Volume 2. London: Lawrence and Wishart, 1974
MARX, K. (1894) *Capital*. Volume 3. London: Lawrence and Wishart, 1959
MARX, K., and ENGELS, F. (1848) *The Communist Manifesto*. Harmondsworth: Penguin, 1967
MATHIAS, P. (1969) *The First Industrial Nation*. London: Methuen
MATTICK, P. (1969) *Marx and Keynes*. London: Merlin Press, 1971
MAYO, E. (1949) *The Social Problems of an Industrial Civilization*. London: Routledge and Kegan Paul
MEADE, J. E. (1964) *Efficiency, Equality, and the Ownership of Property*. London: Allen and Unwin
MEANS, G. C. (1930) 'The diffusion of stock ownership in the US', *Quarterly Journal of Economics*, 44
MEANS, G. C. (1964) 'Economic concentration'. Report to Senate Hearings. In Zeitlin (1970)

MEANS, G. C., *et al.* (1939) 'The structure of controls'. Chapter IX in *The Structure of the American Economy*. National Resources Committee of the U S Senate. Washington: Government Printing Office

MEEKS, G., and WHITTINGTON, G. (1975) 'Giant companies in the United Kingdom', *Economic Journal*, 85

MEEKS, G., and WHITTINGTON, G. (1976) *The Financing of Quoted Companies*. Background Paper No. 1. Royal Commission on the Distribution of Income and Wealth. London: H M S O

MEIER, H.-P. (1976) 'Ideology and control of crisis in highly developed capitalist societies'. In Burns and Buckley (1976)

MENNELL, S. (1977) ' "Individual" action and its "social" consequences in the work of Norbert Elias'. In Gleichmann *et al.* (1977)

MENSHIKOV, S. (1969) *Millionaires and Managers*. Moscow: Progress Publishers

MERTON, R. K. (1936) 'The unanticipated consequences of purposive social action', *American Sociological Review*, 1

MEYNAUD, J. (1964) *Technocracy*. London: Faber and Faber, 1968

MICHALET, C. A. (1976) *Le Capitalisme mondiale* ('World Capitalism'). Paris: Presses Universitaires de France

MILIBAND, R. (1968) 'Professor Galbraith and American capitalism'. In Mankoff (1972)

MILIBAND, R. (1969) *The State in Capitalist Society*. London: Quartet edition, 1973

MILIBAND, R. (1970) 'The capitalist state', *New Left Review*, 59

MILIBAND, R. (1973) 'Poulantzas and the capitalist state', *New Left Review*, 82

MILIBAND, R. (1977) *Marxism and Politics*. Oxford University Press

MILLER, H. P. (1966) 'Income distribution in the United States'. In Atkinson (1973*b*)

MILLER, S. M. (1975) 'Notes on neo-capitalism', *Theory and Society*, 2/1

MILLS, C. W. (1956) *The Power Elite*. New York: Oxford University Press

MINTZ, B. (1975) 'The president's cabinet, 1897–1972', *Insurgent Sociologist*, 5/3

MINTZ, B., and SCHWARTZ, M. (1978) 'The role of financial institutions in interlock networks'. Paper to European Consortium for Political Research, Grenoble

MINTZ, B., *et al.* (1976) 'Problems of proof in elite research', *Social Problems*, 23/3

MOKKEN, R. J., and STOKMAN, F. N. (1974) 'Interlocking directorates between large corporations'. Paper to European Consortium for Political Research, Strasbourg

MOKKEN, R. J., and STOKMAN, F. N. (1976) 'Power and influence as political phenomena'. In Barry (1976)

MOLLENKOPF, J. (1975) 'Theories of the state and power structure research', *Insurgent Sociologist*, 5/3

MONJARDET, D. (1972) 'Carrière des dirigeants et contrôle de l'entreprise' ('Managerial careers and the control of enterprises'), *Sociologie du travail*, 14/2

MONSEN, R. J., and DOWNS, A. (1965) 'A theory of large managerial firms', *Journal of Political Economy*, 73

MONSEN, R. J., et al. (1968) 'The effect of separation of ownership and control on the performance of the large firm', *Quarterly Journal of Economics*, 82/1

MOORE, B. (1966) *Social Origins of Dictatorship and Democracy.* Harmondsworth: Penguin, 1967

MORIN, F. (1974) *La Structure financière du capitalisme français* ('The Financial Structure of French Capitalism'). Paris: Calmann–Lévy

MORIN, F. (1977) *La Banque et les groupes industriels à l'heure des nationalisations* ('Banking and Industrial Groups on the Eve of Nationalisation'). Paris: Calmann–Lévy

MORVAN, Y. (1972) *La Concentration de l'industrie en France* ('The Concentration of Industry in France'). Paris: Librairie Armand Colin

MOYLE, J. (1971) *The Pattern of Ordinary Share Ownership.* Cambridge University Press

MUELLER, W. F. (1964) 'Economic Concentration'. Report to Senate Hearings. In Zeitlin (1970)

MURRAY, R. (1971) 'The internationalization of capital and the nation state'. In *Multinational Companies and Nation States.* Nottingham: Spokesman Books

NAIRN, T. (1972) *The Left Against Europe.* Harmondsworth: Penguin, 1973

NETTL, J. P. (1965) 'Consensus or elite domination', *Political Studies*, 13

NICHOLLS, D. (1974) *Three Varieties of Pluralism.* London: Macmillan

NICHOLS, T. (1969) *Ownership, Control, and Ideology.* London: Allen and Unwin

NICHOLSON, R. J. (1967) 'The distribution of personal income in the UK'. In Urry and Wakeford (1973)

NOBLE, T. (1975) *Modern Britain.* London: Batsford

NOGUCHI, T. (1973) 'Japanese monopoly capital and the state', *Kapitalistate*, 1

NYMAN, S., and SILBERSTON, A. (1978) 'The ownership and control of industry', *Oxford Economic Papers*, 30/1

O'CONNOR, J. (1971) 'Who rules the corporations? The ruling class', *Socialist Revolution*, 7

O'CONNOR, J. (1973) *The Fiscal Crisis of the State.* New York: St Martins Press

OFFE, C. (1970) *Industry and Inequality.* London: Edward Arnold, 1976

OFFE, C. (1972*a*) 'The abolition of market control and the problem of legitimacy'. Chapter 2 on Offe (1972*d*). Translation in *Kapitalistate*, 1 and 2 (1973)

OFFE, C. (1972*b*) 'Structural problems of the capitalist state'. Chapter 3 in Offe (1972*d*). Translation in *German Political Studies*, 1 (1974)

OFFE, C. (1972*c*) 'Further comments on Müller and Neusüss'. Chapter 7 in Offe (1972*d*). Translation in *Telos*, 25 (1975)

OFFE, C. (1972*d*) *Strukturprobleme des kapitalistischen Staates* ('Structural Problems of the Capitalist State'). Frankfurt: Suhrkamp

OFFE, C. (1972*e*) 'Advanced capitalism and the welfare state', *Politics and Society*, 2/4

OFFE, C. (1972*f*) 'Class authority and the political system', *International Journal of Sociology*, 2/1

OFFE, C. (1975*a*) Introduction to 'Legitimacy versus efficiency'. In Lindberg *et al.* (1975)

OFFE, C. (1975*b*) 'The theory of the capitalist state and the problem of policy formation'. In Lindberg *et al.* (1975)

OFFE, C., and RONGE, V. (1975) 'Theses on the theory of the state', *New German Critique*, 6

OLLMAN, B. (1971) *Alienation*. Cambridge University Press

O'NEILL, J. (ed.) (1973) *Modes of Individualism and Collectivism*. London: Heinemann

OSSOWSKI, S. (1956) 'Old notions and new problems'. In Beteille (1969)

OWEN, R., and SUTCLIFFE, B. (eds.) (1972) *Studies in the Theory of Imperialism*. London: Longman

PAHL, R. E. (1977*a*) 'Stratification, the relation between states and urban and regional development', *International Journal of Urban and Regional Research*, 1/1

PAHL, R. E. (1977*b*) ' "Collective consumption" and the state in capitalist and state socialist societies'. In Scase (1977)

PAHL, R. E., and WINKLER, J. (1974) 'The economic elite: theory and practice'. In Stanworth and Giddens (1974*b*)

PAISH, F. (1967) *Benham's Economics*. London: Pitman

PALLOIX, C. (1969) 'Impérialisme et mode de production capitaliste' ('Imperialism and the capitalist mode of production'), *L'Homme et la société*, 12

PALLOIX, C. (1973) 'The internationalisation of capital and the circuit of social capital'. In Radice (1975)

PALMER, J. P. (1972) 'The separation of ownership from control in large US industrial corporations', *Quarterly Review of Economics and Business*, 12/3

PAPANDREOU, A. G. (1973) 'Multinational corporations and empire', *Social Praxis*, 1/2

PARKER TRIBUNAL (1957) *Proceedings of the Tribunal Appointed to Inquire into Allegations that Information about the Raising of the Bank Rate was Improperly Disclosed*. Cmnd. 350. London: HMSO

PARKIN, F. (1974a) 'Strategies of social closure in class formation'. In Parkin (1974b)

PARKIN, F. (ed.) (1974b) *The Social Analysis of Class Structure*. London: Tavistock

PARKINSON, H. (1951) *Ownership of Industry*. London: Eyre and Spottiswoode

PARRY, G. (1969) *Political Elites*. London: Allen and Unwin

PARSONS, T. (1940) 'The motivation of economic activity'. In Parsons (1954b)

PARSONS, T. (1954a) 'A revised analytical approach to the theory of social stratification'. In Parsons (1954b)

PARSONS, T. (1954b) *Essays in Sociological Theory*. Glencoe, Ill.: Free Press

PARSONS, T. (1956) 'A sociological approach to the theory of organizations'. In Parsons (1960)

PARSONS, T. (1958) 'The institutional framework of economic development.' In Parsons (1960)

PARSONS, T. (1960) *Structure and Process in Modern Societies*. Glencoe, Ill.: Free Press

PARSONS, T., and SMELSER, N. J. (1957) *Economy and Society*. London: Routledge and Kegan Paul

PAŠUKANIS, E. (1924) *La Théorie générale du droit* ('The General Theory of Law'). Paris: EDI, 1970

PATMAN REPORT (1966) *Bank Stock Ownership and Control*. Reprinted in Patman Report (1968)

PATMAN REPORT (1967) *Control of Commercial Banks and Interlocks Among Financial Institutions*. Reprinted in Patman Report (1968)

PATMAN REPORT (1968) *Commercial Banks and Their Trust Activities*. Staff Report for the Subcommittee on Domestic Finance, Committee on Banking and Currency, House of Representatives, 90th Congress, 2nd Session. Washington: Government Printing Office. Includes reprints of Patman Report (1966) and Patman Report (1967)

PAVITT, K., and WORBOYS, M. (1977) *Science, Technology and the Modern Industrial State*. London: Butterworth

PAYNE, P. L. (1967) 'The emergence of the large-scale company in Great Britain', *Economic History Review*, 20

PAYNE, P. L. (1974) *British Entrepreneurship in the Nineteenth Century*. London: Macmillan

PERLO, V. (1957) *The Empire of High Finance*. New York: International Publishers

PERLO, V. (1958) ' "People's Capitalism" and stock ownership', *American Economic Review*, 48. References are to the reprint in Mankoff (1972)

PERROW, C. (1970) *Organizational Analysis*. London: Tavistock
PERRUCCI, R., and PILISUK, M. (1970) 'Leaders and Ruling Elites', *American Sociological Review*, 35
PERRY, R. W., and GILLESPIE, D. F. (1976) 'A controversial non-controversy', *Scottish Journal of Sociology*, 1/1
PETERSON, S. (1965) 'Corporate control and capitalism', *Quarterly Journal of Economics*, 79/1
PFEFFER, J. (1972) 'Size and composition of corporate boards of directors', *Administrative Science Quarterly*, 17
PICCIOTTO, S., and RADICE, H. (1973) 'Capital and state in the world economy', *Kapitalistate*, 1
PICKVANCE, C. G. (ed.) (1976) *Urban Sociology*. London: Methuen
POLAND, E. (1939) 'Interlocking directorates among the largest American corporations, 1935'. Appendix 12 to *The Structure of the American Economy*. National Resources Committee of the US Senate. Washington: Government Printing Office
POLANYI, G., and WOOD, J. B. (1974) *How Much Inequality?* London: Institute of Economic Affairs
POLLARD, S. (1962) *The Development of the British Economy*. London: Edward Arnold
PORTER, J. (1965) *The Vertical Mosaic*. University of Toronto Press
POULANTZAS, N. (1968) *Political Power and Social Classes*. London: New Left Books, 1973
POULANTZAS, N. (1969) 'The problem of the capitalist state', *New Left Review*, 58
POULANTZAS, N. (1974) *Classes in Contemporary Capitalism*. London: New Left Books, 1975
POULANTZAS, N. (1976) 'The capitalist state: a reply to Miliband and Laclau', *New Left Review*, 95
POULANTZAS, N. (ed.) (1977) *La Crise de l'état*. Paris: Presses Universitaires de France
PRAIS, S. J. (1976) *The Evolution of Giant Firms in Britain*. Cambridge University Press.
PRATT, S. S. (1905) 'Our financial oligarchy', *Worlds Work*, 10
PRESTHUS, R. (1973) *Elites in the Policy Process*. Cambridge University Press
PUJO REPORT (1913) *Money Trust Investigation*. House Subcommittee on Banking and Currency. Washington: Government Printing Office

RADCLIFFE REPORT (1959) *Report of the Committee on the Working of the Monetary System*. Cmnd. 827. London: HMSO
RADICE, H. (1971) 'Control type, profitability and growth in large firms: an empirical study', *Economic Journal*, 81
RADICE, H. (ed.) (1975) *International Firms and Modern Imperialism*. Harmondsworth: Penguin

RAMSOY, N. (ed.) (1968) *Norwegian Society*. London: Hurst, 1974

RAW, C. *et al.* (1971) *Do You Sincerely Want To Be Rich?* London: André Deutsch

RENN, H. (1975) 'Einfluss-strukturen in der Wirtschaft' ('Influence structures in the economy'). Universität von Hamburg

RENNER, K. (1904) *The Institutions of Private Law and their Social Function*. London: Routledge and Kegan Paul, 1949. A translation of the 1928, revised edition

REVELL, J. R. (1960) 'An analysis of personal holders of wealth', *British Association for the Advancement of Science*, 17

REVELL, J. R. (1965) 'Changes in the social distribution of property in Britain during the twentieth century', *Actes du Troisième Congrès International d'Histoire Économique*, Munich

REVELL, J. R. (1973) *The British Financial System*. London: Macmillan

REX, J. A. (ed.) (1974a) *Approaches to Sociology*. London: Routledge and Kegan Paul

REX, J. A. (1974b) 'Capitalism, elites and the ruling class'. In Stanworth and Giddens (1974b)

REY, P.-P. (1976) *Les Alliances de classes* ('Class Alliances'). Paris: Maspero

RHODES, R. I. (ed.) (1970) *Imperialism and Underdevelopment*. New York: Monthly Review Press

ROBINSON, J. (1933) *The Economics of Imperfect Competition*. London: Macmillan

ROCHESTER, A. (1936) *Rulers of America*. New York: International Publishers

ROLFE, H. (1967) *The Controllers*. Melbourne: Cheshire

ROSE, A. (1967) *The Power Structure*. New York: Oxford University Press

ROSTOW, W. W. (1960) *The Stages of Economic Growth*. Cambridge University Press

ROWTHORN, R. (1971) *International Big Business*. Cambridge University Press

ROWTHORN, R. (1976) 'Late Capitalism', *New Left Review*, 98

RUBINSTEIN, W. D. (1974) 'Men of property'. In Stanworth and Giddens (1974b)

RUBINSTEIN, W. D. (1976) 'Wealth, elites, and the class structure of modern Britain'. *Past and Present*, 70

RYNDINA, M., and CHERNIKOV, G. (eds.) (1974) *The Political Economy of Capitalism*. Moscow: Progress Publishers

SAFARIAN, A. E. (1966) *Foreign Ownership of Canadian Industry*. Toronto: McGraw Hill

SAHAY, A. (1974) 'Weber's Definition of Capitalism: History and Sociology', *Sociological Analysis and Theory*, 4/1

SAMPSON, A. (1962) *Anatomy of Britain*. London: Hodder and Stoughton

SAMPSON, A. (1973) *The Sovereign State*. London: Hodder and Stoughton

SAMPSON, A. (1975) *The Seven Sisters*. London: Hodder and Stoughton

SARDEI-BIERMANN, S., *et al.* (1973) 'Class domination and the political system', *Kapitalistate*, 2

SAYER, D. (1975) 'Method and dogma in historical materialism', *Sociological Review*, 23/4

SCASE, R. (ed.) (1976) *Readings in the Swedish Class Structure*. London: Pergamon

SCASE, R. (ed.) (1977) *Industrial Society: Class, Cleavage and Control* London: Allen and Unwin

SCHROYER, T. (1975) 'The repoliticization of the relations of production', *New German Critique*, 5

SCHUMPETER, J. (1927) 'Social classes in an ethnically homogeneous environment'. In Schumpeter (1951)

SCHUMPETER, J. (1943) *Capitalism, Socialism and Democracy*. London: Allen and Unwin, 1976

SCHUMPETER, J. (1951) *Imperialism and Social Classes*. Oxford: Basil Blackwell

SCOTT, J. P. (1978) 'Critical social theory: an introduction and critique', *British Journal of Sociology*, 29/1

SCOTT, J. P., and HUGHES, M. D. (1976) 'Ownership and control in a satellite economy: a discussion from Scottish data', *Sociology*, 10/1

SCOTT, J. P., *et al.* (1976) 'Patterns of ownership in top Scottish companies', *Scottish Journal of Sociology*, 1/1

SEIDER, M. S. (1974) 'American business ideology: a content analysis of executive speeches', *American Sociological Review*, 39

SEIDER, M. S. (1977) 'Corporate ownership, control and ideology', *Sociology and Social Research*, 62

SEIERSTAD, S. (1968) 'The Norwegian economy'. In Ramsoy (1968)

SERVAN-SCHREIBER, J. J. (1968) *The American Challenge*. London: Hamish Hamilton

SHEEHAN, R. (1967) 'Proprietors in the world of big business', *Fortune* 15 June

SHONFIELD, M. (1965) *Modern Capitalism*. Oxford University Press

SIMON, R. (1962) *Light on the City*. London: Labour Research Department

SMIGEL, E. O. (1964) *The Wall Street Lawyer*. Glencoe, Ill.: Free Press

SMITH, E. P. (1970) 'Interlocking directorates among the "Fortune 500" ', *Antitrust, Law and Economic Review*, 3

SMITH, E. P., and DESFOSSES, L. R. (1972) 'Interlocking directorates: a study of influence', *Mississippi Valley Journal of Business and Economics*, 7

SMITH, J. D. and CALVERT, S. K. (1965) 'Estimating the wealth of top wealth-holders from estate tax returns', *Proceedings of the American Statistical Association*

SOLTOW, L. (1968) 'Long run changes in British income inequality'. In Atkinson (1973*b*)

SONQUIST, J. A., *et al.* (1975) 'Interlocking directorships in the top US corporations', *Insurgent Sociologist*, 5/3

SONQUIST, J. A., *et al.* (1976) 'Examining corporate interconnections through interlocking directorates'. In Burns and Buckley (1976)

SOREF, M. (1976) 'Social class and a division of labour within the corporate elite', *Sociological Quarterly*, 17/3

STANWORTH, P. (1974) 'Property, class and the corporate elite'. In Crewe (1974)

STANWORTH, P., and GIDDENS, A. C. (1974a) 'An economic elite: a demographic profile of company chairmen'. In Stanworth and Giddens (1974b)

STANWORTH, P., and GIDDENS, A. C. (eds.) (1974b) *Elites and Power in British Society*. Cambridge University Press

STANWORTH, P., and GIDDENS, A. C. (1975) 'The modern corporate economy', *Sociological Review*, 23/1

STARBUCK, W. (ed.) (1978) *Handbook of Organizational Design*. Volume 1

STEUER, M. D., *et al.* (1973) *The Impact of Foreign Direct Investment on the United Kingdom*. London: HMSO

STOCK EXCHANGE (1977) *The Provision of Funds for Industry and Trade*. London: Stock Exchange

STONE, R., *et al.* (1966) *The Owners of Quoted Ordinary Shares*. London: Chapman and Hall

STRINATI, D. (1978) 'Capitalism, the state and industrial relations'. In Crouch (1978)

SUTCLIFFE, B. (1972) 'Imperialism and industrialisation in the Third World'. In Owen and Sutcliffe (1972)

SWEEZY, P. M. (1939) 'Interest groups in the American economy'. In Sweezy (1953)

SWEEZY, P. M. (1940) 'The heyday of the investment banker'. In Sweezy (1953)

SWEEZY, P. M. (1941) 'The decline of the investment banker'. In Sweezy (1953)

SWEEZY, P. M. (1942) *The Theory of Capitalist Development*. London: Dennis Dobson

SWEEZY, P. M. (1951) 'The American ruling class'. In Sweezy (1953)

SWEEZY, P. M. (1953) *The Present as History*. New York: Monthly Review Press

SWEEZY, P. M. (1971) 'The resurgence of financial control: fact or fancy', *Monthly Review*, 23/6

SZYMANSKI, A. (1973) 'Marx and the laws of competitive and monopoly capitalism', *Social Praxis*, 1/3

TAUSSIG, F. W., and JOSLYN, C. S. (1932) *American Business Leaders*. New York: Macmillan

TAWNEY, R. H. (1920) *The Acquisitive Society*. London: Bell

TAWNEY, R. H. (1931) *Equality*. 4th ed. London: George Allen and Unwin, 1952

THERBORN, G. (1976) 'The Swedish class structure, 1930–65: a Marxist analysis'. In Scase (1976)

THOMPSON, D. N. (1978) 'Mergers and acquisitions: motives and effects'. London: Canada House Lecture Series, No. 3

THOMPSON, G. (1976) 'Some issues in the development of accountancy'. Paper to Conference of Socialist Economists, London

THOMPSON, G. (1977) 'The relationship between the financial and industrial sector of the United Kingdom economy', *Economy and Society*, 6/3

TITMUSS, R. (1962) *Income Distribution and Social Change*. London: Allen and Unwin

TITSCHER, E. (1977) 'Personelle Verflechtungen von Unternehmensleitungen' ('Personal interlocks of business management'). Working Paper, University of Vienna

TOMASSON, R. F. (1970) *Sweden: Prototype of Modern Society*. New York: Random House

TOURAINE, A. (1969) *The Post-Industrial Society*. London: Wildwood House, 1971

TURNER, B. (1975) *Industrialism*. Harlow: Longman

TURNER, L. (1970) *Invisible Empires*. London: Hamish Hamilton

URRY, J. (1977) 'Capital and the State'. Paper to the British Sociological Association, Sheffield

URRY, J., and WAKEFORD, J. (eds.) (1973) *Power in Britain*. London: Heinemann

USEEM, M. (1978) 'The inner group of the American capitalist class', *Social Problems*, 25

UTTON, M. A. (1970) *Industrial Concentration*. Harmondsworth: Penguin

VARGA, E. (1928) *The Decline of Capitalism*. London: Dorrit Press

VEBLEN, T. (1904) *The Theory of Business Enterprise*. New York: Scribner, 1915

VEBLEN, T. (1924) *Absentee Ownership and Business Enterprise in Recent Times*. London: Allen and Unwin

VERNON, J. R. (1970) 'Ownership and control among large member banks', *Journal of Finance*, 25

VERNON, R. (1971*a*) *Sovereignty at Bay*. New York: Basic Books

VERNON, R. (1971*b*) 'Multinational business and national economic goals', *International Organization*, 25/3

VERNON, R. (1974*a*) 'Enterprise and government in western Europe'. In Vernon (1974*b*)

VERNON, R. (1974*b*) *Big Business and the State*. London: Macmillan

VERNON, R. (ed.) (1976) *The Oil Crisis*. New York: W. W. Norton

VERNON, R. (1977) *Storm Over the Multinationals*. London: Macmillan

VILLAREJO, D. (1961a) 'Stock ownership and the control of corporations', Parts I and II, *New University Thought*, 2/1

VILLAREJO, D. (1961b) 'Stock ownership and the control of corporations', Part III, *New University Thought*, 2/2

WALLERSTEIN, I. (1974a) *The Modern World System*. New York: Academic Press

WALLERSTEIN, I. (1974b) 'The rise and future demise of the world capitalist system', *Comparative Studies in Society and History*, 16/4

WALSHE, G. (1973) *Recent Trends in Monopoly in Great Britain*. Cambridge University Press

WARMINGTON, A., *et al*. (1977) *Organisational Behaviour and Performance*. London: Macmillan

WARNER, W. L. (ed.) (1967) *The Emergent American Society*. Volume 1. Yale University Press

WARNER, W. L., and ABEGGLEN, J. C. (1955) *Big Business Leaders in America*. New York: Harper Brothers

WARNER, W. L., and UNWALLA, D. B. (1967) 'The system of interlocking directorates'. In Warner (1967)

WARREN, B. (1971) 'How international is capital?' In Radice (1975)

WARREN, B. (1972) 'Capitalist planning and the state', *New Left Review*, 72

WEBER, M. (1921) *Economy and Society*. 3 vols. New York: Bedminster Press, 1968

WEBER, M. (1923) *General Economic History*. Glencoe, Ill.: Free Press, 1950

WEINSTEIN, F. B. (1976) 'Multinational corporations and the Third World: the case of Japan and South East Asia', *International Organisation*, 30/3

WESOLOWSKI, W. (1967) 'The notions of strata and class in socialist society'. In Beteille (1969)

WESTERGAARD, J. H. (1977) 'Class, inequality, and 'corporatism''. In Hunt (1977)

WESTERGAARD, J. H., and RESLER, H. (1975) *Class in a Capitalist Society*. London: Heinemann

WHEELWRIGHT, E. L. (1957) *Ownership and Control of Australian Companies*. Sydney: Law Book Company

WHEELWRIGHT, E. L. (1974) *Radical Political Economy*. Sydney: Australia and New Zealand Book Company

WHEELWRIGHT, E. L., and MISKELLY, J. (1967) *Anatomy of Australian Manufacturing Industry*. Sydney: Law Book Co.

WHITLEY, R. (1973) 'Commonalities and connections among directors of large financial institutions', *Sociological Review*, 21/4

WHITLEY, R. (1974) 'The City and industry'. In Stanworth and Giddens (1974b)

WILLIAMS, R. (1960) *American Society*. New York: Alfred Knopf

212   *Bibliography*

WILLIAMS, R., *et al.* (1968) *May Day Manifesto*. Harmondsworth: Penguin

WILSON REPORT (1977) *Progress Report on the Financing of Industry and Trade*. Committee to Review the Functioning of Financial Institutions. London: HMSO

WINKLER, J. (1976) 'Corporatism', *European Journal of Sociology*, 17/1

WINKLER, J. (1977) 'The corporatist economy: theory and administration'. In Scase (1977)

WIRTH, M. (1973) 'Towards a critique of the theory of state monopoly capitalism', *Economy and Society*, 6/3 (1977)

WOLFE, A. (1974) 'New directions in the Marxist theory of politics', *Politics and Society*, 4/2

WRIGHT, E. O. (1976) 'Class boundaries in advanced capitalist societies', *New Left Review*, 98

YAFFE, D. S. (1973) 'The Marxian theory of crisis, capital, and the state', *Economy and Society*, 2/2

ZALD, M. N. (1969) 'The power and functions of boards of directors', *American Journal of Sociology*, 75

ZEITLIN, M. (ed.) (1970) *American Society Inc.* Chicago: Markham

ZEITLIN, M. (1974) 'Corporate ownership and control: the large corporation and the capitalist class', *American Journal of Sociology*, 79/5

ZEITLIN, M. (1976) 'On class theory of the large corporation', *American Journal of Sociology*, 81/4

ZEITLIN, M., *et al.* (1975) ' "New princes" for old? The large corporation and the capitalist class in Chile', *American Journal of Sociology*, 80/1

ZEITLIN, M., *et al.* (1976) 'Class segments: agrarian property and political leadership in the capitalist class of Chile', *American Sociological Review*, 41

ZOLLSCHAN, G. K., and HIRSH, W. (eds.) (1964) *Explorations in Social Change*. London: Routledge and Kegan Paul

Index

There are no entries under frequently recurring words such as 'company', 'corporation', 'capitalism', etc. Similarly, references are not indexed, only substantial discussions of a writer's work.